# Teaching, learning and assessment of law in social work education

Suzy Braye and Michael Preston-Shoot with
Lesley-Ann Cull, Robert Johns and Jeremy Roche

First published in Great Britain in April 2005
by the Social Care Institute for Excellence

© University of Sussex and University of Luton 2005

Written by Suzy Braye (University of Sussex, formerly
at University of Liverpool) and Michael Preston-Shoot
(University of Luton) with
Lesley-Ann Cull (The Open University), Robert Johns (University
of East London) and Jeremy Roche (The Open University)

ISBN 1-904812-20-1

Produced by The Policy Press
Fourth Floor, Beacon House
Queen's Road
Bristol BS8 1QU
tel 0117 331 4054
fax 0117 331 4093
tpp-info@bristol.ac.uk
www.policypress.org.uk

**This report is available in print and online
www.scie.org.uk**

Social Care Institute for Excellence
Goldings House
2 Hay's Lane
London SE1 2HB
tel 020 7089 6840
fax 020 7089 6841
textphone 020 7089 6893
www.scie.org.uk

# Acknowledgements

We would like to thank all those who contributed to this knowledge review, by:

- providing information on research and publications pertinent to the field
- completing questionnaires, sending programme documentation and examples of education practice
- participating in telephone interviews
- participating in focus group discussions
- attending the two consultation events
- reading and commenting on materials and data.

The following individuals and organisations participated in consultation on the research, either through correspondence or through attendance at the two events. We were immensely heartened by the commitment and creativity expressed by all who took part, making an invaluable contribution to our thinking, and to the outcomes of the review.

**Sherrell Barnett**, Young Care Leavers' Consultancy Group, Goldsmiths College

**Sheila Bersin**, Knowsley Older People's Voice

**Bill Blunn**, Moving On With Learning

**Alison Brammer**, University of Keele

**Louise Brown**, University of Bath

**Kevin Chettle**, Advocacy in Action

**Jo Cleary,** Luton Borough Council

**Lesley-Ann Cull**, The Open University

**Charlotte Dodson**, Parents Fight Back

**Jacqui Dodson**, Parents Fight Back

**Alison Dundas**, Young Independent People Presenting Educational Entertainment

**Janet Fabb**, University of Paisley

**Ronny Flynn**, The Open University

**Janet Foulds**, British Association of Social Workers

**William Gandy**, Moving On With Learning

**Julie Gosling**, Advocacy in Action

**Roger Greeff**, British Association of Social Workers/Sheffield Hallam University

**Liz Green**, Goldsmiths College, University of London

**Ann James**, University of Bangor

**Robert Johns**, University of East London

**John Keep**, Chair, Disabled Parents' Network

**Terry Kelly**, Moving On With Learning

**Brian Kelsey**, Young Care Leavers' Consultancy Group, Goldsmiths College

**Heidi Kenworthy**, Moving On With Learning

**Enid Levin**, Social Care Institute for Excellence

**Sue Lightup**, St Helens Council

**Christina Lyon**, University of Liverpool

**Colette McAuley**, Queen's University Belfast

**Ann McDonald**, Social Work Law Association/University of East Anglia

**Fiona MacLeod**, Social Care Institute for Excellence

**Mark Martin**, Kingston University

**Anne Mercer**, Department of Health

**Grace Quinn**, Parents Fight Back

**Gwyneth Roberts**, Social Work Law Association/University of Bangor

**Jeremy Roche**, The Open University

**Hilary Tompsett**, Joint Universities Council Social Work Education Committee

**Helen Wenman**, General Social Care Council

**Michele Wates**, Disabled Parents' Network

**Tom Wilks**, Goldsmiths College, University of London

**Joan Williams**, Suresearch

We are grateful to the many colleagues who have submitted original material for use as practice examples, and have been prepared to share their work in the spirit of working collaboratively to develop education practice:

Canterbury Christ Church University College: **Philip Heasman**; **Su Paurelle**

Cornwall College: **Roy Ledger**; **Barbara Wright**

Glasgow Caledonian University: **Janice West**

Glasgow School of Social Work: **Kate Cameron**; **Fergus McNeill**

Havering College of Further & Higher Education: **Anne Bates**; **Pip Crilly**; **Andrew Thomas**

Liverpool Community College: **Dave Hicks**

Liverpool John Moores University: **Simon Rahilly**

London South Bank University: **Trish Hafford-Letchfield**

Middlesex University: **Christine Cocker**; **Helen Cosis Brown**; **Paul Dugmore**; **Brian O'Gorman**

North-East Worcestershire College: **Jenny Close**

University of Bangor: **Aled Griffiths**; **Ann James**; **Gwyneth Roberts**

University of Bristol: **Bill Beaumont**; **Sarah Cemlyn**; **Gill Hague**; **Liz Lloyd**; **the social work staff group**

University of Cardiff: **Sally Holland**

University of East Anglia: **Carol Dawson**; **Jonathan Dickens**; **Ann McDonald**

University of East London: **Robert Johns**

University of Edinburgh: **Janice McGhee**

University of Hull: **Greta Bradley**; **the programme team**

University of Illinois at Urbana-Champaign: **Sandra Kopels**

University of Kent at Medway: **Cliff Thomas**

University of Lincoln: **Leonne Griggs**; **the Service User Participation Advisory Group**

University of Luton: **Amanda Thorpe**

University of Manchester: **Carole Smith**

University of Paisley: **Janet Fabb**

University of Wales Institute Cardiff: **Dave Miller**; **Dave Lock**

University of the West of England: **Sarah Coldrick**; **Jane Dalrymple**

Our thanks go to the Care Council for Wales, the Scottish Social Services Council, the Northern Ireland Social Care Council and the General Social Care Council (GSCC) for their contribution of summary data from external assessors' reports, and to Helen Wenman, GSCC, for consultation in relation to the reporting of assessors' views.

We are grateful also to Dawn Haysom and Alan Bullimore (University of Luton) for work on literature searches, to Louise Brown (University of Bath) and Dave Hicks (Liverpool Community College) for questionnaire pilots, to Anne Pope and Ruth Melville (University of Liverpool) for work on the questionnaire, focus groups and consultation events, to Amanda Thorpe (University of Luton) for work on focus groups, to Nicki Brown (Transcribeit) for transcription services and to Maria Leitner (University of Liverpool) for advice on methodology.

Fiona Macleod, Enid Levin and Mike Fisher at the Social Care Institute for Excellence (SCIE) have provided invaluable support, consultation and advice throughout the course of the project, and we are grateful also to the anonymous reviewers who offered helpful and constructive comments on the draft report.

**Suzy Braye and Michael Preston-Shoot**

# Executive summary

## Suzy Braye and Michael Preston-Shoot

## Introduction

Legal knowledge and skills in its application are central to social work practice. Lack of knowledge of the legal rules, or shortcomings in how they inform decision making, can have serious consequences for service users, practitioners and managers.

Requirements for social work degrees in the UK strongly emphasise teaching, learning and assessment of law. This knowledge review aimed to identify good practice in the teaching, learning and assessment of law in social work education through:

- a systematic review of international published and unpublished research
- a survey of current education practice on social work qualification programmes in the UK
- consultation with a wide range of stakeholders, including service users and carers.

## Key findings

The literature on teaching, learning and assessment of law in social work education offers predominantly descriptive accounts of teaching and assessment, or conceptual analysis of the relationship between law and social work, and of components within social work law education and practice. There are some empirical studies that include in their analysis the outcomes of law teaching on social work programmes or that report on the effectiveness particularly of methods of assessment. A number of themes emerge, to which can be linked the findings from the practice survey and the consultation with stakeholders, including service users.

## Aim and focus of law teaching

Besides being a requirement of professional bodies in the UK, practice is legally regulated and social work intervention is often shaped or influenced by legal rules in statute and guidance. Irrespective of the setting in which they practise, social workers require familiarity with statute and guidance in order to advise and advocate effectively for clients, to fulfil their legal duties and responsibilities, and to communicate appropriately with other professionals and agencies. The literature also reminds social workers of their social change responsibilities and of the role of legal knowledge and skills in promoting social justice.

The literature indicates that, when teaching law to social workers, the professional requirement that practitioners are able to operate within statutory frameworks must be considered alongside the development of critical competence. By this is meant the ability to question agency procedures, professional roles, and the interface between legal rules and social issues.

In practice, programmes commonly aim to promote knowledge of legal systems and of mandates for social work provision and for this knowledge to be applied to practice. Some programmes identify critical analysis of the legal framework as an aim also. Less consistent mention is made of knowledge of broader legal frameworks; promoting service users' rights; using the law to counter discrimination and support ethical practice.

Sought outcomes for students are: to integrate legal knowledge within their practice; make legally-informed decisions; develop legal research and updating skills; and manage the dilemmas of practice. The focus is on both knowledge and skills, and on being able to use both in a partnership with the service users who experience the impact of legal decisions.

Service users and other stakeholders believe students need to combine critical thinking in relation to the law with hands-on skills.

## Core content

In the literature, there is an emphasis on both knowledge for practice and knowledge in practice. The former includes the functions of law in society and how legal rules are used in response to social issues. The latter focuses on substantive law about particular client groups and practice issues. This must make explicit the location of social work law in primary and secondary legislation, policy and practice guidance, and case law. These should be distinguished from agency procedures, which can be audited for the degree to which they accurately interpret the legal rules. The balanced focus also requires an emphasis on skills for practice and skills in practice. The former embraces policy analysis and advocacy, and researching legal issues to inform decision making. The latter covers core social work skills, such as recording, advocacy, report writing and problem solving.

In practice, a common core is included by most programmes, focusing upon community care, childcare and mental health legislation. Criminal justice is frequently excluded in England and Wales, but is included in Scotland and Northern Ireland. Other common exclusions are legislation relating to housing, healthcare and employment. Lack of timetable space is one reason for exclusion, and in this context programmes sometimes make a deliberate decision to concentrate on depth rather than breadth. Others prefer to be inclusive, because this 'maps the territory' of the broad relevant framework, enabling students to know the breadth of the field. A key concern is to ensure that students are able to draw on and integrate a range of mandates to meet the complexity of people's lives.

Service users and other stakeholders similarly believe students must learn to integrate their knowledge about different aspects of legislation (for example, childcare, mental health and community care) to enable them to respond to the complexity of people's lived experience, because 'families don't fall into boxes'.

## Law, rights and ethics

The literature is beginning to recognise the increasing centrality of ethical issues in the regulation of practice, and the increasing impact of the

European Convention on Human Rights and Fundamental Freedoms on decision making by social work agencies.

In practice, many programmes indicate that there is a strong values component to their law teaching. All indicate that they include coverage of the Human Rights Act 1998, although the depth and intensity of this coverage is variable.

There is a clear invitation from service users for practitioners to work alongside them to ensure that law is used proactively to uphold people's rights. Human rights and citizenship are key principles to be observed when applying the law.

## Curriculum organisation

One key debate in the literature is whether law teaching should be organised around discrete modules and/or integrated alongside other learning. Some research casts doubt on integrated models of curriculum design, suggesting that this results in lack of depth. However, discrete modules must avoid divorcing knowledge of the legal rules from the social work context in which they might be applied.

The literature provides examples of discrete and integrated curriculum design, together with limited discussion on the timing of teaching of the academic law curriculum in relation to practice learning opportunities. There is divergence in the literature relating to the degree to which some, more specialist, client-group law should be covered in qualifying education.

In practice, law is delivered predominantly through discrete modules of teaching early in the programme. This learning is usually expanded upon later by law content integrated within other subject modules. Student contact hours dedicated to law vary between 20 and 105. Averages are similar between types of programme, with the exception of postgraduate programmes with no discrete law teaching, where average hours are lower.

Educators believe discrete modules have the advantage of identifying and controlling the distinctive law content of students' learning, but they challenge their stamina and perseverance. Integrated teaching is believed to facilitate links with the practical application of law in professional roles.

Service users and other stakeholders believe the teaching hours allocated to law should reflect the importance of this subject in the lives of service users. Law should be integrated throughout the programme, rather than be taught just in one year, and should be linked with skills in working with people, rather than seen as isolated knowledge.

## Content and context

The literature indicates that integration of knowledge and skills requires teaching and learning to focus not just on substantive law but also on the contexts where decision making will be required. Students are thought to need an appreciation of how legal rules can impact on, inform, but also empower their decision making.

In practice, there is an emphasis on teaching and learning methods that make explicit the application of law in practice. Students and practice teachers report that the transition of law learning to the practice context of the placement agency is problematic for many students, and that learning can be eroded by a procedural emphasis in agency practice.

Service users want practitioners who are skilled in advocating for rights and challenging practices that are not lawful.

## Methods of teaching and learning in the academic curriculum

A range of methods will help students to learn the content of the legal rules and to connect this knowledge with skills to apply it to decision making. The literature describes, but less often evaluates, the outcome of these methods.

The literature reports positive student evaluations for methods that encourage active involvement and deeper learning. However, detail of data collection is often patchy and more rigorous outcome-focused research designs are rare. More common are descriptive and theory-building conceptual accounts, for example of using case studies, problem-based learning, and ecological or decision-making approaches to law learning.

In practice, lectures, combined with group exercises, are the most commonly used method, but extensive use is also made of seminars and guided independent research, and to a lesser extent of skills workshops and e-learning. Students are very anxious about the law, and a key concern of teachers is to allay students' fears, to make it more manageable and to ensure it has a strong practice focus. Case study approaches are very common. The use of virtual learning environments is likely to increase, with significant work being undertaken to develop their use in law learning.

Problem-based learning is popular with both educators and students, and is increasingly used alongside taught content to encourage students to become active learners. Students appreciate a combination of approaches, including lectures.

It is uncommon for service users and carers to be involved in law teaching, but this is considered an essential development. Service users have a wealth of experience to contribute, and wish to work alongside educators and practice teachers to ensure that students understand and learn from their perspectives.

## Who teaches?

The literature here ranges from unequivocal recommendations that lawyers must be involved, through examples of joint teaching by legal and social work academics, to the paramount need of ensuring that whoever facilitates learning and teaching has knowledge and empathic understanding of both law and social work. A careful use of guest speakers is encouraged but there is limited outcome focused research on what combination best facilitates social work law learning.

In practice, a wide range of staff contributes to law teaching, with an emphasis on ensuring that teaching by lawyers addresses the application of law in practice.

Service users and other stakeholders believe both lawyers and social work staff have important perspectives to contribute to law teaching. Service user involvement was seen as essential, to ensure that students' perspectives are broadened to include awareness of the impact of law in service users' lives.

## Assessment of law learning in the academic curriculum

The key theme to emerge from the literature on assessment is alignment. Methods of assessment should mirror the types of activities and judgements required of social workers in practice. Case studies, extended scenarios, oral assessment and project work are all described as offering alignment; so too is student involvement in self and peer assessment of both knowledge and contribution to group analysis of case material.

The literature contains student evaluations of assessment methods and, less frequently, detailed evaluations of the effectiveness of different methods in assessing knowledge. Missing is research to investigate the most effective means of enabling students to retain knowledge learned. There is a small literature on the timing of assessment, more conceptual than empirical.

In practice, law learning is most commonly assessed through coursework, but examinations also figure in a significant minority of programmes, and it is relatively common to find both methods being used. In both, case studies commonly feature, allowing students to demonstrate they can apply the law to practice. All programmes assess students' legal knowledge and their ability to apply it to practice scenarios. Some are also looking for critical analysis and integration with social work values.

## Connecting law and social work

Relationships between social workers and lawyers can be strained. Students frequently are apprehensive about law learning and interaction with legal systems and processes. The basic objective of law teaching and learning is not to create legal experts but to enable students to operate effectively in their context – social work – using a thorough knowledge of legal concepts and rules.

The US literature in particular contains reports of successful joint working between legal and social work practitioners. Some writers identify a practice or role continuum, at different points along which law or social work will be more influential in contributing to decision making. Others explore commonality of approaches and skills used by legal and social work practitioners.

Published accounts of law and social work students learning together are few, despite the increasing policy emphasis on inter-agency and inter-professional collaboration, with papers offering descriptive and conceptual accounts rather than evaluated outcomes.

Service users and other stakeholders believe it is important for practitioners to see law as a positive element of their practice, rather than as something to be afraid of, or defended against. It is vital that lawyers and social workers make better connections in practice, rather than social workers be excluded from legal debates and negotiations.

## Practice curriculum

The practice curriculum is under-theorised, despite research studies that demonstrate that practice teachers are apprehensive about their competence to facilitate student learning of law and concerned about their own knowledge of the legal rules. Agency support appears crucial in facilitating this aspect of practice teaching and assessment.

The literature links core social work skills and competences with different elements of legal knowledge and skills. It distinguishes between interim and final competence, and offers examples of teaching and assessment methods. There is an emerging concern with preparing students with knowledge and skills to maintain practice that is both lawful and ethical.

In practice, only a minority of programmes set any law-related learning objectives for students on placement. However, it is common to expect that practice teachers will help students be aware of the legal context for their casework, and written placement assignments commonly require some legal content. There are concerns about how consistently students experience the law in placement agencies; students are not satisfied with this aspect of their learning experience. Practice teachers see there being ample opportunity to develop law learning, and encourage students to use the law proactively to challenge poor agency practice. They find students struggling, however, to translate their academic understandings of the law into practice.

Service users and other stakeholders believe it is important that programmes take responsibility for the quality of students' practice learning opportunities related to law. Placements represent a real opportunity to get to grips with the law in practice, and to learn how to negotiate the challenges that practice presents. Accurate guidance on the law in practice is believed to be essential, because the law does not provide crystal-clear rules, it has to be interpreted. The law gives people rights, and it gives social workers discretion, and students need to learn to be accountable for how they use this. Sound use of law can be another step on the way to getting things right for people.

## Conclusion

The majority of literature offers descriptive and conceptual accounts, and practice wisdom rather than research-based evidence of inputs and outcomes. Empirical evidence on the effectiveness of different approaches is limited.

In education practice, learning, teaching and assessment appear well aligned, in that methods are clearly linked to sought outcomes, but educators do not have clear research evidence for the effectiveness of different approaches in practice. Law appears to lend itself to multi-faceted approaches, and no strong emphasis on one best way emerges. Law teaching is relevant to the roles that social workers carry out, with a focus on practice application, but the curriculum varies between programmes beyond a relatively small common core. Where educators succeed in engaging students' interest and effort, the rewards in terms of experienced learning outcomes are high. Some students, however, experience critical analysis, ethical issues and application of the law as an ongoing difficulty. Law in practice learning remains a major challenge and there cannot be full alignment until the neglect of law as a component of practice is addressed.

The knowledge review indicates that theory building in respect of law in social work education now should move beyond delineating the field of study to researching more systematically what enables students to acquire and to retain knowledge of the legal rules and skills in practising social work law.

# Introduction

Suzy Braye and Michael Preston-Shoot

## 1.1 Background to the knowledge review

This publication presents the findings from a systematic review of knowledge relating to current practice in the teaching, learning and assessment of law in social work education. The work was commissioned by the Social Care Institute for Excellence (SCIE) as part of its research programme to support the introduction from 2003 onwards of new social work degree qualifications in the UK.

The review is comprised of two pieces of research: an international research review and a UK-based practice survey. The research review has evaluated relevant published and unpublished materials. The practice survey has identified the range of approaches taken within programmes, and the views of those involved in teaching, learning and assessment, including educators, students and practice teachers.

The views of a wider range of stakeholders, including service users, carers and practitioners, have also been sought through two consultation events to discuss and advise on both aspects of the study. Guidance from SCIE[1] clearly identifies the value of participation by a wide range of stakeholders in its commissioned work. Equally, the participation of service users and carers, and of employers, is a core requirement for the social work degree across the UK. The research has adopted a broad and inclusive approach.

An integrative analysis brings together and comments upon the findings from all sources.

## 1.2 Law in social work education

### 1.2.1 Background

The relationship between social work and the law is disputed. The Beckford Report[2] positioned the legal rules as social work's defining mandate, prompting Stevenson[3] to counter with an ethical duty of care as the cornerstone of intervention. Braye and Preston-Shoot,[4] when reviewing the relationship, suggested that practitioners and managers must strike a balance between these two positions in each case.

This disputed relationship resurfaces in what practitioners and managers distinguish as essential social work skills. Practitioners emphasise process and interpersonal skills, such as advocacy, listening and counselling; managers identify procedural and instrumental skills, such as record keeping. Practitioners stress empirical research and methods of intervention; managers emphasise knowledge of the law and related procedures.[5,6] What appears clear, however, is that social work students and practitioners experience contact with the law and the legal system as stressful. They are concerned about their lack of familiarity with legal settings, language and procedures, and about the frequency with which the legal rules change. They express uncertainty about how the law interfaces with social work values and organisational procedures. Furthermore, legal accountability, which might benefit service users, can be unsettling for social work practitioners.[7] They conceptualise the law as intimidating, conflictual, and more likely to be obstructive rather than empowering.[8,9]

Nor is this a feature just of social work practice. Clarke[10] reports that nurses are more likely to see the law as a weapon to be used against them rather than a tool or framework to facilitate their work. Ridley[11] has found a lack of comprehension among accounting students when they are required to study law. Teaching law to social workers can, therefore, involve a challenge of mobilising students' enthusiasm and of clarifying the interface between legal knowledge, social work values and practice.

### 1.2.2 Social work degree

Law was the only subject for which the rules and requirements for the Diploma in Social Work[12] provided explicit direction on teaching and assessment. For the new degree, governments in all four countries of the UK have specified the inclusion of law within their requirements.[13-16] Knowledge of the legal rules and skills in their application are prominent in the social work subject benchmark statement,[17] which informs all four sets of requirements, and in the National Occupational Standards.[13,16,18,19]

The implication is clear: if social workers are to protect and provide for troubled and troubling individuals,[14] they must understand the relationship between law and practice, and know how to respond as that interface changes and develops. They should also be able to transfer their knowledge and skills into new organisational configurations consequent upon legislative changes designed to ensure coordination between services such as health and social services. Moreover, to the extent that students and practitioners enter situations and engage with service users without an adequate knowledge of how to proceed, they open up themselves and their employing agencies to liability for negligence. This possibility resides in the Mental Health Act 1983, the European Convention on Human Rights and Fundamental Freedoms, and in the Human Rights Act 1998. They may also call into question their continuing registration (Care Standards Act 2000). Note should be taken, therefore, of research, judicial findings and service user and carer experiences of law in practice. Such sources have found restrictive assessments, inappropriate care planning, lack of understanding, failure to follow statutory duties and policy guidance,[20] and evidence of how organisational (resource) pressures can distort practice.[21]

### 1.2.3 Standards of teaching and learning

Law in social work education in the UK has been a particular focus of scrutiny since research[22] identified shortcomings in students' knowledge and understanding of the law. From a survey of 296 newly qualified social workers, only 18% rated as effective or very effective methods of assessing their social work law knowledge and skills. Only 35% rated as good or very good the quality of teaching received, with a further 28%

believing it to be quite good. The Law Report brought the problem into sharp relief but the issue was not new. Grace and Wilkinson,[23] for example, had already identified practitioners' inability to verbalise the legal nature of their cases coherently, together with the ongoing concern that their outlook and understanding of their work is determined by agency procedures and resources that could distort statutory requirements. Phillips[8] had been critical of social workers' dismissal of the legal basis for sound professional practice.

Subsequent theory-building in respect of teaching, learning and assessment of law in academic and practice curricula appears to have had a beneficial impact on how students experience their education. A survey of 545 students leaving qualifying courses[24] found that 80% rated their law learning as relevant or very relevant. The study found an encouraging increase in the range of topics taught and improvement in student perceptions and satisfaction ratings of teaching and assessment.

To a degree this upward trend has continued. Wallis-Jones and Lyons[25] found the teaching of law to be highly rated among 1999 and 2001 qualifying students. In the 2001 employment survey, 48% ($n=700$) rated their knowledge and skills acquired through training as excellent or very good.

Two UK studies, however, offer cautionary tales. Marsh and Triseliotis[5] and Preston-Shoot et al[26] both reported worryingly high levels of lack of confidence among newly qualified and more experienced social workers, coupled with a steep decline in social work law knowledge that was not being routinely used in practice. In the former study, 44% of respondents ($n=385$) thought that too little time had been spent on law. Twenty-eight per cent were dissatisfied but 27% very pleased with the content and delivery of the academic curriculum in law.

Equally, the challenge of teaching, learning and assessment of law in social work education is not unique to the UK. Literature from the US demonstrates continuing concern about the place, quality and effectiveness of law teaching and assessment on social work programmes.[27-31]

These research studies provide an overview of the quality and effectiveness of teaching, learning and assessment of law in social work education. Less clear are the relative merits of different approaches to teaching, learning and assessment.

## 1.2.4 Standards of practising law

In the UK and elsewhere,[32] social workers' competence and practice skills have been questioned. Inquiry reports not infrequently point to the training implications of their findings. These sometimes refer to practitioners' and managers' understanding and implementation of their legal mandates. For example, both the Beckford Report[2] and the Carlile Report[33] were sharply critical of social workers' knowledge of childcare law and made recommendations for rectifying what the reports saw as training deficits. Similarly, in the area of mental health law, inquiries by the Mental Welfare Commission in Scotland have found a need for training and for guidance about when to consult with legal advisors. The Commission has suggested that training deficits apply not just to social workers but also hospital management and clinical staff. It also recommended that government should require the reapproval of Mental Health Officers and that the process of reapproval should establish social workers' competent knowledge of relevant legislation.

However, reviews of inquiry reports, particularly in the field of mental health, have found social workers offering expert legal and procedural knowledge, and observing the principles underlying law.[34-5] A review of inquiry reports in cases of children in need and child protection in contrast has emphasised practice and training deficits in many areas, including risk management, interagency communication, information handling, the use of authority, case conferencing, and managing the emotional impact of the work. However, in clear acknowledgement of the importance of post-qualifying education, changing legislation requires continued relearning.[36]

## 1.2.5 Theory building

Publication of the Law Report[22] sparked a process of theory building that has resulted in the delineation of social work law as a discrete area of academic and practice study. This theory building has provided a recognised body of knowledge, operating in a defined area of activity, and permeated with social work values and principles of administrative law.[37] Guidance on curriculum content for England and Wales was issued,[24] followed by a specific edition for Northern Ireland.[38] An increasing body of knowledge has developed around this new discipline. This includes textbooks (for example,[39-42]) and research studies on law in practice teaching.[26] It includes approaches to teaching and learning social work law[43-5] and further amplification of the different elements within social work law (for example[46-7]).

Despite this activity, there has been a limited focus on systematically drawing together evidence to support best practice in learning, teaching and assessment, and little cross-fertilisation of learning from the teaching of law within cognate disciplines, for example in the professions allied to health, or indeed within legal education. The developing body of research on broad learning, teaching and assessment methodologies within social work education, while important in generic terms, has not been scrutinised systematically for content specific to law. There has until now been no published review of education practice in the UK in the context of the theoretical and curriculum development work undertaken following the Law Report.

## 1.3 Aims and objectives of the knowledge review

The overall aim for both the research review and the practice survey was to identify good practice in the teaching, learning and assessment of law in social work education.

The contributory objectives were to:

- give an overview of approaches to teaching, learning and assessment
- examine evidence on the effectiveness of different approaches
- explore the extent to which current education practice reflects evidence on effectiveness
- identify future directions for research-informed organisation of teaching, learning and assessment.

The research review and the practice survey have made different but complementary contributions to meeting these objectives.

## 1.4 Consultation events

A broad range of stakeholder perspectives was gathered through two consultation events, which aimed to ensure the active participation of the following groups in the research:

- service users and carers
- General Social Care Council
- Department of Health
- Social Work Law Association (to incorporate the perspective of tutors of law in social work education)
- National Organisation of Practice Teachers (to provide a practice teaching perspective)
- British Association of Social Workers (to provide a perspective from the professional association)
- Joint University Council Social Work Education Committee (to include a perspective from higher education institutions)
- Association of Directors of Social Services (to ensure representation of managers and staff development officers in social services departments and new organisational configurations)
- voluntary organisations (ensuring again that both children's services and adult services are represented).

In the event, all but the Association of Directors of Social Services sent representatives to the consultation events. There was broad representation from a wide range of individual service users and organisations of service users. While practice teachers could to some extent represent agency perspectives, it was recognised that these may differ from the view of those in other organisational roles. In order to ensure that employers' and managers' perspectives could be incorporated, the draft reports were sent to two directors of social services for comment.

The consultation events themselves provided opportunities for the convened group to act in two very important ways. First, participants became a reference group to which the researchers presented their plans for the research and later their findings for review. Second, participants contributed their perspectives on the relationship between the law and social work, how they see social workers practising within the legal framework, and what this means for student learning. Within these broad terms of reference, each of the two events had specific objectives.

- The purpose of the first consultation was to seek stakeholder views on the content and process of the study, consider stakeholder views on what law should be taught, learned and assessed in social work training and obtain perspectives on the impact of learning on social workers' practice.

- The second consultation evaluated the data obtained by that point, and identified key themes for inclusion in the draft reports on both the research review and the practice survey.

The perspectives on teaching, learning and assessment of law in social work education that were developed through discussion at the consultation events are reported as part of the practice survey included in this knowledge review.

# Research review

Michael Preston-Shoot, Suzy Braye, Lesley-Ann Cull,
Robert Johns and Jeremy Roche

## 2.1 Methodology

### 2.1.1 Search strategy

The identification of materials that would contribute knowledge relevant to teaching, learning and assessment of law in social work education, literature dating back to 1988, the date of the Law Report, was sought initially in relation to social work education. In relation to legal education, literature was sought from 1967, the year of publication by Twining[48] of an influential paper on the task of educating lawyers, which stimulated debate about whether the purpose of legal education was technical competence in, or critical thinking about, legal rules. This theme will reappear later in the review of evidence. The literature on teaching law in professions allied to health was initially searched back to 1990, since which date there has been increasing emphasis on the interface between health and social care.

In the event, because of the North American literature, which had begun to publish articles on teaching, learning and assessment of law in social work education in the 1960s, the search of the social work literature was extended back to 1967. Similarly, because of the low volume of material relating to teaching law in professions allied to health, this search reached further back than 1990 and was extended to include other professions such as business and sport.

The search was not limited to literature from any specific geographic context but was restricted to English language papers due to limited resources for translation. The search targeted published papers; unpublished, grey literature; research reports; conference papers; and inspection and enquiry reports.

## 2.1.2 Electronic databases

Sector specific databases were searched:

- Lawtel
- Westlaw
- Lexis-Nexis
- Legal Journals Index
- Kluwer
- Social Work abstracts
- Social Services abstracts
- International Bibliography of the Social Sciences (IBSS)
- Sociological abstracts
- Social Sciences Citation Index
- SOSIG
- MEDLINE
- Embase
- PsycINFO
- CINAHL
- Caredata

General databases were also searched:

- SIGLE
- BIDS
- ASSIA
- EBSCO
- JSTOR
- Synergy
- Ingenta
- Metapress
- Science Direct
- Highwire
- Ovid: Bibliographic Records
- Conference papers Index
- British National Bibliography for Report Literature
- British Library Catalogue
- British Library (Dissertation Abstracts).

Search terms were used that combined law and social work or professions allied to health and linked these discipline fields with literature relevant to teaching, learning and assessment. The search terms used can be found in Appendix 1.

### 2.1.3 Hand searching

Manual searching of selected law, social work and nursing journals and abstracts was undertaken. This generally confirmed the thoroughness of the database searches, with only a few additional materials being identified. In addition, contact was made with three journal editors for identification of papers in press.

### 2.1.4 Other sources

Listservers' archives were searched to identify correspondents who were then contacted for information. Requests for information were posted on:

- UKSOCWORK: www.jiscmail.ac.uk/lists/uksocwork.html
- Social Work Learning, Teaching and Support Network: www.jisc.ac.uk/lists/social-work-ltsn.html
- International or comparative social work: www.jiscmail.ac.uk/lists/intsocwork.html
- ESRC evidence-based
- Child-Maltreatment
- UK Centre for Legal Education.

In addition, relevant websites were searched, such as the King's Fund, MIND, Sainsbury Centre for Mental Health, and the Joseph Rowntree Foundation. However, little was found that was directly relevant to teaching social work law.

### 2.1.5 Selection criteria

All titles and abstracts were selected for review where they discussed social work, law and/or a profession allied to health, and focused on teaching, learning and/or assessment of law and/or legal knowledge and skills. Throughout, a distinction was made between law in practice and law in social work education. Thus, perspectives from inquiry reports, from service user organisations and from statutory and voluntary organisations, have been included where they refer to teaching, learning and assessment of law in social work education, rather than how social work practitioners and managers are implementing or should use the law in practice.

Reference to teaching, learning and assessment of law in (social work) education thus formed the initial screening question for this research review.[49] Using the framework proposed by the National Health Service Centre for Reviews and Dissemination (NHSCRD),[50] the initial selection criteria were expressed as follows:

| Selection criteria | Inclusion criteria | Exclusion criteria |
|---|---|---|
| Population | Students in social work, law and/or allied health professions | Students in medicine or other disciplines |
| Intervention | Teaching, learning or assessment of law, legal knowledge or legal skills | Using law in practice Teaching, learning or assessment in post-qualifying education or vocational training |
| Outcome | Acquisition of knowledge or skills Curriculum development | Professional practice outcomes |
| Study design/type of paper | Empirical papers Conceptual papers Descriptive papers | |

In the event, the significant volume of materials on legal education required some refinement of the inclusion criteria. A differentiation was made that included material where the focus was on the teaching, learning and assessment of law, legal knowledge and skills rather than debates over the content of the law curriculum and doctrinal developments in law that did not link to themes relevant to the research. Material that considered students studying for professional qualifications other than law was also included.

Reference has already been made to the broadening of the inclusion criteria to embrace materials on teaching law to some other disciplines.

## 2.1.6 Results

The various search strategies produced 976 publications for initial consideration. At this stage, 690 were excluded, principally because they focused on law in practice without addressing implications for education. Detailed reading of the remainder yielded the following results (although the analysis presented in subsequent chapters draws on a slightly wider range of literature than the included papers).

Included (see Appendix 2)   117
Excluded                    169

One bibliography of research was located[51] that included law among the many fields covered. However, the bibliography only listed seven references, despite emphasising the need for developing research use in social work education and the importance of basing courses and curricula on adequate evaluation of the qualities and impact of existing programmes. This partiality highlights the importance of this research review.

Few empirical papers were located. The relative absence of empirical studies may be the result of the initial requirement to map the territory of social work law, to engage in theory building in order to establish the discipline and articulate the relationship between law and social work practice and education. It may also be the result of educators drawing implicitly on teaching and learning methodologies, such as problem-based learning, that have been researched elsewhere prior to their adoption in teaching and assessing social work law.

In the protocol developed for this review, a distinction was drawn between descriptive and conceptual papers. In the event, many papers included in the review both described approaches to teaching, learning and/or assessment of law in social work education, and developed or reviewed ideas about it and the interface between law and professional practice. Papers that focused on service user and carer contributions to this subject area were noticeable by their absence.

## 2.1.7 Quality assessment

Normally central to the approach to systematic review is the articulation of a hierarchy of evidence based on quality research methodology standards, which include an account of the theoretical framework, aims and objectives of a study, and description of context, sample and methodology.[52] The limited number of empirically based papers relating to the themes of this research review meant that any hierarchy of evidence had to be sufficiently broad to include descriptive and conceptual as well as empirical papers.

Materials were classified according to quality criteria agreed in advance to enable a clear summary and rationale for the decisions made. The quality assessment criteria were derived in part from the dimensions identified by Pawson and colleagues[53] as being robust standards for any piece of knowledge, regardless of source and capable of extension across the three types of papers identified. This accords with Boaz and Ashby,[54] who argue for a broad notion that is concerned not just with methodological quality but also relevance and fitness for purpose.

Thus, assessment and decision making about the material to be included was concerned with the degree to which papers were characterised by:

- transparency (explicit aims, frameworks, methods and conclusions)
- accuracy (credible findings and conclusions)
- purposivity (methods fit for purpose)
- utility (knowledge produced that is fit for use by others)
- propriety (ethical standards met)
- accessibility (presentation appropriate for the audience intended).

## 2.1.8 Consultation events

Two conferences were held to seek stakeholder views. At the first, their perspectives were sought on what should be taught, learned and assessed, and on the range of materials that might be accessed. At the second, their responses were sought to the initial themes and analysis of the data extracted from the included materials in order to assure the validity and reliability of the findings.

### 2.1.9 Synthesis of evidence

Boaz and colleagues[52] refer to narrative synthesis in order to outline and explore the extent, nature and quality of available evidence, in fields where studies and outcome measures are likely to be diverse in nature. Such an approach can be used to explore similarities and differences within a group of studies. Campbell and colleagues[49] describe an approach to synthesis of qualitative research, which enables lines of argument to be identified.

In-depth data extraction was undertaken from which a manual analysis achieved a synthesis of the available material and enabled the identification of themes. Key concepts and themes, together with areas of debate and disagreement, were identified from repeated reading of the material and discussion among the research team. This constant interrogation of concepts and themes within the material enabled the creation of a whole picture that was greater than the sum of the parts.[49] In other words, synthesis went beyond simple summarising or aggregation of individual papers towards the articulation of lines of argument emerging from them. As Campbell and colleagues[49] argue, such an approach offers insights for conceptual development within a particular field of study.

Each of the themes derived from this synthesis will now be presented in turn.

## 2.2 What is the purpose of law teaching for social workers?

### 2.2.1 Pericles and the plumber

Twining[48] first raised this fundamental question about the purpose of legal education. He contrasted the idea of the 'plumber', the mere technician of 'law', with Pericles, the enlightened lawyer of 'integrity'. With obvious parallels to debates in social work about the distinction between education and training, he argued that simply providing law students with specialist knowledge and technical skills (plumbing) was insufficient. Students require a liberal education in law that fosters a breadth of perspective and critical approach, thus permitting a questioning of the origin, organisation and purpose of legal rules and promoting independence of thought and judgement. Bradney[55] uses the analogy of ivory towers and satanic mills to refer to the ensuing debate that took place in legal education. This debate is usefully summarised by Boon[56] who draws attention to the underlying conflict between university law schools and professional bodies such as the Law Society.

Other legal commentators have also warned of the dangers of mechanistic jurisprudence and of teaching methods that divorce law from its social context. For example, advocates of clinical legal education argue that it introduces students to the real world of practice and thus better prepares them for practice.[57] Diesfeld[58] argues that clinical legal education enables students to bridge the gap between theory and practice, promotes the acquisition of important skills, for example interviewing and collaborative working, and empowers students by fostering their participation. Jones[59] differentiates between learning to work (process knowledge and skills developed in the workplace) and learning about work (knowledge). Neglecting the former, competence in practice, results in the practice element being marginalised or under-theorised. Yet for the latter, competence for practice is also important. This means challenging technocratic or exclusively competence-based approaches to education that create unhelpful divisions between theory and practice.[60] Jones suggests that law students must be more than technically proficient since their work requires insight and intuition.

Hinett[61] comments similarly, referring to learning that enables students to develop not just a perspective on action but enquiry into that action. Deciding how and where to intervene requires more than technical competence in legal knowledge: it requires reflection on the underlying rationale for action, including consideration of motivation and ethics, in recognition that law is open to interpretation. She suggests that evidence for such critical thinking skills can be found in student learning logs, critical incident journals, diaries and portfolios.

Writing from a perspective of teaching law to non-lawyers, Byles and Soetendorp[62] link what law is to be taught with the benchmarks and requirements of the professional body for the discipline involved. Applying this to social work, Howe[63] explores the relationship between political, economic and ideological orders in shaping legal rules, and how law affects social work practice. He suggests that if social workers are to respond to individual need and to promote social justice, they must be able to examine state machinery critically. They must be competent in understanding and commenting on how law as implemented by agencies defines and limits practice. For this, he suggests, rote learning is insufficient.

Madden and Wayne[64] and King and Trowell[65] take the analysis further, pointing to how legal processes can lead to harmful or anti-therapeutic outcomes. Social workers should consider this possibility when considering intervention in people's lives, using their skills to influence the legal process in individual cases, questioning how law is used to resolve social issues and advocating for policy change at a macro level. Thus, social workers need to differentiate between a critique of substantive law and of law in process, in order to distinguish between available duties and powers, on the one hand, and reflections on procedures, interpretation and use of law on the other.

Indeed, the literature provides several examples of why social workers should reflect on and critically evaluate how the law regulates and affects institutions and different social groups.[66-7] Some authors argue that social workers should both understand discourses that shape legal rules, often to the disadvantage of particular social divisions, and develop skills to take corrective action.[29,58,68-70] Applying this analysis to social work law in the practice curriculum, qualified practitioners must be able to operate within statutory frameworks but question agency procedures and professional roles. They must be able to recognise legal mandates but also manage the dilemmas and tensions that this will involve.[24]

The logical conclusion is that educational objectives should be both critical and vocational. Social workers should be competent technicians but also well rounded professionals with knowledge and skills to question the context in which they work. Thus, Preston-Shoot[9] refers to the need for competent practitioners who are confident, credible, critical and creative:

- **confident** to challenge inappropriate interpretations or use of the legal rules
- **credible** when presenting the rationale for their decision making
- **critical** to make their professional practice and the legal rules acces-

sible to those with whom they work, to assess the impact of policies on people's lives and to navigate through questions of ethics, rights and needs

* **creative** in order to exploit the opportunities that the legal rules present and to manage the practice dilemmas and conflicting imperatives that the interface between law and social work practice generates.

### 2.2.2 Core content

Twining[48] argued that the law curriculum as a liberal education should be characterised by central values such as free enquiry and intellectual discipline, and within such an approach should emphasise legal knowledge and skills. Toddington[71] elaborated on this by setting out a comprehensive guide to what should be included in universities' law curricula. Within legal education, there has been much recent discussion of skills,[57] with a renewed emphasis on making the learning of skills a central element in legal education and training.[72]

Cull and Roche,[73] however, argue that health and social welfare professionals do not need to study law in exactly the same way as lawyers, although there are some common needs. These include: an understanding and familiarity with legal language and key legal concepts; knowledge of the law-making process; an understanding of the fluidity and discretion inherent in all human decision-making processes; the critical policy debates underpinning major legislative change impacting on social work practice; and the development of a critical sense about the law.

They argue that the social work law student does not study law for its own sake but in order to better understand the many and complex ways in which practice and interactions with service users are regulated. Thus, social work students have to engage with the complexity of the law–practice interface – not acquire the habit of always 'thinking like a lawyer'.[74-6]

Writers on social work law also refer to knowledge and skills. Their proposals can be classified to reflect the distinction between technical competence in, and critical understanding of, the roles and tasks for which they are responsible.

Thus, knowledge for practice includes the legal content of social policy, the functions of law in society, and sources of law.[29,77-8] It embraces the legal rights of various groups and how legal rules are used in respect of social issues.[27,31,70,79] Alcock[80] refers to students understanding how law develops and asking critical questions of this developmental process. These questions include whether the law could be better adapted to the situations in which it is used, whether legal rules ameliorate or solve particular social issues, and whether alternative constructions of such issues suggest different legal and other solutions.

Knowledge in practice includes substantive law about particular client groups, about abuse and neglect, and particular practice issues such as confidentiality, self-determination, consent, access to records, due process and liability and accountability.[27,30-1,78-9,81-3]

Skills for practice include competence to argue cases and fight decisions,[27,31] developing research-informed flexible use of legal rules and challenging how other agencies might seek to apply them.[26] They include policy analysis and influencing, and researching legal issues to inform individual case decision making and wider campaigning.[31,64,79]

Skills in practice include recording, advocacy, accessing rights and problem solving, and report preparation and writing. They involve asking questions, research, analysis and synthesis of information, mediation and negotiation, providing evidence, and decision making in complex and pressured situations.[29-31,64,79,84]

Thus, for social workers[32] and other non-lawyers studying law,[11,85] teaching and learning should focus on acquisition and application of knowledge, and on skill development. However, this should be from the perspective of everyday practice and the social and political context in which it operates, so that the relevance of law and the law-making process are highlighted.

If these areas represent the core content of the curriculum for teaching, learning and assessment of law in social work education, a further step is to clarify the different levels of learning outcomes as students progress through their studies. Byles and Soetendorp[62] distinguish helpfully between learning outcomes that require students to identify and recognise; to describe and list; to apply, use, analyse and explain; and to reflect and theorise. Woodcock[85] writes of ensuring relevance to the student's main subject area, which can now be done by reference to social work's benchmark statement[17] and occupational standards.[13,16,18,19]

It is clear from the growing number of social work law textbooks that a consensus exists over the law that needs to be covered in the curriculum (see, for example[39,41,86]). This consensus embraces primary and secondary legislation, policy and practice guidance, and case law as the legal basis for social work authority. It distinguishes the legal rules from how local authorities, through their organisational policies and procedures, interpret the mandate. However, while there is broad agreement over the content of the curriculum, organisation of the material varies. Some texts adopt a thematic approach, placing greater emphasis on how law can be used by social workers, rather than outlining the powers and duties that social workers have in a given situation (for example[42,77]).

## 2.2.3 Law and ethics

Several writers, for example Stevenson,[3] explicitly link law and ethics in both practice and education for practice. This is partly because practice can be lawful and ethical, lawful and unethical, unlawful yet ethical, or unlawful and unethical.[87] However, it is also because practitioners must have the knowledge and skills to respond appropriately when asked to practise in a manner they consider to be either unlawful and/or unethical.[20]

Roche[88] argues for greater attention to the role of ethics as a component of law teaching. Specifically the argument he sets out is that social work law teaching is an ideal vehicle through which to explore issues of ethics that underpin both law and social work practice. Particular attention can be paid to issues of empowerment and principles that govern social work law teaching and practice. This broader conceptualisation of law, focusing on key concepts such as rights, can also enable students to consider the relationship between social work values and the law.[7,47]

Writing in a Canadian context, Watkinson[89] suggests that the best means of addressing this broader approach is to pay greater attention to human rights cases. Using a number of human rights case law examples, the author argues that human rights education should be central to social work education. With the increasing impact of the Human Rights Act 1998 on law and social work practice, such an approach might also be valuable in the UK context.[66]

Within legal education there has been renewed interest in the relationship between law and ethics and the importance of ethics being part of the law curriculum.[90-2] One key theme within this literature is the need to understand the significance and complexity of professional power. Webb[91] acknowledges the marginal place of ethics in the discipline of law and sees a number of challenges to the development of an ethical curriculum. One of these, 'from seeing right to doing right', focuses on the limitation of seeing ethics as simply a knowledge attribute. Ethical decision making requires the ability to not only recognise an ethical issue and to prioritise ethical considerations but also the ability to convert ethical thought into ethical action. The literature suggests that free-standing courses on ethics alone will not be sufficient to inculcate appropriate values and are easily marginalised; Rhode[90] argues that a pervasive approach is required which supplements discrete modules on ethics.

She suggests that all too often students will view a separate mandatory course as an 'add-on' and a digression from what is really important (see also[93]). Rhode[90] does not dismiss the difficulties of developing an integrated curriculum but argues that, if well constructed, it can increase recognition of ethical issues, enhance skills in ethical analysis and build awareness of the structural conditions and regulatory failures that contribute to issues arising in practice. An integrated curriculum is one where the pervasive method should be seen as supplementing rather than substituting for a separate course focusing specifically on ethics. A single required course inevitably has limitations. The pervasive method enables and encourages students to address ethical issues throughout the curriculum as they arise and makes it clear that they are crucial constituents of practice.[88,90,93]

Consideration of law and ethics, however, also needs to incorporate the social control aspects of the social work task. Here, professional values are concerned with protection of self and/or others from risk and harm, and with situations where the proportional intervention may involve restricting someone's self-determination, liberty, or right to privacy and family life. Practitioners regularly encounter situations where the legal mandate emphasises control as well as care, and where practice dilemmas require social workers to determine the balance to be struck between rights and risk, prevention and protection, and welfare and justice. This requires social workers to know when to use their legal authority, and to feel comfortable in its use. Research and inquiry evidence (for example[94-5]), indicates that social workers experience discomfort with the exercise of authority, perhaps in part because their working environment does not provide through supervision and workload management an experience that they are 'held'. Indeed, Parkinson and Thompson[96] suggest that social work students need to acquire skills in decision making when they are working amidst uncertainty and when they are having to manage anxiety or fear. Social work education, then, needs to provide learning opportunities in managing authority and in resolving practice dilemmas by reference to values, knowledge, risk assessment, and decision-making frameworks.[77,97]

The requirement under the Care Standards Act 2000 that practitioners register in order to continue to practise as social workers brings into sharp relief the centrality of ethics and law in social work education and practice. Arguably, neither an ethical standard nor knowledge of the legal rules alone will prove sufficient to guide effective practice.[3,87] A similar juxtaposition of legal questions and ethical issues is also argued for mental health nurses[98] since their work focuses in part around issues of consent to treatment, freedom of movement, and integrity of the person. The Human Rights Act 1998, it is argued,[99] will have the effect of requiring decision making in health care to be more transparent.

## 2.2.4 Why law?

From a US and UK context, similar responses appear to this question. One answer centres on professional accountability.[46,62,100] Harvey,[101] for example, points to the potentially dire consequences when people do not receive informed advice based on an ability to identify what the law offers and what it imposes. Phillips[8] observes that social workers must know when to refer situations on, how to identify problems that have a legal component, and what information to give. Yet, he and Terry[102] found widespread ignorance of legal powers and duties. Nurses and doctors have come in for similar criticism. Tingle[103] and Cowley and Andrews[104] suggest that legal knowledge can empower nurses, enabling them to develop their capacity for making judgements and for identifying practice standards, for which they are accountable. However, Cox[99] suggests that many doctors and nurses have a poor understanding of the law as it applies to health care and that there is little evidence to suggest that this educational deficit has been recognised or filled.

Another answer, especially in the UK context, centres on the requirements of professional bodies[62,98,105] and the legal regulation of practice through registration and licensing.[27] A third answer recognises that much social work practice is shaped, regulated or influenced by legal rules.[29,37,62,79,106] The majority of social workers are employed in settings where they hold specific statutory powers and duties, such that a discipline called social work law may be recognised.[37] This requires social workers to know and be skilled in applying the legal powers and duties given to local authorities through childcare, mental health, community care and/or youth justice legislation and guidance. Even where social workers may be working in an environment where they do not hold specific statutory powers and duties, they still require familiarity with statute, regulation and guidance. This is to enable them to advise and advocate effectively for clients and to promote a coordinated organisational response to individual and community issues.[37,107,108]

A fourth answer lies in increasing the effectiveness of communication and collaboration between legal and social work practitioners,[28-9,106,109] with the objective of strengthening social work's contribution and perceived relevance to decision making in legal arenas. A final answer lies in promoting system change and beneficial outcomes for individuals and groups.[31,105] This requires the ability to recognise problems as having legal components, to locate rights and how they link with practice values, and to organise intervention aimed at meeting individual need and promoting social justice in line with the international definition of social work's purpose.[47,110]

Such a rationale might usefully be included in course outlines.

## 2.3  How should law be taught?

### 2.3.1 Discrete modules and integrated curricula

Should the law be taught separately in discrete modules or integrated alongside learning about other knowledge and skills?  Most papers discussing this question, and others relating to how law learning should be promoted, are descriptive rather than evaluative. There appears to be little sound evidence that leads inexorably to a recommendation for one method over another.

In the US context of a crowded curriculum, it appears to have been difficult to find space for non-mandated core discrete modules. Gustavsson and Kopels[108] illustrate how an infusion model might operate in an academic syllabus. Bogolub[82] describes an infusion approach to a practice class where cases were selected to reflect the reality of social work practice. Reflection was developed through the use of experiential exercises, skills through role-play and practice, and knowledge through discussion.

Some US commentators describe both dedicated courses and legal content integrated across the curriculum. Thus, Jankovic and Green[27] describe a foundation course, followed by specialisation around client groups delivered through dedicated courses and integration, and field practice where skills of recording, assessment, use of authority, case presentation and analysis were developed. Sparer[111] suggests the provision of a dedicated course for focus and the use of infusion to expand and extend the treatment of dilemmas and standards for intervention.

Madden[31] cautions about the lack of depth, or the infusion illusion, when legal content is integrated across the curriculum. This reinforces the concern expressed in the Law Report,[22] namely that an integrated approach may underplay the importance of detailed knowledge of the legal rules and provide an insufficient foundation for legally informed practice. However, that report did also recognise the parallel danger of ignoring the social work context, and the dilemmas social workers encounter, by teaching only discrete law. Similarly, from an Australian context, Swain[32] uses feedback from students to caution that an infusion and/or problem-based learning approach can marginalise attention to legal knowledge. By contrast, Ward and Hogg[112] offer an integrated approach that includes a model programme that covers concepts, subject areas, skills and different types of assessment. The integration referred to here, however, is as much that between legal knowledge and social work skills as that between discrete and infusion models of curriculum design.

Clearly, for an infusion, cross-curriculum approach to prove effective, close coordination is required between programme/module leaders and teachers, and cannot be assumed. Katz,[113] writing about the disciplines of law and medicine, recognises the complexity of this task and emphasises the centrality of intensive collaborative working. From the discipline of physical therapy education comes a cautionary tale of considerable variation across programmes relating to the hours devoted to legal issues. Integration of content throughout the curriculum did not appear to achieve the same results as a free-standing course.[114] Indeed, the question of how much time has been a long-running question, in social work[22,32,101] and in nursing,[98] however the curriculum has been organised. Wide variations are obvious and complaints arise about insufficiency of time when having to deal with complex legal and ethical questions.

### 2.3.2 Content and context

Lawyers teaching law to business students are clear that teaching and learning should cover not just specific legal rules but should also place them in the context of decisions that these students, as practitioners, will be expected to take.[11,115] Thus, they are concerned with preparing students for the business world. This enables students to understand the practical application of legal principles, to see the relevance of law, and to become sufficiently curious to research further into the subject matter.[116] Byles and Soetendorp[62] agree that student learning should be focused on context rather than content so that students can appreciate how legal rules might impact on, but also support, their decision making. Too much focus on content isolates the legal rules and appears to promote only surface learning. Balanced with context, students can integrate their experience with legal concepts, relating law to their subject discipline.

Wong[117] states that the need to expose students to authentic work environments and to place the learning of law in a social context is equally compelling in undergraduate law programmes. He argues that this can be achieved via a problem-based learning (PBL) approach, which brings closer together the real world and traditional legal education. Problem-based learning helps students appreciate the open-textured and indeterminate nature of law and to see the law as a social phenomenon. However, use of PBL should be accompanied by other teaching and learning methods in order that students appreciate that real world problems do not come neatly packaged.[118]

This emphasis on context appears in the social work law literature also. Eadie and Ward[119] argue that legal competence is as much about questions as answers, and whether a question is relevant will depend on understanding of the context, not simply on knowledge of the law.

### 2.3.3 Methods of teaching and learning

A wide range of methods, aside from lectures and seminars, are recommended for the academic curriculum. Again, however, any evaluation of outcomes and effectiveness is mainly of the student report type.

| Method | Objectives |
|--------|-----------|
| Use of case law | To illustrate legal reasoning and to show that case law is not unambiguous or univocal [31,105,120-1] |
| Use of case studies<br>Use of critical incidents<br>Use of problem-based learning | To analyse issues, locate law and integrate with practice [4,31,61,68,81,105,116,117,122-3] |
| Readings and source materials | To locate legal rules and the discourse surrounding them [9,40,68,79,116] |
| Video and use of films | To develop observation and practice skills [29,68,79,102,124] |
| Project work<br>Social action work | To plan, participate in and evaluate an intervention [68,116] |
| Research Library tasks | To find cases and statutes; to gain research confidence [11,24,79,81] |
| Observation | To experience legal proceedings [29,32,79] |
| Role-play<br>Simulation exercises | To develop practice knowledge and skills, for example through mock courts or tribunals [29,81,122,125-6] |
| Use of web<br>Computer-assisted learning | To develop research skills and knowledge [85,127-9] |
| Distance learning and use of workbooks | To identify legal issues and develop decision-making skills; to highlight and work through dilemmas [9,104,119] |
| Scenarios<br>Extended case studies | To enable students to access law learning [73,130] |

| Critical legal education | To join policy and practice; to apply law to 'everyday' situations [58,131-2] |
|---|---|
| Student presentations | To link knowledge with practice, to research topics, and to communicate professional role to others [81,107,119,133] |
| Service user accounts | To hear and reflect on how service users and carers experience the law in action [96,98,134] |
| Self-audits | To develop reflection [9] |

A number of writers stress the importance of aligning teaching and learning methods with the activities and working methods in which students will engage in practice. Thus, Woodcock[85] uses case studies based on real situations and oppositional exercises, where students research and present different sides of an issue. These learning methods require students to work in groups in order to develop skills of teamwork, interpretation, construction and appraisal. Ridley,[11] who also draws on experience of teaching law to non-lawyers, organises workshops for which students must read materials, including cases, identify and analyse relevant facts, and come prepared to make a presentation. She also advocates role-play of dispute resolution where teams of students develop skills of argument and advocacy, listening and evaluation. However, both authors note the problems of dominance by a few students and different levels of competence among students, with educators needing to be skilled facilitators if they are to enable real student participation and the acquisition of skills in oral communication and interpretation. Nonetheless, they report that students find such learning methods develop their ability to work with others.

Some writers also stress the importance of developing students' reflective skills. Parkinson and Thompson[96] use the presentation of client observation in seminars to develop and assess students' skills in contemplative exploration. Bailey[118] similarly refers to enabling students to reflect on learning, this time seeing the development of such skills through working collaboratively in groups and writing a reflective journal (see also[61]).

Student evaluations appear to suggest that these methods, individually but especially in combination, encourage deeper learning; however, details of how data was collected are often patchy. Sarnoff[129] and Johns[127] report student satisfaction and development when using the Internet in law learning. Eadie and Ward[119] report increased student confidence, demonstrably enhanced enquiry skills, and increased clarity about the nature of law and the complex value issues involved. Braye and Preston-Shoot[135] report that use of case studies enabled students to identify relevant legal issues, clarify their roles and tasks, frame and understand dilemmas and value issues, and be clear about the purposes of intervention. Debreceniova and Kolikova[131] suggest interactive learning through experience is the most effective way of acquiring knowledge. They argue that a law clinic is a good forum for this approach, helping students not only to learn critical and analytical skills, but also to experience what work in teams comprises and how group problem solving works (see also[58,132]).

Endeshaw[115] found that students preferred small-size lectures and interactive sessions, group discussions and learning. Others have found that large and small groups, with students playing an active part, promote deeper learning.[116,133]

In a rigorous research design, Oliver and Huxley[128] found that students valued computer-assisted learning, experiencing it as a valuable way to learn, with direct benefits to their practice in terms of increased knowledge. They also valued it as a means of revision and self-assessment. A later article[136] reports on a controlled experiment with 83 social workers. This demonstrated that students benefited from training using quantitative data and showed positive response to computer-assisted learning. The same authors chart subsequent development in this area of learning and teaching.[137-8] Swain and Evans,[139] writing in Australia, summarise developments in the use of multimedia and relate innovations in teaching, but with only limited discussion and evaluation.

Maharg and Muntjewerff[140] examine the effects of information and communications technologies (ICT) in European law schools and give an account of the types of e-teaching interventions used in European legal education. They report that development of managed learning environments (MLEs) has become a significant force on the teaching and learning environments of law schools, but as yet little research has been undertaken to evaluate their effects on learning or teaching. The authors caution that MLE technology can enable teachers to avoid difficult questions about how they organise their teaching and can be used to support shallow learning. Nonetheless, they argue that the Internet may open up new ways of teaching and learning the law. The article considers in some detail two educational interventions using ICT that have been developed in different jurisdictions, Scotland and the Netherlands.

Allridge and Mumford[141] consider the technical achievements of ICT in the practice and teaching of law in the UK and America. They contend that the most significant changes in law teaching in the first decade of the 21st century will arise from the changes that technology has brought. Their article sets out some of the technical achievements to date, such as datasets, electronic casebooks, and teaching and learning software (for example IOLIS, see[142]) and the advantages that these different tools can bring to the learning experience. The authors argue that skills in ICT are highly transferable and should feature highly in any teaching models. They acknowledge, however, that further research needs to be done to assess the value of learning via ICT over more traditional tutorial and lecture settings. Moodie[142] found that students appreciated the variety of tasks available in workbooks but argues that there is still some way to travel in using ICT and in enabling students to work through this medium in groups.

Less extensive is the literature on the practice curriculum, for both qualifying training and subsequent post-qualifying training in an interagency arena,[143] this despite the importance of understanding and navigating through how legal rules impact on decision making.[115] Indeed, the under-theorising of the content of, and methods for, delivering learning through the practice curriculum is a matter of concern. Practice teachers express uncertainty about their competence to facilitate student learning of law and are themselves often unclear concerning legal issues in social work.[26,102,119,144] Furthermore, student learning is heavily dependent on reinforcement in the practice arena[143,145] without which learning will not be retained.

Some commentators have stressed the need to integrate practice learning into law teaching in the academic curriculum,[146-7] for example by enabling a constructive dialogue between social work law teachers and practice teachers. Others have identified that the practice curriculum needs to expose students to the relevant legislation, to develop their skills in its application, and to experience planning and decision making that involves procedures and processes shaped, in part, by the legal rules.[81]

Ball and colleagues[24] provide an outline practice curriculum, distinguishing between practitioner as self, practitioner and agency, and practitioner and service user. Preston-Shoot[9] provides examples of the types of evidence that students may draw on in practice to demonstrate their competence in such core competences as assessment, communication, intervention and working in organisations. He also distinguishes between interim and final competence in terms of what students should be able to do. Braye[148] also explores this journey towards competence. She charts how students might progress from learning from experience and newly acquired theoretical knowledge to learning from doing; from practice to critical analysis of that practice and its context. She describes transitions that students need to make in practice – from knowing 'what' to managing roles and purposes; from gaining information to deciding what needs to happen and why; and managing the practice and value dilemmas involved. Case studies and learning from critical incidents are useful methods here.

Blumenfield and colleagues[149] provide an example of one approach to practice learning, namely a legal consultation programme in a teaching hospital. Cases were used to illustrate legal content. Case discussion was found to be an effective means of considering legal and ethical issues as workers had to integrate their learning into specific interventions. Although no details are given as to how and from whom data were collected, evaluation was positive, with a view that such groups provided an efficient and productive learning opportunity.

What combination of teaching and learning methods are used, and indeed of assessment strategies, should be related directly to the learning outcomes desired.[62] The key conundrum here is what makes knowledge stick. Evidence suggests that learning about legal duties is often not retained in practice and that loss of learning can occur almost immediately.[26,97,150-1] Indeed, Woodcock[85] found that computer-assisted learning tended to reinforce understanding but that knowledge acquired was not necessarily retained. This may be because academic learning is insufficiently linked to practice, failing to connect the law and social work, or to engage students on a personal level with the context of what they are learning.[135] However, loss of learning may also indicate shortcomings with didactic education whereas the use of case studies alongside skill development workshops and subject-based inputs promotes the integration of knowledge and skills for effective understanding and action.[119,135]

Additionally, as the breadth and depth to be covered is so extensive that, within a time-limited and crowded curriculum not everything can be covered, one focus should be on the process of learning. Students need to take into their own continuing professional development responsibility for updating their knowledge and skills, and the means with which to engage in this activity. Thus, Ward and Salter[121] and Bone and Hinett[152] suggest that skills development should include an emphasis on preparing students to respond to future growth in the law.

### 2.3.4 Who should teach?

Some commentators are clear that teaching, learning and assessment of law in social work education should involve lawyers.[22,119] This appears to be based on research findings that indicate that students are more likely to see themselves as well equipped in relation to legal knowledge where social work academic and law teachers work cooperatively together. Forgey and Colarossi[107] provide an example of joint teaching, in relation to domestic violence, where the law and social work tutors were able to model collaboration, adopt discrete roles in simulation exercises, and appropriately challenge each other and the student group. Stevenson[3] supports a joint teaching approach, arguing that students benefit from exposure to different professional attitudes and approaches, and to modelling inter-professional cooperation that is central to much practice.

However, Ball et al[146] and Terry[102] bemoan the shortage of appropriately qualified law teachers, believing this to be because the content of any social work law curriculum is seen as low status in law schools. Ridley[11] indeed points to the isolation of law teachers teaching non-lawyers from other law lecturers. They and other writers[28,106,149] argue the paramount need to avoid using law teachers with too little knowledge of social work, and social work tutors with too little knowledge of law. In research among mental health nurse tutors, Nash[98] found a lack of understanding of legislation.

Some writers suggest the involvement of guest speakers, who can provide real-world examples of the applications of legal rules and address key issues in practice such as confidentiality and ethics.[29,58,79,125]

However, less adequate would be a curriculum that relies extensively on visiting lecturers.[146]

## 2.3.5 Preparation

Academic staff, particularly in an integrated curriculum model, need to ensure effective inclusion of legal content.[27] When law and social work academics work together preparation will be necessary to ensure that they do not communicate erroneous stereotypes[122] but model professional interaction[107] having addressed in their planning the impact of such issues as power and status.

Practice teachers may lack confidence in their knowledge and competence, and may be anxious about assessing students when they feel out of contact with what students are learning in the academic curriculum. Consideration should be given to the use of seminars, course material and law updates.[26,82,144,147]

From an academic law perspective, Byles and Soetendorp[62] advise that staff should know their own values and experiences but also understand the relevance of law to the discipline they are working in. Preparation should involve identifying the strengths and challenges for the lawyer and for the discipline specialist. Traditional teaching styles and approaches may have to be adjusted to those more familiar for the students concerned.

## 2.3.6 How should students' learning be assessed?

Ball[153] suggested that traditional academic approaches were inadequate for testing students' ability to apply law in practice. However, a variety of methods of assessment are reported in the literature. One emerging principle appears to be that of alignment in order that students perceive as relevant the tasks they are being set. Assessment methods should be related to the practice context and types of activities and judgements that students will engage with in practice.[11,85,151-2] Braye and Preston-Shoot[4,135] use this to support assessment by case study, and it is implicit in Eadie and Ward's[119] use of scenarios. Preston-Shoot and colleagues[97] suggest that the use of case studies enables students to develop and demonstrate an integrated and flexible approach to implementation of the law. Where this involves a modified or evolving case study/scenario, this argument is even stronger since it requires students to demonstrate their ability to handle situations where application of the law does not necessarily follow a neat sequence.[9,84,147] The principle also extends to how students are assessed in the practice curriculum. Here, the suggestion is that the practice curriculum should assess skills in using the law, and the application of values and knowledge to the decision-making process.[151] Braye and Preston-Shoot[135] and Hogg and colleagues[150] provide questions with which practice teachers and students can assess the latter's social work law competence. Other possibilities include the use of a portfolio of legal materials as evidence, including the analysis of cases to identify the law and how or why it was (not) applied.[146]

Henderson and colleagues[84] use oral assessment for the same reason since it places students in a situation that mirrors the practice context. Oral assessment, they argue, allows examiners to gauge a student's knowledge and understanding, problem-solving ability and interpersonal competence. Written examinations, they suggest, divorce knowledge from its practical application.

Carter[106] also recommends oral questioning of students on cases but links this with open book tests and presentation of legal research papers. Other assessment methods include the use of portfolios, comprising project work, case summaries, observation reports and records, and the use of workbooks to guide and structure learning and to bridge learning in academic and practice curricula.[84,147]

Drawing on their experience of teaching accountancy and business students, Ridley[11] and Woodcock[85] use assessed library tasks, to enhance student confidence in using research tools, and peer assessment of seminar tasks, to trigger discussion of criteria used for assessment. Woodcock[85] also presents an evaluation of different assessment techniques. Students appear to value, for example, dispute resolution tasks, where teams take opposing sides, since it is seen as mirroring practice and as assisting the development of their understanding of the legal framework. Oral presentations and assessment of their knowledge of an issue requiring legal knowledge is seen to strengthen their skills in applying the law to practice. Bailey[118] also uses oral examinations to check students' level of understanding.

Some writers present detailed evaluations of assessment methods. For instance, Oliver and Huxley[136-7] researched the use of true/false questions and multiple-choice questions. They found the former to be a valid test of legal aspects of social work knowledge. The latter were especially valued by students and were found to be of predictive value. They also compared computer-assisted learning with paper and pen exercises. The former took less time and obtained a marked student preference for the teaching and testing of mental health law knowledge. Students were less satisfied, however, with trying to extrapolate good practice from computer-assisted learning. True/false questions were more popular among students than multiple-choice questions, but they performed better on the latter. Perhaps this evidence points to the need for several assessment methods to engage students and to test their knowledge and skills.

Henderson and colleagues[84] report student views on the use of oral examinations. Besides student anxiety ahead of assessment, which appears common in relation to social work law, they felt that this method prepared them fairly well for the reality of practice and they appreciated the opportunity to reflect on their decision making. The majority felt that it tested their knowledge of the legal rules but they questioned whether they retained their learning subsequently, a point raised by Braye and Preston-Shoot[4] when searching through the use of case studies for approaches that would make knowledge stick.

Endeshaw[115] found no clear preference among students for particular types of assessment methods, although oral examinations and project work were valued. Byles and Soetendorp[62] suggest the use of both formative and summative assessment and point to how demotivating it can be for students to repeat identical assessment methods in different modules. They suggest that assessment is used to inform the ways in which students learn and that assessment and learning activities should be linked to the outcomes desired. Among the methods they recommend are the use of debates and presentations, multiple choice questions, and reflective logs that require students to engage in self-assessment. They also ask students to review articles, write reports on the legal implications of a case or issue, or pen guidance notes on particular legislative provisions. Blyth and colleagues[81] make a similar proposal, namely that students might write a briefing note for service users on a particular legal point.

Skwarok[116] and Braye and colleagues[133] ask students to prepare for and contribute to class activity surrounding a case. Assessment, which includes a report of their self-assessment, is based on their completion of required reading, their contribution to group learning, their collection of legal documents and arguments, and a written analysis of the legal rules and practice issues in the case concerned. Braye and colleagues[133] include positive student evaluation of the effectiveness of this approach. Forgey and Colarossi[107] also use self-assessment but add peer assessment on the sharing of knowledge and expertise. They too use case examples to enable students to identify the roles and responsibilities of social workers and lawyers, to discuss collaboration and conflicts between the two professions, to link theory with practice, and to analyse such phases as engagement, assessment and investigation. Bone and Hinett[152] advocate self-assessment since it introduces students to making judgements about standards and quality. Ehrlich and Ehrlich[122] suggest the use of pre and post-testing of students to see whether teaching and learning has impacted on the attitudes held about the law and its interface with practice.

There is a small literature on the timing of assessment. Reviewing the evidence, Preston-Shoot[151] concludes that academic assessment is appropriately located just before the final practice learning opportunity. This allows students to benefit from the integration of law into the wider curriculum and from specialist teaching in relation to client groups. However, the introduction of the three-year social work degree opens up the possibility of using assessment at different levels to enable students to demonstrate progression in their learning through the degree.[152] The more innovative methods of assessment can then be introduced as students progress through their degree studies in order to promote responsibility for, and encourage deeper learning, and to widen out and consolidate the skills being promoted.

## 2.4 Connecting law and social work

### 2.4.1 Ambivalence

Both North American and UK commentators agree that relationships between social workers and lawyers can be strained, characterised by antagonism and distrust.[78-9,109,122] They also recognise that students frequently approach law learning and legal systems with fear, lack of confidence and discomfort. This appears related to images of authority, lack of familiarity with legal procedures, language and settings, consciousness of the knowledge required and responsibilities carried, and a fear of ignorance or being exposed as lacking credibility.[5,9,27,29,31,79]

Commentators also agree that students may approach law and its implementation by agencies with a view that barriers to lawful and ethical practice appear intractable. Consequently, they abandon trying to change organisational policies and practices and require the same of their clients. [21,68] Accordingly, they find it hard to locate possibilities for empowerment within the application of the legal rules.

## 2.4.2 Basic objective

In facilitating social work law learning and establishing the linkages between law and social work against this background, several writers articulate a core principle. Thus, Wilson and James[154] see the function of law learning as being to locate the client as the central concern. Social work objectives are primary, with the legal means to achieve these ends secondary. The aim is not to transform social workers into mini lawyers but rather to ensure that they have a thorough knowledge of social work, law and the relationship between them.

Others agree that the aim is not to create legal experts. Rather, it is to know how social work is shaped by law, how legal rules may promote and protect client rights, where legal rules may be found, and under what circumstances individual practitioners might be held accountable for their practice. [27,101,106] Similar observations are offered by those reviewing law teaching to business students[115-16] and across various professional disciplines. [62] Law teaching is best done in the context of the subject area, providing legal education to enable students to operate effectively in their environment using legal concepts and rules. There are parallels here with the discussion about the nature of the relationship between law and social work (see earlier discussion).

## 2.4.3 The relevance of law to social work

A number of commentators have been anxious to demonstrate that the law is pertinent to everyday social work practice, and, at a lesser extent, that social work is relevant to everyday legal practice in its broadest sense. This review has not included articles that are exclusively about practice that engages the knowledge and skills of both legal and social work practitioners working together, but has included a brief overview of those where the educational implications of such joint working has been explored. One surprising finding is that the history of such literature in the US goes back to the early 1970s. For example, Katkin[155] presented an overview of the roles of lawyers and social workers in the youth justice system in the US, from which was derived a critique of the educational curriculum and a proposal for bringing social work and law education together. Likewise, Oneglia and Orlin,[156] again writing in the US, present a model for combined private practice between 'attorneys' and social workers in 'domestic relations'. Building on a theoretical discussion of the relationship between law and social work using a number of case examples, the article argues that the practice of attorneys and social workers should be closer in "domestic relations cases". This means that lawyers should take on board counselling skills and, conversely, social workers should enhance their role in court. A much more recent US article by Slaght[157] explores the relationship between social work and 'law enforcement agents'. It presents an argument that law enforcers need social work skills and that the law enforcement context of much of social work needs to be recognised, a theoretical point that would probably be taken for granted in the UK context. However, the article takes this one stage further and provides examples of places where law enforcement agents are taught alongside social workers.

Other writers take a broader conceptualisation of law and its relevance to social work. Writing in the context of social work in India, Gangoli and Solanki[70] present a feminist critique of the law related to sexuality and sexual offences, with an exploration of the implications for social work and social work education, concluding:

> A social worker educator needs to develop conceptual frameworks that will enable students to critique law, to develop an understanding that there exists a continuum of oppression in civil and criminal law. Simultaneously, students can be trained to use law to benefit oppressed sections of society.

Adopting a narrower focus in an Australian context, Wilson et al[158] deployed quantitative research methods in order to demonstrate that social workers failed to acknowledge the importance of law in their everyday practice with older people. While this research focuses on practice, specifically the entry of older people to residential care, its implications for social work education are self-evident. One of the significant features of this research is that it explored law and the context of work with vulnerable adults, and did so through a robust research strategy that involved both social workers and service users (postal surveys, focus groups and individual interviews with a sample of 377 people).

Smith[120] points to the importance in the UK context of social workers understanding how judges approach childcare cases, define standards of practice, and view the evidential standing and performance of practitioners. Focusing on court work, she argues that social workers need to understand how and why courts might intervene in their work, and be prepared by their employers for the experience of giving evidence. This underlines the need for cooperation between local authorities (that employ social workers) and the courts, and also indicates the need to educate social workers through the use of case law. This is amplified in Vernon et al,[159] who presented a broader analysis of the relationship between social work and the law with a view to establishing what is legally competent professional practice.

Moving to the broadest structural level, Howe[63] presented a macro overview of the relationship between 'welfare law' and social work practice, arguing that social work fails to understand that the state controls social work practice through the operation of the law:

> The occupation does not possess technical skills which allow it to transcend the characteristics ascribed to different client groups by welfare laws, procedures and resources. Practice remains essentially tied and specific to the client group, reflecting the perceptual outlook that the law imposes on each client group.

Thus the law plays a key role in social work. Two implications arise from this. First, social workers need to recognise their roles. For example, Lynch and Brawley[29] consider three roles surrounding court work. There are those who work in the judicial system, those who work outside it but who encounter it when they present evidence and reports, and there are those who require knowledge of how the legal system works in order to advise clients appropriately. Similarly, Preston-Shoot et al[109] identify a social work law continuum as the site for interaction between legal and social work practitioners. The degree to which the environment is the construct of law or social work will depend on the context.

Second, this approach clearly implies recognition of the need to address the broader role of law in regulating social work, and in setting the boundaries and context within which social work is 'allowed' to operate. The broader context of social work is also recognised by Braye and Preston-Shoot[46,160] who explore issues of accountability in social work and argue for a partnership between law and social work in relation to service user rights and community care service provision. The educational implications of this broader context are set out most clearly in Preston-Shoot, Roberts and Vernon[37,109] through the development of a theoretical and conceptual framework that explores commonalities and differences, particularly in relation to the use of language. Here is mapped out the terrain of social work law, with a powerful argument in favour of the acknowledgement of a specific academic discipline called social work law.

More specific implications for social work law teaching are explored in subsequent chapters, which address the specific ways in which legal issues might be incorporated into the curriculum.

## 2.4.4 Learning together

The relevance of law to social work, and social work to law, has led some commentators to explore possibilities of joint education and training. In a US survey, Lemmon[28] found few joint degree programmes and little evidence of law students accessing social work modules. He concluded that the potential for interdisciplinary collaboration was not being realised. Jankovic and Green[27] and Henderson et al[84] argue similarly that ignorance of other professionals' roles impedes joint working.

Weil[161] promotes the merits of interprofessional collaboration between lawyers and social workers by offering continuous professional development training in court work. A result of this collaborative training was that interprofessional practice was viewed more positively and professionals' perceptions of each other changed. Ehrlich and Ehrlich[122] provide an example of law and social work students working jointly with older people. They suggest that joint working enables students to confront stereotypes about which professional group is more effective or objective. However, they emphasise the importance of prior preparation of law and social work staff in order to shift attitudes and develop joint work with students. Madden[31] offers an example of a law clinic where lawyers and social workers work together on cases. Such experience enables students to become aware of their own assumptions (about law and/or social work) and to develop knowledge of other professionals' roles, values and priorities. It also provides an opportunity to coordinate expertise into one helping system that is better able to recognise and respond to individual need and to the legal system.[64]

Focusing on domestic violence, Forgey and Colarossi[107] also consider collaboration between lawyers and social workers, and interdisciplinary knowledge and skills teaching to encourage respect for each other's roles, purposes and codes of practice. They suggest that such joint training should follow once students have obtained a solid grounding in the values, principles, knowledge and skills of their own profession. The potential of joint training, they argue, is to achieve a common knowledge base of legislation and to provide a context for cooperation when seeking to influence policy or to intervene in actual situations. This is achieved through a dialogue that involves exchange of views about roles, and reflection on the influence of attitudes.

From Canada comes a curriculum critique and proposal for bringing social work and law education together. This is presented by Sklar and Torczyner,[162] who report on an innovative programme that offered a joint law/MSW degree. A rationale for the curriculum is supplemented by specific examples of what exactly was taught and how.

Homer[143] discusses issues of inter-professional education at post-qualifying level surrounding child protection. This provides an opportunity to explore role functions and cross-over points, and to counteract negative stereotyping. It enables practitioners and managers from different agencies to know how they might challenge decision making. However, the effectiveness of such opportunities can be limited by the limited time given over to such programmes and by the varying levels of knowledge brought by the participants.

Examples in the literature of law and social work students learning together are few. The literature does not systematically consider or research at what point in their professional education law and social work students might most effectively learn together. However, Forgey and Colarossi[107] do conclude that completion of a foundation social work and law course is advisable before further subject specialisation and joint training. This conclusion is derived from an analysis of students' performance in assessment.

## 2.4.5 Commonalities

Writers who offer examples of social workers and lawyers learning together sometimes highlight that their (individual) roles and tasks contain more similarities than differences. Ehrlich and Ehrlich[122] point to their concern with human relationships, social responsibility and people in stressful situations, and their involvement in investigation and contact with other systems. Barker[100] argues that the two professions serve the same purpose and hold similar respect for people's rights and welfare. Katkin[155] suggests that they hold three orientations in common. An orientation to effectiveness is concerned with skills in problem definition and problem solving. An orientation to communications focuses on oral and written reporting and on documentary analysis. An orientation to evidence is concerned with evaluating facts.

Other writers, such as Forgey and Colarossi,[107] list shared skills. These include advocacy, engagement, problem identification and assessment. They embrace fact finding, system change, and concerns with fairness and social justice. They include research, interviewing, drafting documents and negotiating for particular outcomes. If these skills are concerned with the content of interactions with clients, both professions are also concerned with process skills, particularly empathic listening and genuineness.

White[163] notes that the roles of social workers and legal advisors can overlap, at least in relation to the 'appropriate adult' in the police station, perhaps suggesting that occasionally, at least, policy makers see commonalities when it comes to protecting some people at risk.

However, other writers stress the differences. Phillips[8] observed hostility between lawyers and social workers and believed this to arise from different languages and social workers' images of law's real or imagined purposes. Terry[102] outlines the different relationships that social workers and lawyers have with their clients.

Forgey and Colarossi[107] and Katkin[155] also recognise that there are differences, whether in power and status, roles in legal proceedings, or the confidential nature of their communications with clients, all of which can be barriers to collaboration. Moreover, to the degree that both professions use common terms but mean different things, such as rights or needs,[109] the question remains whether legal and social work practitioners can bridge their different discourses, their different ways of thinking and talking.

The focus in the literature, however, has tended to emphasise linkages from law in the direction of social work. Far less common, but no less important[111] is what social work might have to offer legal education and practice. In this direction, the papers by Brayne[164] and Galowitz[165] are honourable exceptions. Both Nash[98] and Henderson et al[84] point to weaknesses in curricula for nurses, and a lack of knowledge within health professions, about mental health legislation, a gap that experienced mental health social work practitioners and educators would be able to fill.

## 2.5  Shaping the curriculum

### 2.5.1 Foundations for the curriculum

Mirroring discussion in earlier chapters on core content, context and objectives, Dickens[125] itemises four principles of teaching law in social work. Based on a research analysis of childcare law education, including interviews with 54 social services and legal staff in local authorities, the principles are:

- acknowledgement of the wider context
- the need for discrete and integrated law components
- connecting law learning to social work practice
- demonstrating legal competence in practice learning.

In reviewing themes that arose at a conference on social work law teaching and assessment, Preston-Shoot[151] also pinpoints the need to prepare students to manage the practice context. This incorporates negotiation of conflicting imperatives and dilemmas surrounding whether, how, for what purpose and when to intervene in people's lives.

Meanwhile, curriculum guidance[24,146] differentiates between:

- knowledge (of the law relating to practice, of legal structures and processes, and of the relationship between practice and law)
- values (the interface between legal provisions and core social work principles)

- skills (assessment, planning, communication, support, report writing, multi-disciplinary working, and counteracting discrimination).

## 2.5.2 Towards a social work law curriculum – generic and specialist

What should be taught at basic qualifying level and what should be located in more specialist and/or post-qualifying training? Writing from a US perspective, Lemmon[28] proposes an academic curriculum that moves from the general to the specific, with specialist inputs determined by job roles and addressed by continuing education and training. Madden[31] locates a general introduction to law for social workers early in qualifying training, with more specialist client, issue and role-based inputs following on. He, too, emphasises continuing education to cover such matters as involvement in legal proceedings and case handling.

In the UK context, Blyth and colleagues,[81] focusing on education social work, suggest that 20% of curriculum content should be specialised. Ball and colleagues[146] present an extended core curriculum. This begins with the legal context of social work and moves on to client group based content. It embraces work with children and families, disability, older people, mental health, aspects of poverty and discrimination, and criminal justice. They reserve for post-qualifying training reinforcement or consolidation of social work law learning, and practice in courtroom skills and report writing. They specifically ring-fence for post-qualifying education detailed knowledge of the Mental Health Act 1983, adoption, the work of children's guardians, and detailed knowledge of regulations relating to looked-after children and adults in residential care. Later curriculum guidance[24] repeats this formulation.

## 2.5.3 Towards a social work law curriculum – knowledge and skills

From a US context, Lynch and Brawley[29] offer a core curriculum, with particular reference to criminal justice. Jankovic and Green[27] and Kopels and Gustavsson[30] also offer formulations that identify both knowledge to be learned and skills to be acquired and evidenced. Lemmon[28] and Finley and Goldstein[114] offer other comprehensive overviews of the law content in the US social work curriculum. The former presents a national survey of law courses in social work programmes, applying findings on current education practice to a previously devised conceptual model. It contains some reference to continuing professional development and to methods, fieldwork placements and law as social change. The second concentrates on what a survey of courses found in relation to teaching ethics and legal issues.

In the UK context, Blyth and colleagues[81] set out what they regard as the minimum level of legal competence for education social work, covering knowledge, skills, assessment and methods of teaching and learning. More general curriculum guidance[24,146] outlines the legal knowledge base for understanding legal systems and substantive areas of law.

Other writers focus on identifying skills. For example, following implementation of the Children Act 1989, the Family and Child Care Law Training Group[166] identified skill needs. Those covered included communication, partnership working with clients, multi-agency working, assessment and consideration of race and culture. Eadie and Ward[119] are among those who link enquiry skills to substantive legal knowledge – skills in locating and reading legal materials, conceptualising law in social work, identifying and interpreting legal issues, problem solving, and recognising the impact of values.

A further question relates to the timing of law learning. Broadbent and White[105] suggest that input on basic principles of law should be taught early on in qualifying education. Hogg and colleagues[150] recommend that some teaching of general and specific law must take place before the first placement in order to enable students to ask pertinent questions. More detailed understanding of general and specific law can follow.

## 2.5.4 Practice curriculum

By comparison with the academic curriculum, the practice curriculum is under-theorised and less developed. Indeed, it can sometimes be erroneously presented by practitioners as simply knowledge and application of agency procedures.[26,144]

Part of the spotlight here has been on practice teachers' readiness for their role in assessing students' legal competence. Lancashire Polytechnic[147] found practice teachers to be anxious about what law learning they could provide. Hogg et al[150] researched the encounters between practice teachers and students and concluded that there was a lack of knowledge of legislation, confusion about the nature of law, and inconsistency in teaching approaches between college and placement. Practice teachers held widely differing attitudes as to what constituted legal issues in social work. Preston-Shoot et al[26,144] reported on research into practice teachers' views of law content of social work education, summed up in the titles of their two papers. Reporting on a later attempt to address practice teacher concerns through a post-qualifying programme, Preston-Shoot[167] analyses practice teachers' attitudes and the agency context for achieving social work law learning in practice placements.

Part of the spotlight has also focused on how to enable students to acquire resources to sustain resilience amidst the contradiction and uncertainty that is social work practice,[68,125] and to maintain decision making and practice that is both lawful and ethical.[21,105]

There has also been some theory building in respect of the content of the practice curriculum. Ball et al[24] outlined a basic design, proposing a generic knowledge of social work law because of the complexity of people's lives and needs. Thus, an in-depth knowledge of one particular area of law, chosen by reference to the location of the practice learning opportunity, had to be accompanied by the ability to make connections between different areas of social work law. Equally important was the ability to transfer knowledge and skills to new settings. Preston-Shoot[9] develops this guidance by linking core social work competences to legal responsibilities. That is, students must demonstrate the ability to address need, promote inter-agency working, minimise risk, provide information and services, and to know when decisions are required. All this requires the identification and application of relevant law. He also differentiates between interim and final competence.

A research project specifically focusing on the practice curriculum took a similar approach.[147] This project also recognised the problem of providing a curriculum spanning the wide variety of practice learning opportunities. Accordingly, it recommended the identification not of specific legal competences but of competences with legal components; for example, highlighting legal knowledge within advocacy practice or understanding of clients' rights or use by students of supervision. This, it argued, also reflected the integrated way in which social workers were expected to use the law. The project also emphasised the importance of students developing transferable skills, and developing skills with which they could research and update their legal knowledge. In common with writers focusing on the academic curriculum, the skills covered include communication, information provision, problem analysis and resolution, use of authority, recording, and the identification of needs, rights, powers and duties. What this project was looking for in students was legally underpinned, skills-based application of a placement-specific knowledge base.

## 2.5.5 Continuing professional development

Social workers do report on-going law learning needs. A survey of 48 qualified social workers practising in legal services programmes for people on low incomes found that 80% highlighted that continuing professional development should contain workshops on legal issues; 70% identified consultation or supervision with legal practitioners as a learning need.[168] Mental health community agency staff[169] and nurses[10] have also pinpointed the importance of regular updates on legal issues.

Evidence from practitioners and managers in the US and UK suggests, however, that information about new developments in law is not being disseminated to social workers.[26,100,144,153,167] This is potentially very serious given the rapidity with which the legal rules change.[28-9,167] When registered with social care councils, both practitioners and their employers will be responsible for ensuring that individual social workers and the workforce as a whole maintain their knowledge base in order to work lawfully, safely and effectively.[170] This joint responsibility was, however, noted long ago but with variable responses in terms of in-service training.[102]

Reported methods of providing continuing professional development include a legal clinic,[149] computer-assisted distance learning,[137-8] and a post-qualifying programme for practice teachers and academic staff.[167] However, based on research into post-qualifying education programmes, concern has also been reported[28] that universities may not be prioritising the legal dimensions to practice within continuing professional development courses.

Regular refresher training is required to ensure continued competence in relation to legislation[8,96] and to acquire and update more specialist legal knowledge in relation, for example, to the role of Appropriate Adult.[163,171] However, the literature contains criticisms of variable approaches to training for specialist Appropriate Adult and Approved Social Worker roles[145,163] and of short course models of continuing professional development.[143,172] Such models may be insufficient to cover the knowledge required and the complexity of practice demands, or to reinforce the learning process within the work arena. Agencies need to give more attention to how they can enable their employees, for example through Internet access, to maintain competent knowledge during practice and how they can assess the effectiveness of these inputs.[143,171] Read and Clements[173] describe a development aimed at reinforcing the value of in-service training. Training on the law relating to disabled children was part of a process that also included participants reviewing and setting goals for their work with their managers, consultation between trainers and participants relating to these goals, and follow-up. Continuing professional development, therefore, was explicitly linked into a system of performance review. While the long-term impact of this approach is not reported, initial evaluation indicated that participants appreciated the participation of their managers, felt increasingly confident in using the law to reinforce their professional judgements, and valued the peer learning and problem-solving opportunities.

The need is similar for nurses to keep up-to-date with new developments,[103,171] but Cox[99] argues that there has been little recognition of the need to rectify among doctors and nurses poor levels of legal knowledge. However, Fisher[174] provides one example of an educational programme, this time for hospital staff, to raise awareness of the importance of good record keeping. Both lawyers and nurses contribute to this programme and knowledge gained is consolidated by a requirement that participants audit their own practice and return to present the results.

## 2.5.6 Engaging with learners

One thread running throughout the literature concerns how best to ensure that students learn, and with how to engage students with the problems they will meet in practice. Bogolub[82] offers examples of ways in which this might be achieved through case examples and role-play, acknowledging the need to integrate legal knowledge with skills. Braye and Preston-Shoot[4] set out a conceptual framework for teaching and learning social work law that acknowledges the tensions between various competing factors that impinge on the curriculum and the pedagogical process. A powerful argument is presented for teaching social work law in principle and also for adopting a case study approach. By this is meant offering students real or fictitious case examples that facilitate exploration of key points about the law in every day social work practice. This approach can be further developed as a means of assessing students' understanding, either through academic assignments or practice learning. In a similar vein, Eadie and Ward[119] promote a scenario approach to teaching and assessment, offering examples and some student commentary.

More recent developments have included problem-based and enquiry-based learning where the focus is on group learning derived from a shared challenge.[117,123,132-3] Another recent approach adopts an ecological paradigm of practice in childcare, arguing that this encourages a broader approach which enhances high quality, less discriminatory practice.[175] Interest has also been shown recently in online learning specifically in relation to welfare law[129] and law relating to vulnerable adults.[127]

## 2.6   Conclusion: what is the evidence base?

The debate about what constitutes legal education is to some extent mirrored in debates concerning social work. The 'Pericles and the plumber' debate initiated by Twining[48] has resonance with the debate in social work about where responsibility lies for teaching social work skills and practice. For example, it is reflected in the knowledge review on assessment in social work education.[176] A key difference between university social work and law courses is that degrees in the former now constitute professional qualifications in themselves, whereas first degrees in law are primarily academic degrees that students may then use as a passport to entry to professional qualifying courses of various kinds. Hence, the reluctance of law schools both in Britain and the US to engage in legal practice per se (and assessment of key skills such as advocacy) contrasts with social work education in the UK where the practice curriculum is an intrinsic part of the whole pedagogical process.

The literature on legal and social work education needs to be read therefore bearing this in mind. Likewise, it should be remembered that much of the literature referred to here comes from the US, where social work practice is very different, being principally a free-market enterprise dominated by a contractual relationship between social workers and their clients. It is probably for this reason that much of the literature referred to in this review that emanates from the US is preoccupied with demonstrating that law does have more than some tangential relevance to social work. By and large, a British audience would not need to be so convinced, since the majority of social workers in the UK are employed by local authorities or agencies contracted to the statutory sector. Hence the concern is to show, evidently in Australia as much as the UK, that it is the degree of ignorance about the law demonstrated by social workers that needs to be addressed. The point appears to have been well made and in Britain by the early 1990s, the debate essentially centres on how law should be integrated into the social work curriculum rather than whether it should or why it should.

Nevertheless it may be worth summarising the key points that emerge from the debate about the role of law in social work education. First, it appears to be now widely recognised that law sets the context for social work practice, and broader aspects of the law need to be taught so that they include a critique of the law itself. Students need to know about issues of accountability and the role of the law in promoting people's rights and in empowerment generally. Some commentators, for example Roche,[88] go further and argue that a discussion of ethics and rights (jurisprudence) is an important component of law teaching. In essence, students need to be provided with conceptual tools in order to understand law, rather than learning simply what the law says. In this way, students should also be able to understand how the social work role intercepts with, and interconnects with, that of other professionals.

The debate about what should actually be taught and how emerged in the UK in the late 1990s, and there is a growing literature on this topic. Even so, there appears to be comparatively little on methods and processes of teaching, although there are some useful contributions to what should be included in a law curriculum and what social workers need to know about the law. Unsurprisingly, there is not complete consensus on this, and much of the work is descriptive. Indeed, looking at this aspect of the literature there is precious little on evidence-based pedagogy, and a dearth of literature on carer and user involvement. There are some useful contributions in relation to professional learning and some valuable examples of innovative teaching practice, including online learning. Yet, the pressing need appears to be for evidence-based teaching and learning in social work law. This evidence-based approach to teaching, learning and assessment should be constructed in such a way that the everyday experience of service users and carers is integrated into student learning, and assessment takes place not just at universities but also throughout practice learning, both at qualifying and post-qualifying levels.

Since few empirical papers were located, subsequent research projects should focus on a systematic evaluation of the outcomes for practice of different approaches to teaching, learning and assessment of law in social work education. Such projects could research student reactions to different approaches and evaluate the degree to which diverse methods enable knowledge and skill acquisition, influence attitudes and perceptions, and lead to beneficial change for service users and employing organisations.

This review of the literature invites the conclusion that it is difficult to say with any certainty what approaches to curriculum delivery work. Empirical studies in the UK have focused on the general outcome of professional training in social work, including some reference to, and feedback by, students on law teaching.[5,25] By and large, however, the literature does not research the quality and effectiveness of different methods of teaching, learning and assessment of law in social work education. With a few exceptions (for example[22,137-8]), it does not report outcomes in terms of qualifying students' knowledge, skills or attitudes, nor measure change over the duration of a programme. Where an evaluation of student opinion is undertaken, this is usually obtained immediately after completion of a course (for example[84,119,133]). It cannot therefore determine whether changes in knowledge, skills or attitudes are sustained over time. Such gaps in evidence-based pedagogy and outcomes point to next steps in research and theory building of the discipline of social work law.

Finally, research (see, for a summary[21]), and inquiries (for example[95]), continue to demonstrate how good practice can become distorted within agencies. Indeed, Pithouse and Scourfield[177] observe the power of organisational culture to instil its own messages about what is competent practice. Training alone will be insufficient to hold students as qualified social workers to legal and ethical standards. The quality of supervision, management and support will also be critical[95,145] to practice outcomes where knowledge and skilled application of the legal rules is called upon. It is perhaps of concern, therefore, that there appears to remain evidence of the long-standing divergence between employers, service users and carers, students and social work academics regarding what social workers should know and be competent to do.[5,102]

# Practice survey

Suzy Braye and Michael Preston-Shoot

## 3.1 Methodology

### 3.1.1 Aims and scope of the survey

The purpose of the practice survey, in line with guidance from SCIE,[1] was to find, describe and consider examples of current practice in the teaching, learning and assessment of law in social work education. The survey sought to identify current practice in teaching, learning and assessment of law by providers of social work education in all four countries of the UK. As a result of the timing of the survey in relation to implementation of the new social work degree requirements, it elicited information about both the existing Diploma in Social Work (DipSW) and the new degrees. Information was sought on factors such as:

- aims and objectives of law teaching
- learning outcomes
- curriculum content
- teaching and learning strategies
- user and carer involvement
- forms of assessment
- the rationale for all of these.

### 3.1.2 Sources of information

a) A postal questionnaire was distributed to 78 social work programme providers in England, representing the total number of those providing either a DipSW programme, a new degree programme or both. Of those, 32 were returned in time for inclusion in this review, representing a return rate of 41%. The questionnaire was piloted with two programmes, and amended to take account of feedback. A copy of the final version may be found at Appendix 3.

The questionnaire was designed to be completed by the member of staff with the best overview of law teaching on the programmes in each institution. Predominantly responses were from academic staff responsible for providing and convening the law teaching, or programme leaders where no specific law module existed.

The researchers requested follow-up telephone interviews with a sample of 19 respondents. Selection was based on identification by the researchers of approaches that exemplified particular methods of teaching, learning or assessment, or took an apparently innovative, uncommon or otherwise distinctive approach, as judged by the original questionnaire response. Telephone interviews, conducted by a single researcher, took place with 16 respondents, representing a response rate of 84% of those approached.

b) A slightly condensed version of the same questionnaire was used as the basis for telephone interviews with academic staff on programmes in Scotland, Wales and Northern Ireland. The change of approach, from postal questionnaire to telephone interview, arose from the experience of an early low postal response rate in England, and the fact that the much smaller number of providers in Scotland, Wales and Northern Ireland permitted a more individualised approach. All telephone interviews were undertaken by the same single researcher. In Scotland, six out of the nine providers were approached, resulting in six interviews (67% of all programmes). In Wales, five out of the six providers were approached, resulting in three interviews (50% of all programmes). In Northern Ireland, each of the two providers was approached, resulting in one interview (50%). All four countries of the UK were therefore represented in the responses received.

c) Respondents to both the postal questionnaire and the telephone interviews were asked to submit supporting materials, including module outlines, teaching materials and assessment tasks. Approximately 50% of all respondents provided supporting documentation of this kind, which was used to support the qualitative analysis and in some cases provided practice examples for this review.

d) Focus groups were conducted with students convened from two separate programmes in England, involving a total of three researchers and using a standard topic list (which may be found at Appendix 4). The focus groups were attended by a total of 27 DipSW students in both first and second years of their programmes. Ethnicity and gender were mixed (21 women, 6 men; 22 white, 5 black participants). There were 10 postgraduates and 17 undergraduates. Students were asked about their experiences of learning law, in both academic and practice contexts.

e) Focus groups were conducted with practice teachers associated with both programmes, involving a total of three researchers and using a standard topic list (which may be found at Appendix 5). The groups were attended by a total of 33 practice teachers. The groups contained both experienced and new practice teachers, both off-site and agency-based (statutory and independent) and included those supervising first and second placements. The groups were predominantly white (29 participants out of 33) and 27 of the 33 participants were women. Practice teachers were asked about their experiences of using the law in their own practice, and of helping students learn about the law while on practice placement.

f) Inspectors from the Care Councils in the four countries provided summary reports on external assessors' comments on law teaching, learning and assessment, derived from annual programme monitoring reports. Individual programmes were not identified. This information related to DipSW programmes in the academic year 2002-03 (that is, prior to the introduction of the new degree in any of the countries).

g) It was originally intended to undertake searches of university and college websites for teaching and learning material. Early piloting of this approach did not elicit any useful information, and this strategy was abandoned.

h) A broad range of stakeholder perspectives, including those of service users, was gathered through two consultation events, as outlined in the Introduction, working from briefing documents which may be found at Appendices 6 and 7.

### 3.1.3 Confidentiality, bias and ethics

Questionnaire respondents were identified by name and institution on their returns, but all personally identifying information has been removed in analysing and reporting on the data for this review. Where contributors of material (practice examples) are acknowledged by name, this is with their knowledge and consent. Participants in the focus groups remain anonymous within this review. Where participants in the consultation events are named, they have given permission for this.

Because the researchers are themselves teachers of law in social work education, with views and established education practices of their own, particular attention has been paid to the question of possible bias, both in the selection of respondents for follow-up telephone interviews and choice of questions asked, and in the analysis and reporting of the findings from all aspects of the survey. The core research group has been large and diverse enough to provide a range of perspectives on the data, and to ensure that the analysis has been fair and objective. Equally, because the researchers were based and experienced in the England context, consultants from Wales, Scotland and Northern Ireland were asked to read and advise on the data.

Every effort has been made to ensure that service users and carers participating in the consultation events were fully informed about the purposes of the research, that the information provided was accessible and that appropriate support for participation was available. It has been important for the researchers to hear the strength of the messages from service users and carers about both the limitations and potentials of social workers' engagement with the law, and to ensure that those perspectives inform the analysis and conclusions of this review.

### 3.1.4 Data entry and analysis

Data from the postal questionnaires and telephone interviews were entered and analysed using SPSS V.11 (Statistical Package for the Social Sciences), alongside additional manual thematic analysis of qualitative data. All focus groups were tape-recorded and the tapes transcribed, prior to manual thematic analysis of the data. Key themes, concerns and debates were identified from repeated reading of the transcript material, with subsequent organisation of the data within the thematic framework.

At the consultation events, notes were taken by at least two recorders at each event, and subsequently matched in order reliably to identify the themes emerging. The final records of discussions at the events were verified by participants who had attended. The synthesis of the views of external assessors was verified by the Care Council inspectors who provided the original data.

## 3.2 Questionnaire and telephone surveys of programmes

### 3.2.1 Background information on the institutions taking part

The timing of the survey posed some challenges, taking place as it did in the spring of 2004. The 2003-04 academic year was the first in which some institutions in England had introduced the new social work degree. Not all England institutions had done so, however, with a number due to start in 2004-05. In Northern Ireland, Scotland and Wales, new degree programmes were due to start in the academic years 2004-05 or 2005-06. In all four countries, therefore, DipSW programmes were still actively running, and indeed will continue to do so until all existing students have completed. Development work for the new degree was nonetheless well in hand, and in many cases had influenced perceptions of the existing programmes.

In the light of this diverse picture, the researchers decided to offer institutions in England the choice of responding to the survey in relation to either their new degree or their DipSW provision, with the potential differences captured through questions on retrospective or prospective changes. In Northern Ireland, Scotland and Wales, institutions were asked about their existing DipSW provision, with a question about prospective changes.

In England, a total of 32 programmes responded to the postal questionnaire, between them running 44 different social work qualification programmes.

**Figure 1: Proportion of responses relating to programme type (England)**

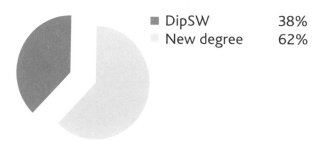

■ DipSW　　38%
□ New degree　62%

Nineteen institutions were between them providing 29 new degree programmes. Of those, 11 had only undergraduate programmes while eight had both undergraduate and postgraduate. Of these eight, at postgraduate Level, 5 were offering only Masters degrees, one was offering postgraduate diploma and two were offering both.

**Figure 2: Institutions and types of new degree programmes (England)**

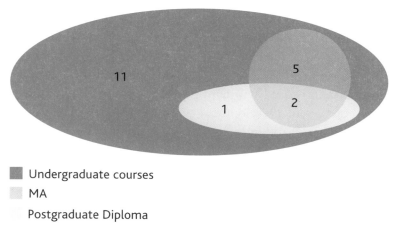

■ Undergraduate courses
□ MA
　Postgraduate Diploma

Thirteen institutions were between them providing 15 DipSW programmes. Of these, nine were involved in just DipHE or undergraduate provision, with three providing just Masters qualifications and one providing both.

## Figure 3: Institutions and types of DipSW programmes (England)

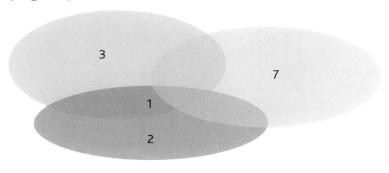

■ Undergraduate courses
■ MA/Postgraduate Diploma
□ Diploma/Higher education

Student numbers (full-time equivalent) varied considerably between programmes (from 18 to 120 on each year of undergraduate programmes and from 20 to 60 on postgraduate programmes), with undergraduate and new degree programmes tending towards larger student cohort sizes. Table 1 shows average student numbers.

## Table 1: Average student numbers on social work programmes (England)

|  | Under-graduate | Post-graduate | Institu-tional | New degree institutional | DipSW institu-tional |
|---|---|---|---|---|---|
| Average | 54 | 39 | 60 | 68 | 49 |

*Note:* Data in this calculation excludes figures from one institution that has 1,000 students, on the grounds that inclusion would skew the figures and give a false picture of programme and institutional numbers.

The six institutions in Scotland were between them running 12 programmes (six undergraduate, six postgraduate), with plans to replace this with five undergraduate and four postgraduate programmes with the introduction of the new degree. Programmes ranged in size, on available data, from eight to 40.

The three institutions in Wales were between them running three programmes (one undergraduate, two postgraduate) with plans for a shift (to two undergraduate, one postgraduate) with the introduction of the new degree. Programmes ranged in size, on available data, from 36 to 70.

The Northern Ireland institution was running a postgraduate programme, with plans to move to a three-year undergraduate programme and a two-year degree programme for graduates with relevant degrees.

### 3.2.2 Location, aims and content of law teaching and learning in the academic curriculum

In England, 28 (87%) of programmes delivered at least some of their law teaching thought discrete modules of learning, in which law was the primary focus.

**Figure 4: Proportion of institutions delivering law through discrete modules (England)**

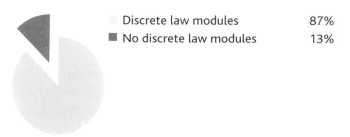

| | |
|---|---|
| Discrete law modules | 87% |
| No discrete law modules | 13% |

Where institutions provide both undergraduate and postgraduate teaching, the approach to this aspect of programme structure appears to remain the same across the levels. The trend with the introduction of the new degree appears to be towards more discrete module law teaching as indicated in Figure 5.

Figure 5: Trend towards discrete teaching in new degrees (England)

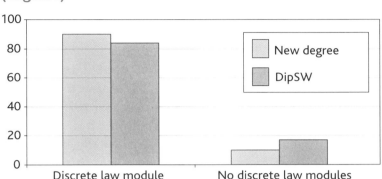

In Scotland, Wales and Northern Ireland, all programmes delivered law teaching in discrete modules.

Discrete law teaching in all countries is most commonly located in the first year of DipSW programmes, the first two years of the undergraduate programmes and the first year of postgraduate programmes, although in one programme law is delivered in a discrete module at all three undergraduate levels and in two-year postgraduate programmes it is not uncommon for certain aspects of law to be integrated with second year teaching.

In England student contact hours relating to law in discrete modules vary over a wide range. Calculation of average hours is more difficult because data were not given by all institutions but on the available data, average hours are as given below. It appears that although postgraduate programmes typically run over two years rather than three, law learning is not reduced by a proportionate amount, but is to some extent preserved within the allocation of timetable space.

Table 2: Student contact hours on law in discrete modules (England)

|  | Undergraduate programmes | Postgraduate programmes |
|---|---|---|
| Range of hours | 24-105 | 24-82 |
| Average hours | 60 | 50 |

In Scotland, Wales and Northern Ireland, the picture on contact hours is very similar. In Scotland, the range is 24-96, with an average of 49. In Wales the range is 20-95, with an average of 65. Contact hours in Northern Ireland were 70.

Of the programmes delivering discrete law modules, 82% of England programmes and all in Scotland, Wales and Northern Ireland also integrate some law teaching within other modules, but it proved impossible to identify the additional law contact hours delivered this way. The trend for integration appears to be increasing with the introduction of the new degree, with a number of programmes, particularly in Scotland, identifying enquiry-based approaches (such as problem-based learning or enquiry and action learning) as a significant development. Even so, it is anticipated that some discrete teaching will remain.

Where law is not delivered at all through discrete modules but is integrated with other subjects across the curriculum (as in four institutions in England, representing six programmes), the organising principles appear to be either:

- service user groupings (such as children or older people). One programme, for example, described having 'salami-sliced' the law module and integrated it with modules of teaching related to service user groups or
- functions of practice (such as assessing need or constructing interventions). In one new degree programme, for example, the academic learning is organised around the six Key Roles in the National Occupational Standards[19], and law teaching is integrated within this system.

Table 3: Student contact hours on law in integrated learning (England)

|  | Undergraduate programmes | Postgraduate programmes |
| --- | --- | --- |
| Range of hours | 22-81 | 24-42 |
| Average hours | 56 | 35 |

Contact hours related to identifiable law learning remain similar to those in discrete teaching models for undergraduate programmes, but drop markedly in postgraduate provision (although it must be noted that there are insufficient cases from which to draw any clear conclusions). The number of modules within which law learning is covered range between one and ten.

Institutions in all countries were asked about the rationale for locating law teaching as they did. Pedagogic advantages of discrete module teaching were seen to be the following:

- it provides a solid foundation of core knowledge that is recognisably 'law'
- it gives programmes a greater degree of control over the content of learning, avoiding the danger of overlaps and gaps in essential content and allaying fears over dilution of content in integrated models
- there can be an explicit focus on a set of skills for acquiring and using a specific kind of knowledge
- for most students, law is a distinctive and new discipline, which requires introduction in itself before it can sit easily alongside other themes of learning. Unless they know what they are looking for, students may not pick up the integrated law content in other modules. A discrete module 'tunes students in' to the importance of law and helps to allay anxiety
- it can act as a 'navigational aid' to which later learning can add complexity and detail
- it ensures that core content is taught by staff with a degree of specialist interest and knowledge, rather than relying on a wider range of colleagues who might be less confident about their competence to deliver the subject
- it ensures that 'formal written assessment' can be focused in the way required by the GSCC Requirements for the DipSW.

There were also other pragmatic reasons. Discrete teaching may be the most efficient way of using the specialist teachers from outside the core teaching team who are commonly involved in law teaching. In Scotland some programmes were working to a common framework set by the West of Scotland Consortium, which prescribed both the location and the format of discrete law teaching in the first year of the programmes, leaving little discretion to vary this, at least at this foundation level.

Despite the perceived advantages, discrete teaching was felt at times to challenge students' stamina and perseverance. In some cases modules were described by questionnaire respondents as being very intense and sometimes dry, making it difficult for students to digest the information and apply it to practice. There were also fears that discrete teaching encourages students in the assumption that law begins and ends with that module, rather than the module acting as a springboard for later developments.

The rationale advanced for integrated teaching was equally well articulated.

- it enables closer links with the reality of practice, because students are finding out about law alongside other knowledge for immediate application to practice themes
- it makes law more relevant and immediate for students
- it encourages a more joined-up approach
- it makes it easier for students to place law within the wider policy and practice context
- it encourages social work tutors to engage with the law as part of their own area of subject-based expertise, whether that is related to specific service user groups or more generic knowledge and skills.

In some cases the rationale for integration was drawn more from adult learning perspectives than from anything to do with the inherent nature of the subject. In programmes where enquiry and action learning or problem-based approaches are believed to be an effective way to learn social work, law is clearly included within that philosophy. Concerns were expressed about some potential loss of focus on law within integrated models of teaching (whether delivered through problem-based learning or not).

A certain amount of natural movement between the two models has to be noted. Programmes which have previously worked in discrete modules are taking the opportunity to develop more integrated or problem-based approaches, while programmes which have operated such systems are introducing discrete modules.

A further question facing institutions in locating their law teaching is the question of its relationship with periods of practice learning. Students were described as finding law learning more interesting once they have been on placement, but needing some exposure to the subject before they go out into agencies. This issue will be raised again later in this knowledge review in the section on law learning on practice placement.

### 3.2.3 Aims and learning outcomes of law teaching and learning

Regardless of whether the teaching is located discretely or not, the aims, objectives and learning outcomes are remarkably similar. The most common themes to emerge in all countries are the need to promote:

- awareness of legal systems in the relevant country of study, and the range and status of different sources of law
- understanding how the law influences social work practice (guides, empowers and controls)
- knowledge of the legal frameworks for social work practice, sometimes termed professional law
- critical analysis of that legal framework, to evaluate it from a political, moral perspective
- understanding of its application to practice.

A number of programmes add more specific objectives, such as:

- understanding the broader legal frameworks (beyond social work mandates) that impact upon the lived experiences of people who use services
- using appropriate legal knowledge for the purposes of advocacy and representation
- knowing how to use legislation to support, defend, represent, challenge and advocate for human rights and justice
- understanding the role of law in countering different forms of discrimination, and recognising the contribution of law to anti-oppressive practice
- understanding the underpinning values and ethical frameworks.

Practice example 1

# Law and ethics – London South Bank University

**Law for Social Work, Ethical Dilemmas and Decision Making:** This unit introduces students to the legal context and statutory responsibilities of social workers in England and Wales. It requires students to integrate a number of components in their learning:

- First, the powers and duties that provide social workers with their core mandates for practice found in legislation, delegated legislation and judicial interpretation in areas such as child care, community care and mental health. Students will also be introduced to a wider range of legislation so that they can respond appropriately and are familiar with areas such as housing, welfare rights, education, employment, family law and discrimination
- Second, aspects of administrative law that regulate the way in which social work is conducted, as well as the organisational context
- Third, the human rights legislative framework, important judicial comment and processes of decision making and practice in health and social care orgnisations.

Alongside technical knowledge, social workers are required to practise ethically on the basis of professional values. The unit will emphasise the complex relationship between law and social work values. Specific dilemmas for practice will be highlighted, for example, how the law can protect or promote rights and mandate actions that oppress and marginalise as well as ethical conflicts in the context of resource constraint and organisation performance management. Legal mechanisms to put values into practice through promotion of partnership working, service user choice and autonomy, will be given priority in teaching.

Outcomes for students include the ability to:

- identify legal issues in practice situations and make legally informed decisions
- research into legal problems and solutions, understand how to access information and update their knowledge
- manage the dilemmas of applying the law to practice, including the complexities of competing rights and demands
- integrate an understanding of law and social policy with social work practice
- be confident in using the law.

As in the practice example above, programmes commonly incorporate outcomes relating to values and ethics within law module descriptors.

Practice example 2

# Law and values – University of Glasgow
(now part of Glasgow School of Social Work)

The law teaching builds on an introduction to social work ethics which is offered to students in their entry unit. That unit sets the scene for debates about values and ethics across all modules. It includes material on codes of ethics, practice and conduct, and social work duties and 'virtues', as a foundation for the law teaching in the Social Work Services 1 unit.

**Social Work Services 1:** The aims for this part of the study scheme are:

- to provide students with a basic and broad knowledge base in relation to the legal context of social work in Scotland
- to enable students to develop a basis for their professional competence by demonstrating their abilities in critical analysis, reflective practice and transferability of knowledge, values and skills

- to facilitate the consideration of ethics, values and issues related to discrimination and racism and specifically in relation to the implications for social work practice.

On completing the module, students should be able to:

- confirm a thorough grounding in statute, delegated legislation and case law pertaining to social work in Scotland relating to children, community care, criminal justice and the underpinning principles and philosophies
- exhibit an awareness of the rights and responsibilities of both social workers in the public and independent sectors and of service users; and recognise and address the complexities of competing rights and demands
- display sufficient familiarity with national objectives and standards for social work in the criminal justice system
- acknowledge the legal context and practice implications of imposing controls and restrictions.

Sometimes there is an emphasis on the dilemmas and conflicts associated with application of the law in practice, overtly related to constraints arising in the organisational contexts within which professional practice takes place.

Practice example 3

## Law and values – Cardiff University

The policy issues raised by social care and social work practice are often controversial. They include the pressure on local authority resources that limits provision of community care services, the abuse scandals that surface regularly in relation to children, older people and those with learning difficulties, and controversy over professional decision making and interventions in family life. This course examines the role of law in regulating the complex range of tasks and issues raised by modern social care and social work practice. We explore how the law influences and shapes social work practice, not forgetting how social work practice can use the law in a positive way, and we consider the different views that service users and professionals have of the role and value of law, examining the practice dilemmas of working in an ethical way.

Practice example 4

## Social work law and the organisational context of practice – University of Bangor

The course will provide a comprehensive overview of the law as it relates to a range of service users, children and adults. The approach is experiential, and demonstrates how the law and social work practice are intertwined at both the strategic and operational levels. It places professional practice within its organisational context by showing how local authorities as statutory bodies are both mandated and empowered to determine the strategic parameters within which social work practice should occur. It demonstrates how decisions at the operational level are shaped by the relevant legal provisions and how the law permeates decision-making processes, from referral to outcomes. It conveys how social workers need to be familiar with substantive law and procedural issues as well as being aware of the professional values that imbue practice. The course illustrates the complex relationship between legal provision and professional values. It also takes into account the importance of social work values in working with service users and how these may coincide and conflict with the values of the bureaucratic setting in which social work is located.

The notion of staged learning is important in a number of programmes, with an emphasis on core knowledge building blocks being located early in programmes to enable more sophisticated knowledge systems and skills to be developed later on. This incorporates the notion that students

Practice example 5

# Staged learning – Liverpool John Moores University

### Level 1: Introduction to Social Work Law

This module aims to provide a general introduction to the English legal system and to key areas of social work law, and a consideration of legal rights and values. After completing the module students should be able to:

- demonstrate an understanding of the legal system
- access and use legal resources
- discuss ways in which the law can provide and protect rights, and counter discrimination
- demonstrate an understanding of the key principles of child care law, community care law, mental health law and criminal justice.

The module is assessed through a 2-hour, seen exam, consisting of case studies for which students are able to gather relevant legal information and plan their answers.

### Level 2: Law for Social Work Practice

This module aims to build on existing knowledge of social work law, to provide a greater insight into the legal context of social work practice and thus help provide the legal skills and understanding expected of a social worker. After completing the module students should be able to:

- demonstrate an ability to apply relevant law in social work practice and have a critical and analytical understanding of service delivery standards and the powers and duties of social workers
- demonstrate a working knowledge and understanding of key areas of welfare law that are significant to service users
- analyse the tensions and dilemmas that arise in the implementation of the law in social work practice

- demonstrate a commitment to the anti-oppressive practice of social work law.

The module is assessed through coursework consisting of two case studies of 1,500 words each.

might gain a little knowledge about a broad range of law, followed by in-depth knowledge of a more restricted range.

Differentiation also exists in relation to learning outcomes at different academic levels within the Quality Assurance Agency Frameworks for Higher Education Qualifications.[178-9] This is most clearly observable in programmes where both undergraduate and postgraduate programmes incorporate law modules with similar content, but different sought outcomes.

Practice example 6

# Learning outcomes and academic levels – Middlesex University

### Law for Social Workers
This module aims to provide students with an understanding of the structure and organisation of the legal system and processes and of relevant areas of law and to develop skills in applying knowledge of the legal position to social work practice. It aims also to help students understand how to use the law positively and effectively.

### Level 3: Learning Outcomes
On successful completion of the module students will have the following knowledge and skills:

- be able to identify the relevant substantive law and apply it appropriately to the facts of the question
- demonstrate an appropriate understanding of the place of ethics and values in social work practice

- be able to explain the purpose of statutory and legal requirements in the practice of social work
- be able to understand the possible impact of the law on service users and carers, and to understand how the law can be used to promote their interests
- demonstrate the role of law in social work decision making.

**Level 4: Learning Outcomes**
- critically evaluate the relevant substantive laws and assess their application to practice
- critically discuss issues of anti-discriminatory practice and oppression as they arise in the practice of social work
- clarify the powers and duties inherent in the social work role and critically discuss their adequacy in achieving social work goals
- demonstrate the impact of law on service users and carers and be able to articulate the dilemmas and problems that this imposes for the social worker
- show the inter-relationship between the law and good social work practice and be able to evaluate each in the light of the other.

Practice example 7

# Learning outcomes and academic levels – Liverpool John Moores University

**Level 2: Law for Social Work Practice**
This module aims to build on existing knowledge of social work law, to provide a greater insight into the legal context of social work practice and thus help provide the legal skills and understanding expected of a social worker. After completing the module students should be able to:

- demonstrate an ability to apply relevant law in social work practice and have a critical and analytical understanding of service delivery standards and the powers and duties of social workers

- demonstrate a working knowledge and understanding of key areas of welfare law that are significant to service users
- analyse the tensions and dilemmas that arise in the implementation of the law in social work practice
- demonstrate a commitment to the anti-oppressive practice of social work law.

## Level 4: Law for Social Work Practice

In this module students will critically examine current social work law and its underlying principles and values, to evaluate the legal context of social work practice and thus help provide the legal skills and critical understanding expected of a social worker. After completing the module students should be able to:

- demonstrate expertise in knowledge and understanding of the significance and limitations of the law in providing and protecting rights and countering discrimination, and the ways in which the law might be used to promote anti-oppressive social work practice
- display competence in handling a complex area of legal knowledge and skills: to understand the key principles and the legal framework for child care law, community care law, mental health law, criminal justice law and key areas of welfare law that are significant to service users; to apply relevant current law to social work practice; and to know how to independently update and research legal knowledge and understanding
- critically analyse the tensions and dilemmas that arise in the implementation of the law in social work practice.

### 3.2.4 Curriculum content

Institutions were asked to identify the presence in their programmes of core content in relation to a range of aspects of the legal framework. The list was compiled using the Law Report,[22] DipSW curriculum guidance,[24,38] and feedback from the questionnaire pilot sites. While it transpired that every pre-determined area of legislation was taught by at least several programmes, there were relatively few that were taught by all. In England, there were some topics that received wider coverage, regardless of whether the programmes were postgraduate or undergraduate:

Table 4: Areas of legal framework offered by a high proportion of institutions (England)

| Provided by 100% of all programmes | Provided by 90%+ of all programmes | Provided by 80%+ of all programmes |
| --- | --- | --- |
| Legal system<br>Human rights<br>Child protection<br>Older people<br>Disability<br>Mental health<br>Youth justice | Court structures<br>Anti-discrimination law<br>Adult protection | Family support/children in need<br>Adoption |

Some areas of the possible relevant legal framework, however, were offered by far fewer institutions, with fewer than 60% of programmes offering teaching on adult criminal justice, healthcare provision and employment. Housing and education are more widespread, but by no means covered in all programmes. Where there are differences between postgraduate and undergraduate programmes, there is no clear rule, with different exclusions apparent in both.

In Scotland, Wales and Northern Ireland, the core legal content followed the same patterns of inclusion and omission, with the exception that adult criminal justice was routinely included in Scotland, and appeared in the Northern Ireland curriculum, while more frequently excluded in Wales and England.

The most common reason given for exclusions was lack of timetable space, and the view that superficial coverage might be more confusing for students than none at all. Some programmes clearly articulated the view that the most relevant aspects of the legal framework were those relating to childcare, community care and mental health. Thus there is a real tension between breadth and depth of coverage. Figure 6 shows the full England picture.

There were also a number of additional topics listed by programmes. The following received one or two mentions each, but it may well be the case that other programmes have assumed some of the following to be included in the main list and therefore did not add them.

- Access to legal services
- Carers
- Children's rights
- Confidentiality
- Court work
- Decision making
- Family law
- Jurisprudence
- Legal liability of local authority and individual social worker
- Looked-after children
- Matrimonial causes
- Mental incapacity
- Registration and inspection
- Sexualities
- Working in legal settings

In relation to anti-discrimination legislation, institutions were asked to specify where their focus lay. This proved to be predominantly upon the Race Relations Act 1976 and Amendment Act 2000, the Sex Discrimination Act 1975 and the Disability Discrimination Act 1995. In Northern Ireland and Wales, legislation specific to the geographical context was also mentioned (the Fair Employment [NI] Acts 1976 and 1989 and the Welsh Language Act 1993). A small minority of programmes mentioned a broader spectrum, including EU directives on sexual orientation and age, the Freedom of Information Act 2000, the Special Educational Needs and Disability Act 2001 and legislation on immigration and asylum. The Human Rights Act 1998 was often also mentioned in the context of legislation supporting anti-discriminatory practice, and in a few cases receives detailed attention in teaching.

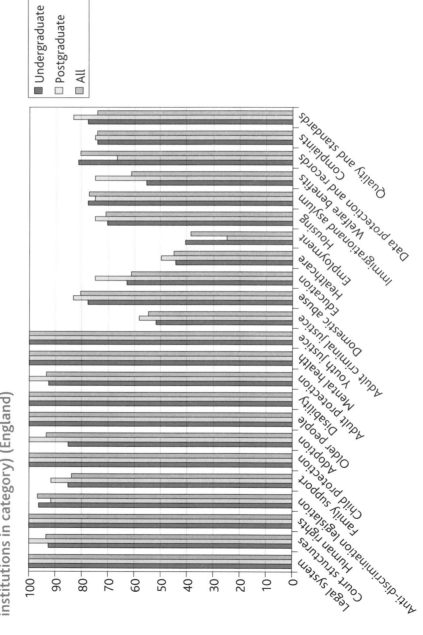

Figure 6: Core law curriculum covered in postgraduate and undergraduate provision (all as % of total institutions in category) (England)

Practice example 8

# Human Rights Act 1998 – University of Manchester

Please work individually on the tasks below. By the end of the 3-week period of guided study you should have a reasonable understanding of the Human Rights Act and the way in which it is judicially applied under particular circumstances.

- Go to www.doh.gov.uk/humanrights/ and click on 'Questions and Answers'. Read the text and consider what is the relationship between the Human Rights Act and the European Convention on Human Rights.
- Follow some of the links provided to explore the Act further. In particular you should visit www.doh.gov.uk/humanrights/ casestudies.htm, which details some important European and domestic cases. You will find further detail on the cases at www.echr.coe.int/. Of particular interest in relation to childcare and protection is *Z and Others v United Kingdom,* 10 May 2001 (Application No 29392/95).
- You can read the Human Rights Act at www.hmso.gov.uk/ acts/1998.htm
- In the newspaper database in the library, find this article – 'Law, the rights stuff' by Clare Dyer in *The Guardian,* 2 October 2001, p 16. What does the article tell you about the impact of the Strasbourg Court on domestic law?
- Again in the newpaper database, find 'Society: social care: free thinking' by Matthew Brown in *The Guardian*, 7 February 2001, p 11. What conclusions does the article draw about the potential impact of the Act?
- You might also find it useful to look at one of the following texts: Hegarty, A. and Leonard, S. (eds) (1999) *Human rights: An agenda for the 21st century*, Cavendish; Swindells, H., Neaves, A., Kushner, M. and Skilbeck, R. (1999) *Family law and the Human Rights Act*, Jordan.
- From your research, can you think of any potentially negative implications of the Human Rights Act?

Now try and answer the questions below. We will discuss what you have learned in a whole group session at the end of this period.

1. When was the Human Rights Act 1998 implemented?
2. Has the Act been implemented fully or only in part?
3. The Act is designed to protect human rights. Where are these rights identified?
4. What does section 3 of the Human Rights Act say?
5. What action can someone take under the Act if they think one or more of their rights has or will be violated? Does the Act cover violations of human rights by any action of the Houses of Parliament?
6. What remedies are available under the Act for someone whose rights have been or will be violated by the actions of a public authority? What is the relevant section of the Act governing remedies.
7. What rights does Article 6 protect?
8. What rights does Article 8 protect?
9. What rights are particularly relevant to social work intervention?
10. Think of some examples where social work intervention might be in danger of violating an individual's human rights.
11. Is the Children Act 1989 compatible with the rights protected by the Human Rights Act? What would a court do if it decided part of the Children Act was incompatible?
12. Can a court be called to account for the violation of someone's human rights?

When it comes to identifying any impacts on curriculum content coinciding with the introduction of the new degree, there are no clear trends, with again different exclusions apparent in both DipSW and new degree programmes. The picture for England is shown in Figure 7, page 80.

Table 5: Difference in areas of legal framework between DipSW and new degree programmes (England)

| Included in equal proportions of DipSW and new degree programmes | Included in higher proportion of DipSW programmes | Included in a higher proportion of new degree programmes |
|---|---|---|
| Legal system<br>Human rights<br>Child protection<br>Older people<br>Disability<br>Mental health<br>Youth justice<br>Complaints<br>Quality and standards | Anti-discrimination law<br>Adult criminal justice<br>Domestic abuse<br>Education<br>Employment<br>Housing<br>Immigration and asylum<br>Welfare benefits<br>Data protection | Court structures<br>Family support/ children in need<br>Adoption<br>Adult protection<br>Healthcare |

However, one trend apparent from programme documentation is an increasing emphasis on ethics as a particular aspect of students' law learning. Many programmes articulate what is probably a longer established awareness of the relationship between law and social work values, drawing attention to practice dilemmas and ethical imperatives in practice. What some programmes are introducing, however, are modules in which law itself is explored in the context of ethical and moral frameworks for action, and the practice dilemmas in its application are explored from an intellectual perspective. This was seen to be part of both a broader inter-professional concern with ethical practice and a more generalised mission for ethics education.

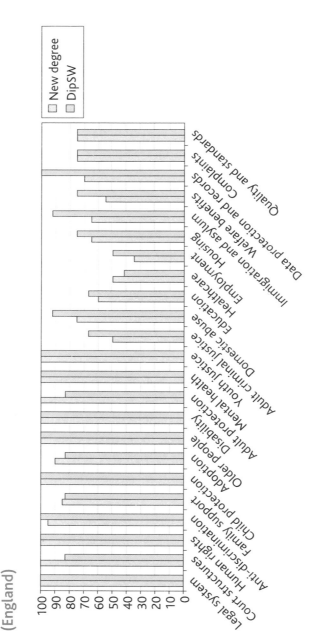

Figure 7: Core legal curriculum: comparisons between new degree and DipSW courses (as % of institutions) (England)

Practice example 9

# Law and ethics – University of Manchester

**Law and Ethical Conduct**: The framework of legal rules, regulations and guidance and ethical/moral obligations provides the basis for social work intervention and informs assessment, intervention and service delivery. This course unit aims to:

1. Enable students to develop a critical understanding of the relationship between law, ethical principles, ethical conduct and social work values
2. Develop students' knowledge and critical understanding of relevant law, regulations and guidance and their ability to apply law and ethical principles intelligently to social work problems, including those relating to risk, autonomy, protection, rights and welfare
3. Develop students' ability to understand complex legal judgements and their relationship with legal principles, ethical conduct and social work practice
4. Develop students' ability to work collaboratively with others to analyse and evaluate relevant research, synthesise information and solve complex problems
5. Develop students' written and oral communication skills.

The course unit introduces issues about law and ethical/moral values at the beginning so that these can be incorporated into subsequent discussions about how the law operates and informs practice. Thus an initial session considers the nature and basis of law and ethics; rules, rights and the role of trust; ethical principles relating to autonomy, benefits and welfare, negative and positive freedom. Subsequent sessions then consider legal powers and duties and social work practice for different service users, employing themes of state intervention, risk, harm, autonomy, protection and rights as a coherent framework. The end session then returns to the question of law as a self-referential system with a particular way of thinking, and its relationship with non-legal (ethical and moral) communications. Students consider the implications of this (legal) perspective for the application of social work values and possibilities for intervention. Additionally, throughout the course unit, students work in groups to prepare a presentation on the relationship between the legal framework and ethical/moral issues and their implications for social work practice.

A related development is the concept of ethical practice and its location within the legal framework.

Practice example 10

# Law and ethics – University of Bristol

**Policy, Law and Ethics**: This element forms part of a unit of teaching that prepares students for practice-based learning. The broad aims of this element are:

- to ensure students are ready to commence practice-based learning
- to introduce students to the legal, policy and ethical framework of social work practice, with reference to European and international law where appropriate.

The sequence of teaching is as follows:

1. Introduction to the policy and legal framework of practice: key issues in the development of the legal and policy frameworks, and the concepts of statutory and non-statutory work
2. Introduction to the policy process and the role of social workers within this: how social problems come to be defined, the process of policy making and implementation, local policy concerns such as resource allocation, role of social workers within the policy process

3. Contemporary trends and issues in policies relating to social work: the complexity of the legal and policy framework, key trends such as mixed markets, consumerism, managerialism and gate-keeping, human rights and anti-discrimination legislation
4. The Children Act 1989 and other key child care legislation
5. The NHS and Community Care Act 1990 and related key legislation
6. Mental health legislation
7. Legislation relating to practice with young people in trouble with the law
8. Ethical practice: key issues in professional ethics, developments (such as registration and protection of title) in the status of social work
9. Ethical practice within contemporary law and policy: a workshop in which groups will work on a scenario to identify key legislation, policy issues, ethical and professional expectations.

In commenting generally on the curriculum, a number of programmes made the point that they were not attempting to make students learn by rote, or to digest great chunks of knowledge. Nor were they training social workers to be mini-lawyers. The emphasis was more on mapping the territory, identifying what social workers needed to know as a foundation and ensuring that students know where to look next when they are facing specific practice situations.

### 3.2.5 Teaching and learning processes

**Teaching skill mix**

In England, the number of people teaching law on social work programmes in each institution varies from one to 12 (or 40 including the programme that has 1,000 students, and uses 40 teachers). Two thirds of institutions have more than three people teaching law. Without having any rigorous measure for comparison with other areas of the curriculum, it seems likely that these figures are higher than in other subjects.

## Figure 8: Number of people teaching law on programme (England)

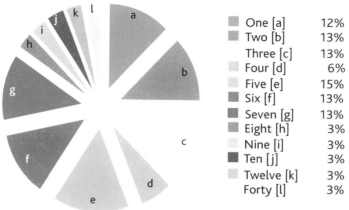

| | | |
|---|---|---|
| ■ | One [a] | 12% |
| ■ | Two [b] | 13% |
| | Three [c] | 13% |
| | Four [d] | 6% |
| | Five [e] | 15% |
| ■ | Six [f] | 13% |
| ■ | Seven [g] | 13% |
| ■ | Eight [h] | 3% |
| | Nine [i] | 3% |
| ■ | Ten [j] | 3% |
| | Twelve [k] | 3% |
| | Forty [l] | 3% |

Law is perhaps also unusual in that in a number of institutions the teaching is resourced predominantly or entirely from outside the core social work staff team.

## Figure 9: Involvement of core social work team in law teaching (England)

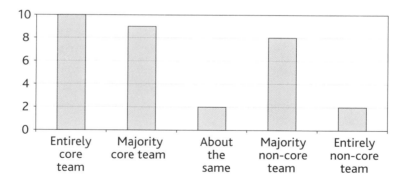

The issue of skill mix within the staff group is clearly important, with both law and social work academics, and practitioners from law, commonly involved in teaching the law curriculum. There is, however, no common pattern. For example, of those institutions who answered the question about the professional background of those teaching law to social workers:

- 13 have practising lawyers (43%)
- 7% have academic lawyers (no practising lawyers)
- one course just has a practising lawyer and one just has an academic lawyer (no social work staff are involved in the law teaching)
- eight institutions (27% of those who answered the question) have no lawyers (academic or practising) among the law teaching team.

In one case, lawyers had been replaced by social work staff, having given insufficient attention to social work practice issues in their teaching, and presented the detail of the law without its application. This had been experienced by students as dull and divorced from the reality of their professional role. In another, a deliberate move had been made to encourage social work tutors to take responsibility for the legal context within their own subject area, as a means of integrating law more securely across the curriculum.

Conversely, several programmes emphasised the importance in involving practising lawyers in the teaching. Their mere presence was believed to assist the development of openness to inter-disciplinarity, and certainly of illuminating for social work students the discourse and processes of law.

The delivery of teaching on programmes in Scotland reflects a similar picture of involving a large number of people (from one to 15), but with perhaps higher representation of social work staff and, occasionally, a deliberate move away from the involvement of lawyers. This may reflect the use of problem-based learning increasingly being used in a number of programmes, or the broad integration of law across the curriculum requiring a higher number of social work staff to engage with core legal content.

In Wales, the numbers of teaching staff ranged from four to eight, with a skill mix more comparable to that in England.

In Northern Ireland the programme involved 20 teachers, split equally between law and social work staff, often practitioners who are close to law in practice. A deliberate decision had been made for the convenor to be social work qualified, to assist in ensuring that material and presentation is relevant for social work students at their stage of professional learning.

In response to a specific question about the involvement of service users and carers in law teaching across all countries, only four institutions considered that such involvement in direct delivery of teaching was well established. A fifth institution mentioned the representation of service user perspectives in distance learning materials, where participation is achieved through audio and written programme content.

Practice example 11

# Service user involvement – University of Lincoln

The Service User Participation Group has contributed to law teaching in a number of ways:

The group has produced a video, from which a 10-minute clip is used in law teaching to focus discussion on the Care Standards Act 2000, and how this might influence services. The video extract shows Alice, who is in her 90s, waiting for her home care assistant, who is late. She talks about how this makes her feel anxious. She also talks about how important it is for her to be able to remain in her own home, as she has lived there for over 50 years. Students are asked to consider the following questions with regard to the Care Standards Act 2000:

1. Alice has a home care assistant. Think of three standards that would be important to ensure her home care is of good quality
2. What systems would you put in place to measure these?
3. If Alice entered a residential care home, think of three standards that would ensure her care in the home is of good quality
4. What systems would you put in place to measure these?

Young people who have had experience of the care system present a session related to the Children (Leaving Care) Act 2000. In the presentation, they interview each other about their experiences, using a script of specific questions (see below). This took a lot of preparation by the young people. Active preparation with the students is necessary also to ensure that their responses to the young people are not intrusive.

Billy, thinking about when you left care …

1. How old were you when you left care?
2. What support did you want when you left care?
3. Did you know what support you were entitled to? Did anyone tell you?
4. What support from your social worker did you actually get when you left care? What about other people?
5. How were decisions made about your life?  How were you involved?
6. When you left care, where did you want to live?  What actually happened?
7. What career did you want when you left care? What training did you want to do? What has happened?

So how are things now …

1. Where do you live now?
2. What about work or training? Do you get any support (financial, or advice, for example)?
3. What about support as a care leaver? How have the changes in the law about care leavers affected you? Do you have a pathway advisor?
4. What about decisions now – are you in control?  How are you involved?
5. What are your career plans and plans for the future now?

Kelly, thinking about how things are now …

1. Where do you live now?
2. What are you doing at college at the moment?
3. Do you have ideas about what you would like to do for a career in the future?
4. What kind of support do you get from your social worker? What about your foster carers?

5. Do you have a pathway plan personal advisor? What sort of things do you talk to him/her about? Are you in control of things, do you make the decisions?

Thinking more about the future ...

1. What do you want to do when you leave care?
2. Where do you want to live?
3. What support do you want to have when you leave care?

Programmes acknowledged that lack of service user participation was a weakness, but saw it as an area for development within the new degree. Plans included asking service users to contribute on the impact of legal interventions from their perspective, to give their own critical analysis of the legal frameworks, and to present specific sessions on aspects such as young carers' legislation.

Where social work practitioners made significant contributions to teaching law, institutions were asked to comment on the particular value added by their involvement. The key benefits here appeared to be, first, the focus on using the law in practice, the issues and dilemmas this raises, and how practitioners manage those in the context of agency ac-countability frameworks. An important aspect of their contribution was seen as their familiarity with how policies and practice frameworks are interpreted and used in daily practice. Second, practitioners contribute knowledge that is seen to reside in specialist areas of practice such as approved social work, adoption, transitions, youth justice, welfare rights, housing and asylum. Third, they assist in preparing teaching materials, acting as critical readers during the development process to ensure case scenarios are topical and relevant. Fourth, they benefit from a certain degree of 'street credibility' as perceived by the students, and thus their contributions to teaching command respect.

### Teaching and learning methods

In relation to teaching and learning methods used, institutions indicated a wide range of approaches both in the classroom and in relation to students' independent learning. In England the picture is as follows:

## Figure 10: Learning and teaching methods used (England)

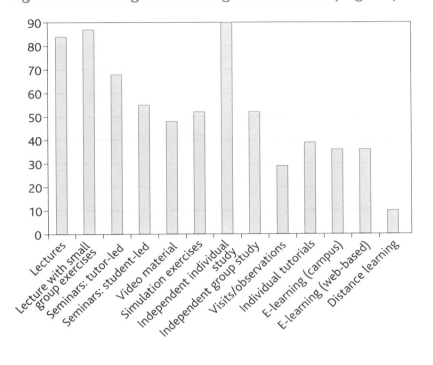

The picture in Scotland, Wales and Northern Ireland showed use of a similarly broad range of methods, with similar emphases on lectures, lectures with small group exercises and independent study.

Respondents were asked to explain their rationale for choosing their teaching and learning methods. Factors that are taken into account are:

- practical constraints of time, group size, space and teaching personnel
- adult learning theory, along with practical knowledge and experience of students' needs, including:
  > respect for the variety of learning styles
  > need for variety in how they learn
  > need to enliven a subject that can be viewed as 'dry'
  > importance of opportunities to contribute their own experience
  > importance of opportunities to learn together
  > encouragement of curiosity and research skills

- the need to develop knowledge, application and skills, which require different approaches
- problem-based learning theories
- concepts of 'deep learning'.

Lectures, including those with small group exercises, are used by a large majority of institutions. Lectures are commonly seen as an efficient way of delivering accurate core knowledge, and of having a degree of control over what is taught, even if it is acknowledged that this may not equate to knowing what is learned. They were also described as a preferred method of learning by some students. Lectures might be designed to build on independent study that students undertake in advance, working to a weekly schedule of tasks.

Practice example 12

# Week-by-week directed study – University of the West of England

**Legal and Policy Frameworks for Social Work Practice (Level 1):** The learning outcomes for the module are the ability to:

- identify major statutory responsibilities of social workers in relation to all user groups
- understand the significance of legislative and policy frameworks and service delivery standards
- demonstrate a critical awareness of legal and policy frameworks and their impact on the users of health and social care services
- understand statutory accountability and the tensions and relationship between statute, policy and practice.

| Module topic | Directed study for the following week |
|---|---|
| Week 1: Introduction to the module | Make notes relating to your observations of a court at work |
| Week 2: Introduction to law and policy | Make notes on discriminatory practices you have encountered, and possible strategies for dealing with them |
| Week 3: Law and policy relating to discrimination | Find out what you can about:<br>The experience of young people as victims of crime<br>Young offenders' views of their experience of youth justice |
| Week 4: Introduction to the criminal justice system, with special reference to youth justice | Find out all you can about different definitions of homelessness |
| Week 5: Family breakdown, homelessness and domestic violence | Make a list of all the government initiatives you can think, of introduced in the last five years, to promote the wellbeing of children under 16 |
| Week 6: Introduction to law and policy relating to children and families | Find out as much as you can about the Victoria Climbié Inquiry |
| Week 7: Children and families legislation (cont'd) | Make notes on what ways vulnerable adults may need protection |
| Week 8: Introduction to law and policy relating to community care and vulnerable adults | Have a look at the MIND website (and other sites) for information and concerns about the new mental health legislation |
| Week 9: Introduction to mental health law | |

Taught input is routinely accompanied by tasks that require students to apply the knowledge to situations described in case studies, or to carry out further research to answer more detailed questions related to the topic in hand. Often case studies are used as a means of ensuring that the application of law in practice is addressed in the classroom, rather than merely delivery of technical knowledge.

Practice example 13

# Developing professional judgement – University of Wales Institute Cardiff

The law is not as clear and prescriptive as may be believed. The dilemma for the practitioner is knowing when to apply a piece of legislation. This requires a breadth of knowledge of what legislation may apply in a given practice situation, and the skills to decide what, if any, legislation is the most appropriate. How will the application of particular pieces of legislation impact upon the service user? How does the legislation help or hinder the work of the social worker in that particular practice situation? There is not always necessarily one right answer. Each situation is different and what is required of the practitioner is that they are clear and accountable about what legislation they applied, and why they chose to apply it in that particular instance.

Independent group study tasks were identified as supporting the development of group research skills and teamwork, as well as helping students to share the task of researching a wide range of legal knowledge. Seminar presentations by students, based on their independent learning, were used as a means of offering practice and feedback on verbal skills in presenting a case for a particular legal interpretation.

Practice example 14

# Student seminar presentations – Glasgow Caledonian University

Each group should prepare a presentation on a case study, lasting approximately 15-20 minutes, which will form the basis for discussion within the class as a whole. When examining the case study, students should attempt to explore the following:

- What legal issues are involved?
- What needs, rights and risks are involved?
- What do you consider to be the most appropriate response?

The aim of the group presentation is to explore the options available within the legislative framework, not to look for practice solutions. Discussion of options should be supported by ideas from across the theoretical framework covered by the programme so far, for example, poverty, family and lifespan, social work practice, key concepts and values. As it is sometimes difficult to grasp ideas quickly from spoken word presentations, groups should consider also using limited visual aids such as flipcharts or acetates. All class members should come to the seminar having read the case studies in advance, and prepared to discuss the issues raised, not merely to listen. Attendance at each seminar is required by the whole student group.

Students work on one of four studies, covering a range of legal issues.

Sample Case 1: Brian (27) has been convicted of assault following a fight with three other men after a local football match. All had been drinking heavily and police charged all four with assault, as each made statements incriminating the others. Brian has a history of violent offences, usually while under the influence of alcohol. He has been unemployed for the past three years, having lost his last job because he was frequently arriving drunk at work. He has, until now, lived with his parents, but they are fed up with his behaviour and have asked him to move out unless he seeks help with his excessive drinking. You have been asked to prepare a social enquiry report for the court to provide information and advice as an aid to sentencing.

In the Wales context, separate study group seminars were an important way of ensuring the rights of Welsh-speaking students to study through the Welsh medium.

A number of programmes use court workshop exercises to train students in working within court systems. Such workshops vary in length from several hours to several days, and commonly take place in a working court, and involve legal practitioners taking the legal roles. A key aim is to give students a realistic experience of the language and culture of such settings. There were, however, no examples given of skills practice in other settings, such as complaints hearings or resource panels, where practitioners may need to use verbal presentation skills to argue a case within a legal framework.

Many tutors were aware of students' fears about the law, and tendency to find it more difficult than other subjects. Respondents emphasised the need for learning and teaching methods to make the law more accessible, and to allay students' anxieties. Some teachers have developed aids to learning, such as algorithms, decision-trees and charts, for students to use as 'maps' when absorbing some of the finer detail of legislation and when working their way through case studies. Such aids typically attempt to break decision making down into a sequence, or to gather together and present coherently information from a range of sources.

Practice example 15

# Statutory Work with Children with Faltering School Attendance (2004) – Liverpool Comunity College

*Note:* A 'parent' as defined in section 576, Education Act 1996 can be a natural father who is not and has never been married to the mother, any other person who has parental responsibility, or any person who 'has care' of the child. Thus mothers should not always and exclusively be the persons who face legal action.

*Note:* This algorithm is under regular development but will, at best, be approximate.

A child is defined in section 17, Children Act 1989 as 'in need' if owing to absence from school or other factors it is likely there is impairment of intellectual, emotional, social or behavioural development, compared with a similar child. Section 17 specifically states that children with disability are children 'in need'.

Underlying problems can often be dealt with via discussion, which may obviate the necessity of legal action. If a child might not be attending school, the Local Education Authority (LEA) must enquire if the child is of compulsory school age and if s/he is registered as a pupil at a school or s/he is otherwise receiving efficient full-time education.

Under sections 444A and 444B, Education Act 1996, inserted by section 23(1), Anti-Social Behaviour Act 2003, penalty notices may be given rather than prosecute. If paid, that will discharge any liability to be convicted for that offence.

An assessment may be carried out by the Social Services Authority (SSA) and services offered via section 17 and Schedule 2, para 10, Children Act 1989.

If the 'threshold criteria' have been satisfied under section 31, Children Act 1989 the SSA may seek a Supervision Order or Care Order via the Family Court, in which instance the child care checklist, welfare principle, 'No Delay' and 'No Order' principle apply.

If the child is registered with a school but s/he does not attend school regularly the LEA has options to:

or

A School Attendance Order may be sought via section 437, Education Act 1996. Liverpool and Sefton LEAs tend to prefer this as the Education Supervision Order has tended to have little effect.

If the child is registered at a school and not otherwise receiving an efficient, full-time education, then the LEA will prosecute under section 7, Education Act 1996.

After consulting social services, the LEA may seek a 12 months Education Supervision Order (which can be extended to three years) via section 36, Children Act 1989 (not available if child is in the care of LA). The child care checklist, welfare principle, 'No Delay' and 'No Order' principle apply.

and then

and only after that

The court may make an interim Supervision Order, Interim Court Order or Care order.

If regular attendance is not achieved within 15 days, a parent may be prosecuted via section 443, Education Act 1996 for failure to comply with a School Attendance Order. A Parenting Order may also be made at the same time.

If regular attendance is not achieved, a parent may be prosecuted for failure to secure regular attendance at school via section 444, Education Act 1996. A Parenting Order may also be made. Parents may be prosecuted for 'aggravated truancy', section 8, Crime and Disorder Act with possibilities of 3 months prison or community service and parenting classes if non-school attendance persists.

As a result of the precedent set in the case *Re O*, when the LEA's use of these measures has failed to secure regular school attendance, the 'threshold criteria' will have been satisfied for a Care Order under section 31, Children Act 1989, the proceedings for which must be brought by the SSA.

If more than one of Supervision Order, Education Supervision Order or Probation Order in effect:
A child may be subject to a Supervision Order, made to a Probation Officer or a SSA, or an Education Supervision Order made to an LEA; and a parent may be subject of a Probation Order. If directions under an order conflict with those under another, a Probation Order has first precedence, a Supervision Order comes next and an Education Supervision Order comes after either or (in the event) both.

Practice example 16

# Decision making under the NHSCCA 1990 and DPA(SCR) 1986 – University of Liverpool

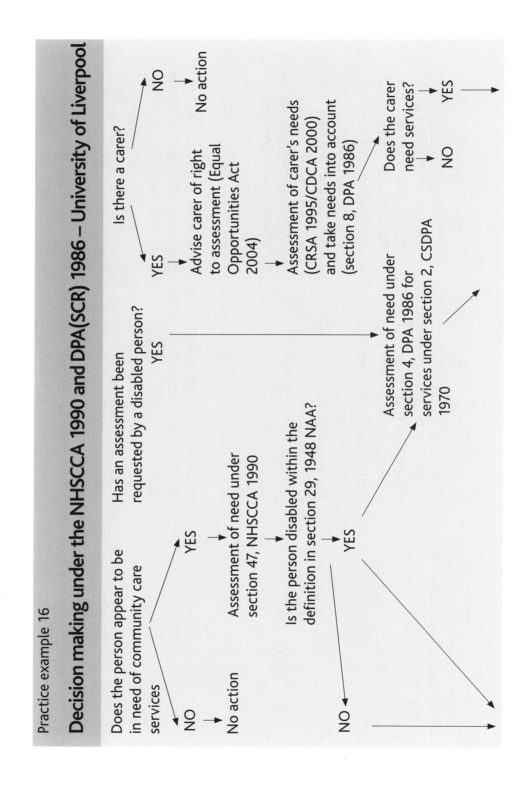

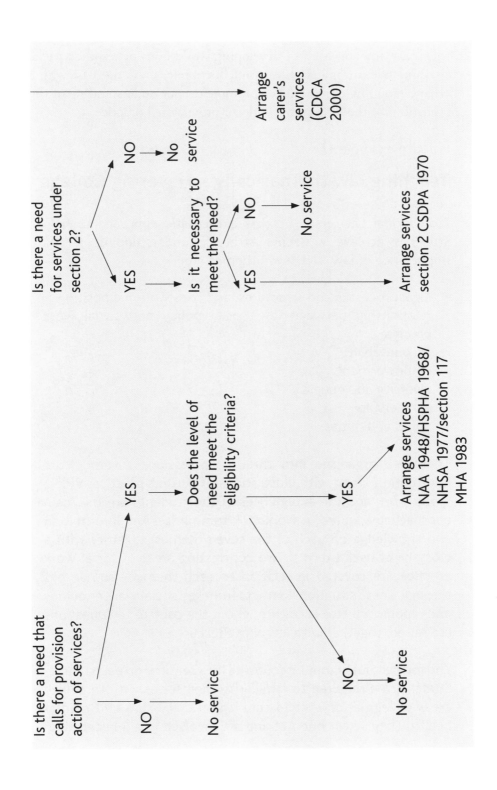

Is there a need that calls for provision action of services?

YES

NO

No service

Does the level of need meet the eligibility criteria?

YES

Arrange services
NAA 1948/HSPHA 1968/
NHSA 1977/section 117
MHA 1983

NO

No service

Is there a need for services under section 2?

NO

No service

YES

Is it necessary to meet the need?

NO

No service

YES

Arrange services section 2 CSDPA 1970

Arrange carer's services (CDCA 2000)

Others take the approach of developing workbooks or resource packs containing relevant materials for students to refer to, in one case with a thematic grouping of material to promote deeper understanding of the implications of the legal framework for professional practice.

Practice example 17

## Teaching law thematically – Havering College

Professional Law, Part 1, takes a thematic approach to help students achieve a deeper strategic understanding of the importance of law. The seven themes are:

- legal processes and structures, and constitutional position
- relationship between law, social policy and social work practice
- accountability
- empowerment
- diversity and equality
- partnership
- rights and duties.

These are organised into three-hour sessions covering core information along with illustrations of current practice. Video, group work and the experiences of the students are the main approaches adopted. A workbook summarises key information and knowledge on each of the seven themes, together with a glossary of useful terms. Two contrasting areas of social work practice are covered in relation to each theme – sometimes through a case situation. Extracts from key social work enquiries and reports are also used throughout the course. Key questions are raised, together with learning checklist.

The formal taught input is followed by a seminar on each theme. Students are required to familiarise themselves with three key areas of legislation – child care, community care and mental health. They select one Act and are involved in a 'Mastermind' session in the seminars where, later in the course, they must answer a series of straightforward questions to check their understanding of the legislation. Investment in the seminars is therefore inbuilt within the programme.

A formative assessment task is linked to the key themes. Students are asked to identify specific duties of social workers and rights of service users, in relation to a case study. In addition, the students select a course theme and are asked to identify key issues and potential conflicts for social work practice.

No respondents specifically commented on what approaches to learning and teaching were designed to assist students with the task of developing a critical perspective on the legal framework, although many had said this was an aim of the teaching.

Respondents in all countries raised interesting questions about the use of enquiry-based approaches such as 'problem-based learning' or 'enquiry and action learning'. These were sometimes seen as an alternative to lectures presenting law as a discrete subject, and often as a development that assists students in applying the law in a more integrated way to practice. Their major strength was seen as replicating the tasks social workers have to undertake in practice and to research what is needed in the complexity of any given situation. Emphasis was also placed on the benefits of transferable skills development in research, group learning and verbal presentation. Group accountability was seen as a significant factor in motivating students to undertake the necessary work.

While programmes exclusively using such approaches to deliver the law teaching were very uncommon, a number of programmes use smaller-scale independent group projects within law modules.

Practice example 18

# Student seminar presentations – University of Manchester

Students work in small groups to undertake the research necessary to make a presentation to the whole group on one of the case studies. Guidance is given as follows:

1. First, decide what are the relevant issues in the case. Allocate between your group members the task of researching particular aspects of law. You will need to list the relevant statutes pertaining to your part of the case study and then work on deciding which Acts and sections are most relevant.
2. When you have completed this phase of the work, you should meet and debate the pros and cons of various interventions. You should think about the requirements of anti-oppressive practice alongside the more philosophical discussions, and try to think what you would really want to do in this case.
3. You should aim to produce a 20-minute presentation that discusses the law and makes some recommendations for action.

Case 1: George D is black British, aged 75. He lives with his daughter Simone and her children Jenny (10) and Joe (15). George is known to the local services for older people with mental health problems. He has had Alzheimer's disease for the past five years and is becoming increasingly anxious and confused. The social services department provide home care for George while Simone is at work. Simone has called social services saying she is very concerned about her father and is not sure whether she can cope any longer. He is becoming verbally and physically abusive and has recently attempted to strike out at Jenny. He has also been getting up in the night and leaving the gas switched on, which means Simone is unable to get any rest.

Case 2: Lisa is white British and 19 years old. Between the ages of 10 and 18 she was looked after by the local authority. She was placed with foster carers for a short time but her behaviour proved too challenging and she was moved to a children's home. Lisa has some learning difficulties and mental health problems, and is supported on medication. She has a history of aggressive behaviour and self-harm which is well controlled as long as she takes her medication. She has minimal contact with her parents, who have never been able to accept or cope with her disability. She is currently living alone in a local authority flat. She is known to the aftercare team and the community mental health team, who provide support to enable her to live independently. Lisa has just discovered she is 16 weeks pregnant, and says she does not know who the baby's father is. Health professionals are concerned she may not be able to cope with the pregnancy and that she may not be capable of looking after a child alone.

Case 3: Gary is 16 years old, and white British. He lives with his mother Anne, who has recently been diagnosed with multiple sclerosis. Gary has recently been excluded from school, following an incident in which he threatened a teacher with a knife. Gary's teachers say he has always been 'a loner', but recently seems to have become very agitated and disorientated at times. Anne says he is "not the boy she knows". He is spending all his time in his bedroom, will not communicate and has shouted at her and pushed her a number of times. This is out of character and Anne is worried that Gary is either on drugs or has inherited his father's mental illness. Gary's father, who no longer lives with the family, has a diagnosis of schizophrenia. Currently Anne's symptoms associated with the MS are quite severe and she is desperate for help.

Useful resources:
www.carersnorth.demon.co.uk/policy.htm
www.careandhealth.com/arch/article_219.asp
www.hmso.gov.uk/acts.htm
http://nchacti01.uuhost.uk.uu.net/carelaw

One programme commented positively on having switched to enquiry-based approaches and finding that students' results improved considerably, with assessments showing better retention of knowledge and application. In Scotland, the introduction of the new degree is likely to be marked by a shift towards enquiry-based learning in a number of programmes, reflecting a belief that this will raise the profile of law at all levels in the new programmes.

Practice example 19

## Skills-based workshops – University of Paisley

We have abandoned the formal lectures with a social work lecturer and a law lecturer at the front of the class and moved to a skills-based workshop approach. We begin with several classes which set the context, looking at key concepts and a framework for understanding and practising social work law. The students are introduced to the legal resources available in our library/learning resource centre. A list of required weekly reading is circulated. Following this, each week students are introduced to a scenario highlighting law and social work practice issues in a specific area of work – for example, in relation to community-based disposals for the courts. A lecturer ensures that students understand the task. The students then work all morning in small sub-groups on answering questions related to the scenario. In the afternoon the class reconvenes with the lecturer present. Each sub-group presents their responses to the scenario questions, with discussion. The lecturer's role is to ensure that the key concepts, themes, issues, etc are emphasised, that the most accurate and up-to-date material is highlighted and the class goes away having met the learning outcomes for the day.

Feedback has been increasingly good. Most students do seem to like to work in this way. Results have not been significantly different as a result of the introduction of this new approach. It is not yet clear how durable is the knowledge acquired in this way, but anecdotally students seem to be able to make good use of the knowledge while on practice placement.

E-learning is another development that is receiving major attention, in line often with institutional developments in electronic resources. The Scottish Institute for Excellence in Social Work Education is focusing on law, among other subjects, in its e-learning development project and a number of e-learning resources are already in use.

Practice example 20

## Rationale for e-learning – University of Strathclyde (now part of Glasgow School of Social Work)

Benefits of computer-assisted learning in the experience of this programme are:

- it encourages and stimulates student-centred learning
- it can help develop students' problem-solving abilities
- it can keep up to date with ever-changing legislation and policy (crucial in the area of law teaching)
- it enables tutors to respond directly to individual students and challenge misunderstandings
- it encourages debate more easily than in traditional methods of delivery.

It should not totally replace other teaching methods, but be seen as one of a range of ways of helping students to increase their knowledge and understanding of the place of law in social work practice.

Practice example 21

# E-learning package – Glasgow Caledonian University

*The Law Relating to Children in Scotland* is a computer-assisted learning package which enables students (and practitioners) to understand the legislative context of work with children and families, and to begin to critically evaluate the legal concepts within practice. It aims to assist students to develop their practice by better understanding the context within which it takes place. It does not seek to provide a comprehensive understanding of the law in relation to children and is therefore an adjunct to learning rather than a substitute for other reading. Indeed, it is vital that students make reference to appropriate statutes and wider reading to gain maximum benefit from the package.

The programme has been constructed in three sections:

1. Information on Child Care in Scotland: this section contains an overview of four key legislative influences on child care decision making – Social Work (Scotland) Act 1968, Children (Scotland) Act 1995, Adoption (Scotland) Act 1978 and the UN Convention on the Rights of the Child. Hypertext links provide access to additional information that illustrates the interrelated nature of the statutory base.
2. Self-assessment: this section is intended to provide a light-hearted test of legal knowledge on the questions set, without implying that successful completion indicates any broader understanding. The user has access to randomised questions about four key aspects of child care legislation, mainly based around the children's hearings system, and must decide whether each option offered is True of False. In the 'easy' version, the user may continue to select responses until the correct response is achieved. In the 'harder' version, the correct answer needs to be selected in order to proceed.

3. Case study and report writing: the case study is based on the structure and content of a fairly typical social background report for a children's hearing. The user must make 'real time' decisions in response to the options posed by the report. The computer then selects an outcome at random, requiring the user to make further choices, culminating in the construction of a report by the user which explains the reasons behind the choices they have made. When working with the case study, the user may access additional information via hypertext links to the legislation section of the programme. The completed report can be saved onto disk for future discussion with student colleagues or tutors.

Students will use the programme in a number of ways:

- accessing information about the law
- testing out their current legal knowledge
- examining existing case law in respect of particular issues
- exploring available legal options
- examining practice dilemmas
- improving report-writing skills
- using the Conference Centre, which allows interactivity among networked users.

The programme is designed to allow the user to make her/his own decision about what they wish to explore and in what order. A student may, for example, decide they have adequate working knowledge of the legislation and decide to begin working at the self-assessment stage in order to test their understanding. It is also possible to begin working on the case study stage, and subsequently decide to refresh one's understanding of the legislation, and retrace one's steps accordingly. The user is able to work at a pace acceptable to them, and suitable to their own style of learning. As steps can be retraced, this allows knowledge to be consolidated more effectively.

Other programmes are using or developing the use of virtual learning environments, such as Blackboard, and see this as an important means of students acquiring formative feedback through self-testing and tutor contact.

Practice example 22

## E-learning – Canterbury Christ Church University College

The use of a virtual learning environment such as Blackboard offers a range of benefits in relation to law teaching and learning:

- A gateway to resources, with links to:
  > journal articles
  > databases
  > websites
- Immediacy of interactive links for consultation with:
  > lecturers
  > other students
- Support to students while off-campus on placement, with the opportunity to:
  > consider legal aspects of placement-related work
  > discuss dilemmas and practice issues encountered.

The numerous iterations of learning that can be achieved through random electronic selection of questions and responses to student input were seen as a major benefit.

Practice example 23

## Social work law e-learning tutorials – University of East London

These tutorials form a discrete part of a second level law module that offers more specialist input on community care and working with vulnerable adults. The web-based tutorials are planned so as to provide supportive learning materials that can be accessed either on-site or from a student's workplace or home through WebCT (password protected). The tutorials are not designed to be self-standing, but are integrated into teaching, so that students can benefit from tutorial support and are not left to feel that this is some kind of distance learning.

The learning outcomes for the module are that students will be able to:

1. demonstrate an understanding of the rights of adults to social work services
2. outline the provision for protection of adults from abuse
3. summarise the duties of social workers in relation to vulnerable adults
4. highlight the main features of anti-discrimination law
5. empower adults in pursuing their legal rights
6. identify the scope of provision for adults in the community
7. explain the developing nature of group care provision in the context of community care
8. explain the distinctive roles in undertaking assessment, care management and direct service provision.

The e-learning tutorials are intended to address 1, 3 and 4 and help with the attainment of 2, 5 and 8. It is not intended that the whole module should be online, since much of this module involves small-group and experiential work, with significant contributions from practitioners and service users. Rather it is designed to make learning about the law more attractive and more interactive, whilst encouraging the use of web-based materials as an essential information tool.

At the same time it is hoped that the tutorials will provide a resource that should remain relatively up-to-date. The use of hyperlinks to reputable web-based sources is considered to be an essential means of achieving this objective. In this respect the tutorials offer skills development in accessing information. The tutorials do not substitute for book-based knowledge, but demonstrate a method of updating knowledge and applying it to the case examples which the web-based tutorials offer. They also offer the potential for interrogating students to ensure that they are making progress; for example, at various stages student cannot proceed with the rest of the tutorial unless they answer specific questions correctly. Current developments include incorporating this aspect in some kind of formative assessment strategy.

Distance learning was mentioned by relatively few respondents, and in one case experience had been that law could not effectively be delivered through this medium, without some form of personal contact between student and law teacher.

**Learning and teaching resources**

Law teachers were also expecting students to draw on a wide range of materials in their learning. In relation to programmes in England, these were as follows:

Figure 11: Material used to support student learning (England)

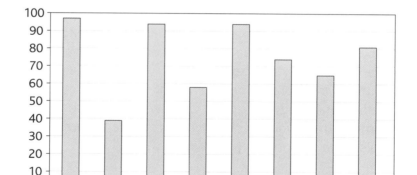

Specific additional mention was made of virtual learning environments such as Blackboard, dedicated law files produced by the institution, and course packs containing all the resources students need to access. Other programmes, however, emphasised the importance of students working independently to become familiar with a range of library resources in order to develop transferable research skills as an investment in their ability to maintain their learning in future. The use of library exercises is common in legal education, and has been adapted by some programmes to address the specific learning needs of social work students.

Practice example 24

# Library exercise – University of Edinburgh

This exercise is an opportunity to look at a range of statutes, guidance and one or two cases, to begin to familiarise yourself with this type of legal material. You need to go to the main library and the law library to examine the material and consider the questions set out below. Choose one of the exercises below and have it completed to bring to class.

### 1. Children and families
### Exclusion order
- Look at the Children (Scotland) Act 1995. What are the grounds for applying for an exclusion order?
- Look at the guidance. What advice does it offer?
- Look at the case report of *Russell v W 1998 FamLR 25*. What are the facts of the case? What was the court's decision?

### Parental responsibilities order
- Look at the Children (Scotland) Act 1995. What are the grounds for applying for a parental responsibilities order?
- Look at the guidance. What advice does it offer?
- Look at the case report of *City of Edinburgh Council v H 2001 SLT (Sh Ct) 51*. What are the facts of the case? What was the court's decision?

## 2. Criminal justice

- Look at the Criminal Procedure (Scotland) Act 1995 – how long can a probation order last? What conditions can be attached to an order?
- Look at the National Objectives and Standards in Social Work Services in the Criminal Justice System – what are the main points the standards address in relation to probation?
- Look at the case *HM Advocate v Smith 1999 SLT 909* which is an appeal by the Lord Advocate against an 'unduly lenient' sentence – what are the facts of the case? Consider the court's reasoning in this case.

## 3. Community Care

- Look at the Adults with Incapacity (Scotland) Act 2000 – what are the general principles to be applied in guiding intervention under the Act?
- Look at the Code of Practice for local authorities regarding the assessment of adults' needs (www.scotland.gov.uk/Topics/Justice/Civil/16360/5176).

In terms of the sources of law that students were expected to access through the use of these resources, most were well represented, but only statutes were mentioned by 100%, and circulars were omitted by a significant minority.

Figure 12: Sources of law (England)

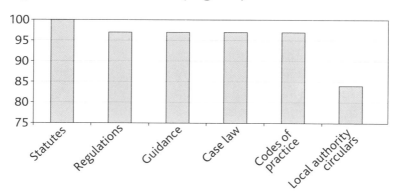

One programme sets a particular learning task to encourage students to encounter the impact of case law, and the role of the courts in developing the legal framework and impacting upon practice.

Practice example 25

## Legal case analysis – University of Manchester

Students are asked to read the following case commentary in preparation for the class:

Smith, C. (2002) 'Case commentary: human rights and the Children Act 1989', *Child and Family Law Quarterly*, vol 14, no 4, pp 427-45.

Students are then asked to discuss in small groups one of a range of questions:

- What were the legal and 'care' issues informing relationships between local authorities and the courts that provided the context for these appeals? (Group 1)
- What were the grounds of appeal to both the Court of Appeal and the House of Lords in these cases? (Group 2)
- What do the appeals tell us about the judicial interpretation of human rights as these are identified in the European Convention on Human Rights and protected by the Human Rights Act? (Group 3)
- What did the Court of Appeal do in relation to these cases and arrangements to protect relevant human rights more generally? (Group 4)
- How did the House of Lords respond to the case(s) and to the decision in the Court of Appeal, and what were the grounds for its reasoning? (Group 5)
- Consider the reasoning in these cases and see if you can identify situations involving adult service users where the law might be informed by similar principles and decisions. (Group 6)

Some programme placed specific emphasis on EU legislation, international conventions, enquiry reports and the European Convention on Human Rights, demonstrating a broadening perspective as perhaps a developing trend in the curriculum.

### 3.2.6 Law and practice learning

Institutions were asked whether there were specific learning objectives relating to law for students while on practice placement.

In Wales, two out of the three programmes had no specific law-related practice learning requirements. In Scotland, programmes commonly made reference to Practice Requirement 3.3 within the GSCC Framework of Requirements for the Diploma in Social Work as an indicator that law was addressed on placement. Practice Requirement 3.3 requires students to demonstrate that they can "work in accordance with statutory and legal requirements" and applies across the four countries (although replaced in the new degrees by requirements specific to the national contexts). In England, just under half the institutions had law-related placement objectives.

**Figure 13: Law learning objectives on placement (England)**

| | |
|---|---|
| No response | 26% |
| No | 29% |
| Yes | 45% |

Those that do have specific objectives mentioned the opportunities for students to consider:

- how law and policy affect provision
- how agencies develop specific procedures to meet legal requirements (for example, data protection)
- how the law is interpreted with reference to specific situations encountered in practice

- the views of practitioners on how they meet legal requirements in their work.

Two programmes differentiated between levels of placement, specifying that law learning in the early levels would focus on awareness of relevant legislation, whereas later there would be more specialist knowledge and application, and evidence of critical analysis and evaluation.

Again looking at trends associated with the introduction of new degrees, it appears that fewer new degree respondents indicated specific placement-related learning objectives for law in new degree programmes than in DipSW programmes, although in two cases respondents indicated that the question had prompted them to consider such a development. A number of respondents in England noted a lack of focus on law in the National Occupational Standards Key Roles,[19] which tend to form the focus of practice learning expectations and assessment.

**Figure 14: Percentages of institutions offering each type of degree who do/do not have specific law learning objectives on placement (England)**

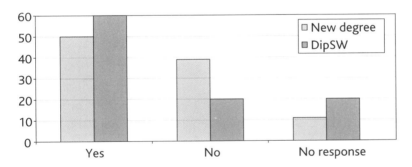

Nonetheless, there are a variety of ways in which law learning is integrated within practice learning: overt inclusion in placement agreements; ensuring that casework supervision highlights the legal mandates for work undertaken; building in specific law-related tasks to be undertaken while on placement; and specifying that the law must be an element of academic work that draws on placement practice.

Figure 15: Incorporation of law learning within practice elements (England)

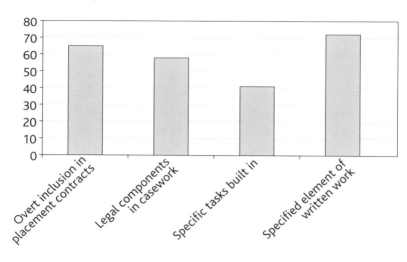

Practice example 26

## Placement-related assignment – Cornwall College

**The Social Worker in the Legal System/Law In Practice:** Following an academic assessment by examination, students are required to undertake a law-related task during their practice learning placement. This is the preparation of an Analytical Learning Diary.

Students should aim to produce about six entries, depending on the nature and depth of the work they are undertaking from a legal perspective. The intention should be for each entry to focus on a different client, and on the way in which the law impinges on the work undertaken with that client. However, it is recognised that some aspects of the law are likely to be common to many pieces of work the student undertakes, for example, working in partnership. In this case, this aspect should be addressed in depth in one entry and can then be referred to in others.

Students are expected to make their diary entries in relation to work they are undertaking themselves. However, as wide a range of entries and opportunities as possible should be sought and these may include observation of or involvement in work that is not the student's own, for example, court work, mental health admissions. More than one such entry would be exceptional and should be discussed in advance with the tutor.

The format for the diary entries should include:

- the date
- a brief overview of the work undertaken
- a summary of the legislation that is relevant to the situation
- the way in which the legislation has an impact, or is likely to have an impact, on the lives of the service user/carer/family
- a detailed description of those aspects of the legislation/ guidance that the student needed to be aware of in order to undertake the work and/or a detailed description of the procedures, systems and guidelines relevant to what was observed
- a description of what the student actually did and/or a description of what they observed happening in response
- an evaluation of their practice and/or of the practice observed:
  - > Was their practice aided by the legislation, or did it impose constraints?
  - > Were guidelines followed and what impact did that have on the service user/carer/family and on the aim and purpose of the intervention?
  - > How did the student view their practice in using the legislation (give examples and critique)?
  - > What were the value issues/conflicts?

Practice example 27

# Placement-related assignment – University of Kent at Medway

**Law for Contemporary Social Work Practice (Level 3):** The main objective for the module is to ensure that students know the law as it pertains to contemporary social work practice in England. Students need a basic understanding of such law across a wide range of service user groups and settings, and a more highly developed or deeper knowledge in their area of current practice.

The module is assessed entirely by coursework. Students will present two 2,000 word essays. The first will be on a topic unrelated to the student's final assessed placement. It will test students' ability to recognise and discuss the significance of legislative and legal frameworks and service delivery standards at a level detached from specific practice constraints. The second will give an account of students' application of the law while on placement, demonstrating that they have considered the relationship between agency policies, legal requirements and professional boundaries in shaping the nature of the service provided.

The use of a summative unseen examination is not considered appropriate for this module. An unseen examination might encourage students to turn such an assessment into a memory test rather than an opportunity to show their ability to process what has been learned, and would thus be counter-productive in androgogic terms.

Independent of the module assessment, and to ensure integration and application of legal knowledge, a capstone assessment of students takes place while they are on the 200 days in practice settings.

One programme sets an assessed assignment prior to students going out into their placement agencies, with a specific expectation that they will use placement resources and dialogue with practitioners to assist in their research for the paper.

Practice example 28

# Short answer paper – University of Luton

**Social Work and the Law:** This module is in part assessed through a Short Answer Paper, which students have six weeks to complete. The paper is set prior to the start of the practice placement, with the intention that students use resources and discussion with personnel on placement to assist their research. The paper consists of 23 questions, of which the following are a sample.

1.    What is the difference between a power and a duty? Give an example of each.
2.    What is meant in law by the 'burden of proof'? Explain the difference in the burden of proof in criminal and civil law?
3.    Ivy is 15 and has cerebral palsy. She lives with her parents, grandmother and brother. What legislation would inform your work in this situation?    What services might be provided? What principles would guide your work?
4.    Ron is 80 and lives alone in a second-floor flat. He is recently widowed. He has difficulties coping at home and is at risk through forgetfulness and falls. What legislation would inform your work with Ron? What conflicting imperatives might be involved?
5.    How would you enable a dissatisfied client to complain about services they had received? What is the legislative base for this procedure?
6.    What duties does the Race Relations (Amendment) Act 2000 place on local authorities?

7. Give a brief analysis of your placement agency's anti-racist and anti-discriminatory policies. How are these connected to the legislation?

8. What is the difference between the nearest relative as defined in the Mental Health Act 1983 and next of kin?

9. A gay man who lives with a long-term partner requires admission under section 2 of the Mental Health Act 1983. His mother lives nearby and sees him regularly. Who is the 'nearest relative'?

10. In what ways does the Children Act 1989 seek to empower children and young people?

11. Under what legislation may the local authority provide residential accommodation and for whom (excluding children)?

12. Give an example of a 'qualified right' under the Human Rights Act 1998.

13. In what way does the Carers and Disabled Children Act 2000 add to the Carers (Recognition and Services) Act 1995?

14. What are the implications of Article 8 of the European Convention on Human Rights for practice in your placement agency?

Institutions in England were additionally asked to identify the respective locations of law teaching and practice placements within their programmes overall. Of the institutions who gave this information (28):

- three (11%) had a placement in the year before the first law course was taught
- six (21%) had a law module in the year before the first placement
- 19 (68%) taught the first law module in the same year as the first placement
- one programme has law modules and placements in all three years.

Figure 16: Correlation between placement and law modules by year (all institutions) (England)

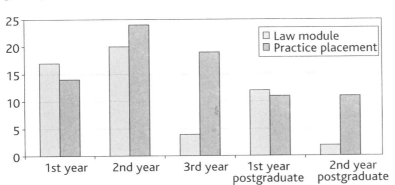

While law teaching is most commonly located in the first two years of the undergraduate programmes and the first year of postgraduate programmes, practice placements are more evenly spread but tend to be later in the programme. This trend intensifies as a result of changes in programme structures with the introduction of the new degrees.

Figure 17: Correlation between placement and law modules by year: DipSW respondents (England)

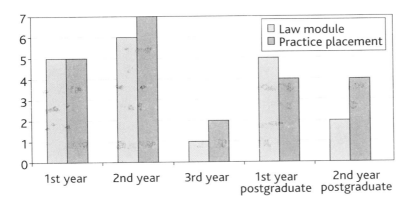

Figure 18: Correlation between placement and law modules by year: new respondents (England)

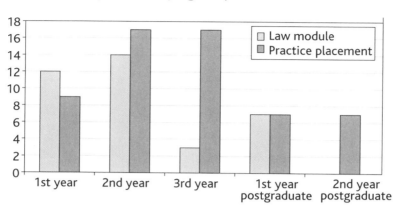

In the debate on the timing of law teaching relative to practice learning, it appears that knowledge is more commonly delivered before practice, and that final integration, if it is to take place, will commonly be a task that students must undertake on placement.

Programmes in England were asked to comment on how they were interpreting the new degree requirement that students gain experience of statutory work in at least one of their placements. Programmes were split here between two positions. Some interpreted the requirement as meaning that the placement had to take place in a statutory agency. Others interpreted it as requiring students to undertake work that is explicitly defined and regulated through statute, but which might be taking place within an independent agency, in some cases acting under contract to a statutory authority. The work should require students to understand and act under the legislation. One programme specified that they would be interpreting the requirement as meaning students must experience the 'strong control' elements of the legislation.

Notwithstanding the recognition that practice learning could make an important contribution to students' understanding of law, concerns were expressed in all countries about how effectively and consistently this could be achieved. Practice teachers' and agencies' own knowledge and understanding of the legal frameworks for practice were not considered to be reliable across the board. One programme had taken some specific steps to work with and develop a more consistent approach by practice learning agencies, through producing written materials that identified the legal frameworks relevant to non-statutory agencies.

The question was also raised of whether institutions provided specific guidance or resources for practice teachers to support them in the task of facilitating students' law learning on placement. While recognising that this was important, the majority of programmes do not currently provide specific law-related support. In England, only 41% of institutions provide anything of this nature, and in Scotland, Wales and Northern Ireland the picture was similar, with the majority of programmes indicating that they did not undertake specific, law-related activities with practice teachers.

Those who do, provide it in a number of ways:

- law revision sessions for students during the course of the placement, which practice teachers are invited to attend
- practice teachers invited to participate in some of the concurrent taught sessions, in which the focus is on investigating the legal and procedural issues related to situations arising on placement
- written guidance given on the legal frameworks for agency practice (seen as particularly important in relation to placements in voluntary agencies)
- practice teacher roles in relation to law learning included in the written guidance offered to practice teachers
- workshops for practice teachers on their role in relation to specific law-related tasks undertaken by students on placement.

Another approach is to offer resources to practice teachers more generally through, for example, offering taught sessions on practice teacher training or refresher programmes, mentioned in three cases.

One programme undertook a significant amount of liaison with practice teachers over one elective module, running workshops for practice teachers on the links between the module and the students' placements, and providing detailed written guidance on the legal and policy context.

### 3.2.7 Assessment

Coursework is the most commonly used method of assessing students' law learning. It is the sole method used by over half of institutions in England, and is combined with examinations by a further third. With the introduction of the new degree, there is a slight shift in favour either of coursework or examinations, rather than combined methods.

**Figure 19: Methods of assessment by institutions (England)**

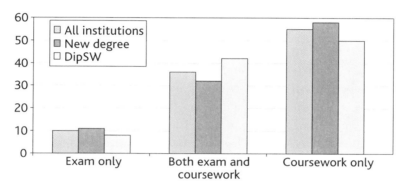

In Scotland and Wales, the picture is similar, with coursework or examination and coursework being employed as the method of assessment for the majority of programmes, albeit with occasional plans to introduce examinations or assessed seminars within the new degrees. In Northern Ireland, however, there has been a move away from coursework in favour of examinations (computer-based). In all countries, law commonly figures as one aspect of assessment criteria in other assignments elsewhere in the programme.

These broad categories of examinations and coursework contain a range of different types of assessment. Coursework might include case study commentaries, essays, assessed seminars, assessed presentations or other law project work. Project work might involve students in acting independently to secure access to a learning opportunity outside of the college.

Practice example 29

# Courtroom observation report – University of Illinois at Urbana-Champaign, School of Social Work

For this paper, students will attend court for at least two hours as an observer. If you are involved in a case as a witness or a party, you should not report on this experience. You may select federal or state court in any locality that is convenient for you. Please describe your experience and what you observed, thought and felt.

Weave into your paper answers to the following questions:

- When and where did your observation occur?
- What kind of case did you see?
- What was the legal issue that the court was deciding?
- Who was present in the courtroom?
- How did the people involved treat one another?
- How did the case relate to social work?
- Did it invoke for you any issues related to social work values or ethics?
- How did you feel about what you observed?
- How do you think a vulnerable client would feel in the same situation?

Your paper should be 2 to 3 pages long, typed and double-spaced. It should not report on the content of the case (other than where indicated above) but instead should focus on your attitudes, beliefs, feelings and reflective thoughts about what you observed. It should be written in a clear, concise and comprehensive manner.

The most commonly used approach to assessment is content based around case studies, used by 67% of all England programmes using coursework or combined methods of assessment, and by the majority of

Scotland and Wales programmes. Students are given detailed guidance about what is expected in case study-based coursework, and typically the 'cases' set require integration of a range of legislation, crossing childcare, community care, criminal justice and mental health boundaries.

Practice example 30

# Coursework case study – University of Bangor

This assignment is in two parts, both of which are based on the following case study.

This case has been assigned to you following referral by a Health Visitor, who is concerned about Josie and her children. Josie has just been discharged from hospital having had the initial diagnosis of multiple sclerosis confirmed. She is the single parent of four children aged between 3 and 14, since her husband died in an accident on a building site 12 months ago. Over the last few months Josie has been feeling ill and very depressed by the possibility of long-term sickness. Her mother, Marguerite, has been travelling 10 miles by bus three times a week to help her with housework and shopping. Delroy (14) and Elaine (12) have taken over much of the responsibility of looking after their younger siblings Sandra (3) and Milly (7).

The Health Visitor is concerned particularly in relation to Josie's physical and emotional condition and the effects of those upon her parenting skills. She is also very suspicious that Josie is smoking cannabis to relieve the pain of multiple sclerosis (MS). However, Josie denies this and also denies she is unable to cope with looking after herself and the children. The Health Visitor is also concerned about the pressures on Marguerite, who is in her early 70s and suffers from asthma, and about Delroy and Elaine, who have been missing school. Delroy is under threat of exclusion because of his frequent absences and his aggressive behaviour in the classroom when he does attend.

Part 1 (2,000 words): this part of the assignment asks you specific questions about the law, which you should answer fully, citing the relevant legislation (including sections of Acts) and making reference where appropriate to regulations, policy and practice documents and judicial cases.

- List the main duties and powers, if any, that a social work authority may have in relation to Josie, and discuss how and why you might use them in this case.
- List the main duties and powers, if any, that a social work authority may have in relation to Marguerite, and discuss how and why you might use them in this case.
- List the main duties and powers, if any, that a social work authority may have in relation to Delroy, Elaine, Milly and Sandra, and discuss how and why you might use them in this case.

Part 2 (1,500 words): for this part of the assignment you should choose any member of this family and offer a critical discussion about his/her situation, relating the use of law to practice. Your answer should fully consider the following issues:

- conflicting imperatives
- compulsion and negotiation
- partnership and empowerment.

Practice example 31

# Coursework case study – Glasgow Caledonian University

It is not enough for social workers to have some knowledge of the legislation which governs their work, without that knowledge being tempered by an awareness of the potential range of its discretion and the potential consequences of its use. This exercise is intended to give students the opportunity to explore some of the complexities of the social work task within the legal framework. It is not therefore sufficient for students to quote the statutory basis without placing this within the overall social policy context, taking full account of issues of racism and discrimination. In short, therefore, students must not only say what legislation applies to the particular matter they are discussing, but why they have chosen it and what its potential consequences might be.

Select one of the following case studies (choice of 2) and in your answer address the following three issues. These are of equal importance in terms of the requirement to demonstrate an understanding, but this does not mean they will be of exactly equal length. The overall word limit is 3,000 words.

- **The statutory law and the range of possible options available to the social worker within the legislation:** select the legislation you consider to be the most appropriate response to the situation. This should also involve some discussion of the wider context within which this decision has been made. For example, if you are suggesting that the child in Case Study 1 should be the subject of compulsory social work intervention, what does research tell us about the possible outcomes of such an action? Are there gender issues? How might the mother's learning difficulties affect her choices? On the basis of this information, why are you making a particular choice of legislative option?

- **Roles and responsibilities imposed by the legislation:** having selected the legislative option, you are then required to examine the roles and responsibilities of the social worker and those agencies that are involved. There will be combinations of roles and responsibilities imposed by the legislation. For example, preparing a report for a court is a statutory responsibility, which you would be expected to state. There are also social roles involved in the collation of the report. How these are discharged in any given situation will be affected by other issues, including the potential for racism and discrimination.
- **The rights of those involved:** in deciding upon a particular course of action, a social worker would have to be alert to the rights of service users, their families and perhaps the community. This again will be influenced by external factors, which you will draw from wider reading.

Anti-racist and anti-discriminatory perspectives should permeate your work, rather than be 'tagged on' at the end. The way to approach this is to examine the decisions you are taking and the options you are choosing from an understanding that different groups in different situations experience the legal context differently. For example, how might this affect decision making in relation to a young woman with a disability? What do we know about the impact of poverty on people's access to the law?

In order to examine the range of issues raised within the questions, you will be well advised to look beyond the basic legal texts. Try to link in with the teaching on other modules to provide a broader range of analysis for your work. If a residential option is inappropriate in terms of a legal option, why is this the case? Would it matter if the person were of a different age, sex, culture, income level? What does the literature say about the issues?

Obviously within the word limit set for this assignment you will not be able to explore everything in detail. Where sacrifices need to be made, try to reduce the description and retain the analysis.

**Sample Case Study 1**: Alan Brown (47) and Sue Smith (23) were referred to the Social Work Department by their GP when Sue was eight months pregnant with their first child. The GP was concerned about Sue's ability to understand the implications of her pregnancy and the responsibilities of parenthood, as she has learning difficulties. She attends the Resource Centre run by the local authority.

When the social worker visited, she found the family home sparsely furnished with poor standards of hygiene and no apparent signs of preparation for the baby. The flat is on the 14th floor of a local authority high-rise block, soon to be renovated but currently damp and draughty. Alan Brown was hostile, insisting they did not need any 'interference' – they had everything under control and would be able to provide adequately for the child.

Three weeks later the social worker received a call from the hospital, expressing concerns about Sue's handling of her baby son, born two days previously. They felt she was not feeding or handling the baby properly and was not responding to attempts to help her. Now Sue had been seen by staff to smack the baby because he was not feeding quickly enough when her favourite TV programme was about to start. She had become agitated and frustrated with her son, and staff had had to intervene. When Alan Brown had arrived he had been told of the referral and had become very angry. He stated his intention to remove Sue and the baby from hospital immediately, and had said he wanted to ensure his child did not end up in care 'like the others'. A check of child protection records had revealed that he had two children from a previous relationship with whom he was denied contact, having committed a Schedule 1 offence against one of those children. His behaviour at the hospital had become so difficult that the police were called and he was charged with breach of the peace and assault. Sue had told hospital staff she did not feel ready to go home just yet.

Case studies also figure frequently within examination-style assessments also, alongside, to a lesser extent, essays, multiple choice and short answer questions.

Figure 20: Content of examinations (England)

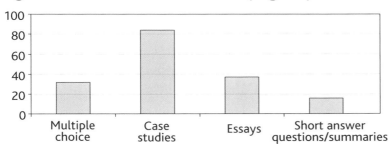

Whether tested through case study or multiple choice, the emphasis is often upon accurate technical legal knowledge, correctly applied, in the case of case study approaches, to the situation in hand.

Practice example 32

## Multiple choice examination (November 2003) – University of Hull

| The duty which is placed on local authorities by Section 47(1)(A) of the NHS and Community Care Act 1990 requires them to | |
|---|---|
| | a Assess everyone who asks for assessment |
| | b Assess everyone who appears to them to be in need of a service which they may provide or arrange |
| | c Assess everyone who is referred by a doctor or other professional |
| | d Screen all applicants in order to decide whether to assess them |

| | |
|---|---|
| **Which of the attached statements best describes the decision of the House of Lords in *R v Gloucestershire CC ex parte Barry*?** | a Local authority resources were not to be taken into account when assessing need<br><br>b Resources were not to be taken into account when the local authority had exhausted them<br><br>c Need for services cannot be assessed without some regard for the cost of providing them<br><br>d Need is an absolute concept and qualitatively different from questions of resource |
| **A person wishing to challenge a local authority by requesting Judicial Review must normally first** | a Apply to the Local Government Ombudsman<br><br>b Exhaust the local authority Complaints Procedure<br><br>c Apply to the Social Care Tribunal<br><br>d Ask the social worker for a formal review and reassessment of care package |
| **Under section 4, Disabled Persons (Services, Consultation and Representation) Act 1986, disabled people are** | a Entitled to a service<br><br>b Entitled to practical assistance in the home<br><br>c Entitled to an assessment<br><br>d Entitled to a holiday |
| **Under the Carers (Recognition and Services) Act 1995 carers have** | a An entitlement to a service<br><br>b A right to have their needs assessed alongside that of the person for whom they are caring<br><br>c An entitlement to have their needs assessed<br><br>d A right to an independent assessment |

| | |
|---|---|
| **Under section 114(1), Mental Health Act 1983, approved social workers are appointed by** | a A local health authority |
| | b A local social services authority |
| | c The government |
| | d The mental health tribunal |
| **Admission for assessment (Section 2, Mental Health Act 1983) lasts for a period not exceeding** | a 72 hours |
| | b 28 days |
| | c 6 months |
| | d 6 hours |
| **Before compulsory admission for treatment under section 3, Mental Health Act 1983, the patient must be seen by at least** | a One consultant psychiatrist |
| | b An approved social worker |
| | c An approved social worker and a doctor |
| | d Two doctors and an approved social worker |
| **Admission for assessment in cases of emergency (section 4, Mental Health Act 1983) may be made by** | a A hospital manager |
| | b A magistrate |
| | c An approved social worker or nearest relative |
| | d The police |

Practice example 33

# Case study examination – University of East Anglia (UEA)

Candidates have already received the case scenarios excluding the questions and will answer questions from two out of three sections. The percentage of available marks is shown at the end of each question. Copies of UEA Law Files may be brought into the examination. Students are examined in three distinct areas of law – mental health, childcare and community care. An example of the type of questions set is given below.

### Section 1 – Mental Health Law

1. Tamsin (23) has lived with her half sister Alison (28) for the last year. Both women have fallen out with their mother, Sheila, since she disapproves of their partners. Tamsin is involved with her employer Mike, who has a wife and two children aged three and five years. Alison has a relationship with Maria (25) who works in London during the week and returns to her parents' home every weekend.

Under the Mental Health Act 1983 who is the nearest relative for:
(a) Tamsin; (b) Alison; (c) Maria?
Give your reasons                                                    (10%)

2. Tamsin's relationship with Mike is volatile and causes her much distress. She has walked out of her place of work following arguments, has gone missing with no memory of where she has been, and has slept all night in his garden to be near him. Mike has suggested the relationship should end but Tamsin has refused to accept this and has threatened to harm herself. She has a history of self-harm. Mike's wife, on learning of the relationship, has telephoned Tamsin telling her to stay away from her husband. She says that he wants nothing more to do with her. Tamsin has cut her wrists. Although the injury is slight she appears to

be out of control, threatening to kill Mike's wife and children, or herself. Alison is used to Tamsin's outbursts but is frightened as she feels that this episode is more pronounced than others. She has called Maria's parents who are now at the house preventing Tamsin from leaving. Alison phones the GP who judges that Tamsin's mental state requires assessment under the Mental Health Act 1983.

Which professionals may be involved?
What are their roles? (20 %)

3. The professionals arrive and undertake an assessment.

What must the Approved Social Worker do in order to assess Tamsin under the Mental Health Act 1983? (10 %)

4. It is decided to admit Tamsin to hospital.

Under which section of the Mental Health Act 1983 might it be appropriate to admit Tamsin?
Give your reasons and explain why you consider other sections to be inappropriate (20 %)

5. When Sheila learns of the situation, she arrives at the hospital in a fury and demands that Tamsin be discharged immediately.

What rights do (a) Sheila and (b) Alison have under the Mental Health Act 1983? (20%)

6. Tamsin remains in hospital and it is agreed that she requires treatment for a mental illness.

What treatments may be given to Tamsin without her consent? Describe the legal bases and processes under which these treatments may be given. (20 %)

The balance of examination content is similar where examinations are used in Scotland, and Wales. In Northern Ireland, multiple choice questions are used to test essential and precise legal knowledge in all areas of relevant law that practitioners are believed to need readily accessible in their mind for daily practice.

In setting criteria for assessment of students' learning, institutions in all countries were looking for a range of evidence, with two aspects sought by all – knowledge of the legal framework and application of the law to practice. There is a broad measure of agreement between programmes about what they deem important for students to evidence, although no programme seeks evidence across the whole range. Additional criteria included the correct citation of legal sources, the use of law to analyse agency practice and the ability to access information on specialist areas of law.

**Figure 21: What is being looked for in students' assessed work (England)?**

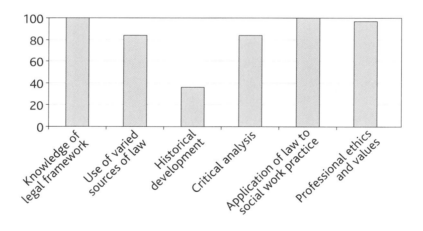

In Scotland and Wales, there was a similar range of expectation, although with perhaps a more consistent expectation in relation to critical analysis of the legal framework, which was mentioned by all institutions. In Scotland, most respondents referred to an additional consideration – the requirement to test students' knowledge across a comprehensive range of legislation in the key areas of community care, childcare and criminal justice. In Northern Ireland, the emphasis was placed on accurate legal knowledge and its application in practice.

Most programmes articulated a clear rationale for the choice of assessment methods, although it has to be said that equally strong and sometimes the same justifications were advanced for very different methods. Examinations were seen to have the following strengths:

- they can clearly be judged as students' own work, eliminating concerns about plagiarism, because students take them under controlled conditions
- they create a motive for students to retain knowledge
- they test time management and the ability to work under pressure.

Open book and closed book examinations both had advocates. Allowing students to take resources and materials into the examination was thought to set a task more akin to the reality of practice, where it is arguably more important to know where to look something up than to have memorised every legal detail. Respondents were satisfied that students still did work in preparation, recognising that they could not use texts competently under examination conditions if they had not previously established familiarity with the content. Having texts available made it possible for students to quote legislation accurately, reinforcing their learning.

Closed book examinations were seen not as a memory test, or as a way of showing off legal knowledge, but as a way of assessing students' ability to write about the interface between the law and practice. The choice in one case was justified by experience of student performance, which had improved over open book examination approaches. Closed book examinations were also to some extent seen to be the most robust way of addressing the verification dilemmas of knowing students have done the work themselves.

Similarly, seen and unseen examaniations both drew support. Having the paper in advance at least gave students a chance to engage in some targeted research around the topics, thus testing their use of sources and ability to integrate information over a period of time. Unseen papers, in contrast, tested the ability quickly to identify the key legal issues in a given situation and to apply relevant knowledge to problem-solving activity within time constraints. They were judged more reliably to test the students' own understanding rather than the results of collaborative work.

Typically, institutions using examinations operated some combination of open/closed, seen/unseen papers, with the least common being unseen, closed-book tests.

Coursework was seen as having the following strengths as a method of assessment:

- It replicates the practice reality of being faced with a task and needing to find and apply appropriate knowledge. Students need to use appropriate enquiry skills to seek out relevant knowledge, and integrate it within their response, as they would in practice.
- It preserves the approach that is taken in teaching where formative assessment is used to help students develop the knowledge and skills that are then summatively assessed.
- It prevents students feeling they are merely required to pass a memory test in the assessment.
- It was felt to be a more appropriate assessment medium for students demonstrating Masters-level (postgraduate) learning outcomes, allowing greater opportunity for reflection and critical analysis and for integration with other areas such as ethics and values.

Particular types of assessment tasks were thought to offer different opportunities, whether located in examinations or in coursework.

- Multiple-choice questions, for example, were thought to assess detailed points of law and to encourage students to engage with some core knowledge. They have been positively evaluated by students. Some respondents were critical, feeling that the knowledge tested is superficial.
- Case studies were believed to assess ability to apply the law to practice situations, ensuring that professional values are considered and decision-making processes are evidenced. They were thought appropriate for testing understanding as well as knowledge. They enable several areas of law to be tested, reflecting the breadth of knowledge that would be needed to respond to one situation in practice. One respondent, however, felt students had difficulty structuring their answers, necessitating either very structured guidance or tutorial support to ensure a more coherent response.
- Essays were thought to enable students to consider more fully the dilemmas and philosophy of the underpinning legislation. Students

could be expected to integrate and critically evaluate information from different sources. Others felt that the concrete legal knowledge evidenced could be thin, and that a discursive 'academic' essay did not test accuracy of legal knowledge or ability to apply it in practice.

- Group tasks were believed to encourage key skills of cooperative learning, encouraging students to use collective organisation to cover a wide range of material in a short space of time. Group dynamics are unpredictable, however, and can sometimes interfere with students' learning.
- Assessed presentations enable verbal skills in discussing the legal framework to be developed. However, they are time intensive, particularly if done in small groups, and pose the challenge of how to moderate the results.

In programmes where law is learned in a wholly integrated fashion, emphasis was placed on the integration of knowledge and understanding across all assignments. One programme attached the criterion "uses and critically evaluates relevant policy and legislation" to all assessed work. One difficulty attached to the practice of integrated law assessment (not raised by this programme, but by another) is that of identifying that the law component is of sufficient quality. It was thought important to construct assessment criteria that avoid the possibility of weak performance in law being compensated by stronger performance in another component of the assessment task. One programme using an enquiry-based approach sets a two-part assessment, where law must appear in both.

Practice example 34

# Integrated law assessment – University of Bristol

The Unit 'Society, Social Need and Social Work' aims to provide students with a beginning understanding of the development of social work, a critical analysis of the ways in which social problems may be constructed and social need and social welfare conceptualised, and an awareness of how these issues link with expectations about social workers' professional tasks. The unit introduces students to the legislative framework within which social work operates, the major functions of social work agencies in different settings and the profession's value base. The Unit consists of a series of study group themes and a programme of lectures. Working with a facilitator in study groups of about 12, students will explore issues of social need in society, the role of social welfare agencies in relation to three groups – children and families, older people and offenders. For each group a study theme is provided, which includes study outlines on which to plan a study programme using a range of resources including books, articles, videos and consultations. The study group meets twice a week for 1½ hours.

Assessment of the legal component is undertaken through:

a) an assignment in which law must be integrated alongside other components
b) a law assessment task.

**a) Sample assignment titles**
1. Write an essay outlining the reasons why homeless families are housed in temporary accommodation, the problems and needs they face and the role of social work and social welfare agencies in providing assistance
2. Write an essay outlining the impact of disability on family life, the needs of such families and the role of social work and social welfare agencies in providing assistance
3. Write an essay about older people with medical and social needs who live alone. Outline how and why their needs arise, and the range of ways in which these can be met, including the different roles and perspectives of health and social services. You should indicate how older people's rights to self-determination and independence could be balanced with the duty to provide care
4. Write an essay about the issues in family-based care for older people. This should include relevant policies, the needs of older people and their carers, the relationship between

those in need of care and carers, and the role of social work and social welfare agencies in providing assistance

5. Write an essay on the way the criminal justice system deals with women offenders. Outline the problems and difficulties faced by women as a consequence of imprisonment and the role of social work and social welfare agencies in providing assistance

6. A voluntary agency has expressed an interest in starting up a project for unemployed young people on an estate. Write an essay setting out possible reasons why young people offend, and the potential role of probation and social welfare agencies in providing assistance. Your essay should include an outline of the form the project could take.

Marking criteria are that the assignment should:

- meet the requirements of the question
- use clear and accurate English
- be well organised with an appropriate structure
- use and critically evaluate relevant theory, research and literature
- use and critically evaluate relevant policy and legislation
- make effective use of relevant experience and/or practice
- integrate core social work values, including anti-oppressive practice.

### b) Sample law assessment tasks
Division of the task within the study group is encouraged. However, each student's submission must be an individual one.

Question 1

In relation to the assessment matrix on pages 134/135 of the Area Child Protection Committee's Multi-Agency Procedures (of which all groups will have a copy), assume you have undertaken an initial assessment on the child/children described there and answer the following:

a) What need code would you allocate and why?
b) What level of response/priority would you decide on? What evidence would you require to demonstrate this? Are there any other relevant factors not included in the matrix?
c) What would be the 'range and level of services' appropriate to the needs identified and who might provide them?
d) Discuss the extent to which the matrix facilitates a holistic assessment of the needs of children and their families.

Question 2

a) Outline the legal requirements on social services departments to produce individual care plans for people assessed as in need under the NHS and Community Care Act 1990
b) Identify the difficulties likely to be faced by a care manager in drawing up such care plans
c) Discuss the significance of the above for anti-oppressive practice for older people.

Question 3

a) As a group, produce a summary of the contents of the Crime and Disorder Act 1998 and discuss its provisions. Include in the summary and discussion your responses to questions (b) and (c) below
b) Outline the overall aims and provisions of the Act and provide more detail on the sections of the Act which provide for 'detention and training orders' and 'anti-social behaviour orders'
c) The Crime and Disorder Act attempted to establish a coherent new approach to work with young offenders. Outline that new approach. Discuss the extent to which it enacts the government's policy commitment to be 'tough on crime and tough on the causes of crime'.

Overall it was common for programmes to use mixed method assessment of law – perhaps an examination in one year, followed by essays or case studies later in the programme. This was linked overtly by some to the required development in students' learning from knowledge acquisition, through application, to evaluation and critical analysis. By others it was linked to the need to test different levels of learning – surface layers (technical knowledge), application, conceptual and deep learning which would enable students to adapt their understanding when technical knowledge changed as the legal framework developed.

Practice example 35

## Mixed assessment methods – North-East Worcestershire College

**Law for Social Work Practice (Level 2):** The academic assessment comprises two elements:

- open book examination to test legal knowledge
- written assignment in which students choose one piece of social welfare legislation and plot its route from inception to enactment. They will research its origins (from Private Member's Bill or Parliamentary Committee) through its passage to statute, looking at objections and amendments to its final stages. They will be required to critically evaluate its intent and purpose, whether the final Act achieves the original aims and whether it is controlling or empowering to service users.

Students also carry out a practice exercise on placement, the result of which will be included in their portfolio of evidence of learning from the placement. Students will be required to build a 'tool kit' of information and resources. This may consist of a list of agencies, independent advisors and experts in particular fields, who can provide objective, good advice on the legal dilemmas presented by service users' needs. It is envisaged that this 'tool kit' will grow as students move into different placements with different service user groups.

Practice example 36

# Mixed assessment methods – University of Lincoln

**Professional Practice and the Legal Framework (Level 1):** This unit concentrates on giving students practice-relevant knowledge of key aspects of the legal framework, a critical understanding of the debates on applying the law, and skills in finding out about and understanding new and existing legislation. The unit will examine the key philosophy and principles underpinning the legal framework. There is particular emphasis on applying the law in an anti-oppressive way that promotes service user participation at the highest possible level.

The assessment will be in two parts:

- a series of three multiple-choice class-based tests testing students' knowledge of specific legislation
- a written assignment of not more than 2,500 words in which students are asked to demonstrate their understanding of the legal framework for professional practice through a response to case material. The assessment criteria reflect the learning outcomes for the unit, rewarding evidence of:
  - > understanding the key philosophy and principles underpinning legislation
  - > selection and accurate description of relevant legislation
  - > knowledge of statutory responsibilities and powers of social workers
  - > description of how the legal framework affects decision making in social work practice
  - > identification of legal dilemmas and relating these to professional practice
  - > consideration of how the law can be used anti-oppressively in order to promote service user participation.

Even a single form of assessment could have several different components – for example, an examination requiring students to tackle some multiple choice or short answer questions, plus an essay or case study question; or a two-part assessment comprising both examination and coursework. For some programmes, this reflected the recognition that different forms of assessment favour different students and that variety was therefore fairer to all. Allied to this was the recognition that law assessment can become rather formulaic, with students knowing what to expect, and an associated intention to develop assessments that test legal research skills rather than rote learning. One respondent described a system in which testing was incremental throughout a whole semester of teaching, targeting different knowledge and skills as time went by. This was thought to have the advantage of breaking down the learning into smaller, manageable portions for students, and to enable them to build in improvement over time in the light of formal feedback. Another programme has changed the timing of assessment to locate it after the final placement, to allow students time to incorporate their learning from practice within their overall understanding of the subject. Another has constructed a portfolio approach to enable students to demonstrate their law learning in a range of different ways.

Practice example 37

# Mixed assessment methods – London South Bank University

**Law for Social Work, Ethical Dilemmas and Decision Making:** There are three elements to the assessment, which together will form a portfolio of work:

- Tutor assessed seminars: each student will be a member of a small group which researches two case studies (one in adult law and one in child care law). The final seminar discussion (20 minutes) resulting from this research will be assessed. Marks will be awarded for:
  > evidence of preparation for the seminar
  > scope and accuracy of the information presented
  > contribution to the seminar discussion

> showing familiarity with the material
> listening and building on the contributions of others
- A formal write-up of each case study, with evidence of understanding how the material relates to social work values and is relevant to social work practice (1,000 words)
- A self-assessment showing reflective commentary on the learning process and how this has assisted the student in their practice setting (1,000 words).

Acknowledgement: Tutor-assessed seminars draw on published material[133].

For the future, several programmes are developing online assessment mechanisms. Computer technology was seen to provide the benefit of multiple opportunities for students to achieve a sound level of achievement, using early attempts at tests as formative experiences, on the basis of which higher scores can be achieved at subsequent attempts.

The introduction of the new degree has also clearly offered opportunities to make changes, and a number of respondents mentioned that the assessment systems in their new degree were, or would be, different from their existing custom and practice. There is, however, no dominant trend associated with the changes. Institutions currently using examinations are moving to coursework; institutions currently using coursework are introducing examinations. This mirrors the exchange of practice in teaching and learning, with institutions using integrated models introducing discrete modules, and those favoring discrete modules, while not abandoning these, moving towards greater integration elsewhere in the curriculum.

## 3.2.8 Evaluation of law teaching learning and assessment

The survey sought to identify how law teachers on social work programmes evaluate the teaching learning and assessment activity. It is clear that students and external examiners/assessors are influential, alongside the perceptions of teaching staff.

**Figure 22: Sources of evaluation of law teaching learning and assessment (England)**

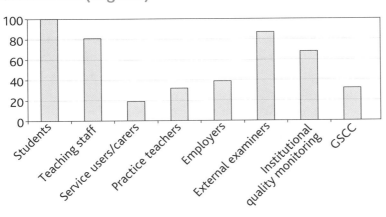

Students' perceptions of their law learning were reported as being predominantly positive, with the proviso that students say they find law difficult and that it makes them nervous. They sometimes struggle to read legal texts without additional explanation. The level of satisfaction appears in some cases to be related to the amount of effort that students invest to achieve their learning outcomes – along the lines of "the more you put in the more you get out". Some students were reported as finding the topic more interesting than they had anticipated. For others, it is a necessary evil, to be endured rather than enjoyed. A common complaint made to programmes is that of not enough time being allocated to this subject. Another is that law teaching by lawyers does not always address the complex task of applying the law in practice. Group learning is often appreciated, as are seminars where there is an opportunity to test out ideas and ask questions. Presentations by practitioners with 'real' experience draw positive comment from students, as does discussion of the principles and values underpinning the law. The combination of lectures and enquiry-based approaches works well for many students. Class handouts that achieve some synthesis of the complex legal frameworks and thus make them more accessible, rather than merely reproduce what can be found in textbooks, are seen as very helpful.

Some programmes reported good feedback from their agency partners, appreciative of being able to recruit practitioners with a sound working knowledge of law.

A majority of respondents in England (74%) indicated that external guidance had influenced their approach to their law teaching. The sources of guidance included curriculum guidance from the Central Council for Education and Training in Social Work (CCETSW) law project,[22] feedback and advice from colleagues in other universities, feedback from agencies in the programme partnership, the Quality Assurance Agency (QAA) benchmark statement for social work[17] and comments from practice assessors, external assessors, service users and carers.

Respondents were asked to comment on other sources of influence on their approaches to learning teaching and assessing law. Nine institutions indicated that they had been influenced by research, quoting examples of journal articles that had been helpful, the SWAPltsn website, and the Law Report.[22] Eight institutions mentioned other broader literature that had influenced them, including a number of social work law textbooks, inquiry reports and a series of journal special issues on law in social work education. Two respondents mentioned the enduring influence of their own original law learning and the enthusiasm it had given them for the subject, which in turn influences their own approach to teaching.

Across the four countries there were no concrete examples of evaluations that have been conducted as formal outcome studies, the emphasis being, as in England, on evaluation of teaching input, and satisfaction with learning outcomes.

In conclusion, institutions were asked how satisfied they were with their current approach to learning teaching and assessing law. In Scotland and in Wales, all but one of the programmes expressed reasonable satisfaction, although none was very satisfied. In England, the majority of programmes were reasonably satisfied also.

Figure 23: Satisfaction with law teaching learning and assessment (England)

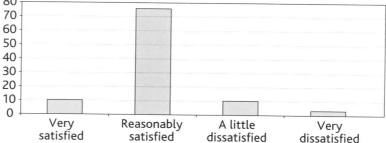

Dissatisfactions in the four countries reflected similar themes, including:

- a wish to move away from over-reliance on rote learning
- pressure on the curriculum that leaves certain topics under-emphasised
- pressure on the curriculum following devolution, particularly in Scotland
- shortage of resources such as appropriate texts, again particularly in Scotland
- the tension between breadth and depth
- pressures to employ quick fix, instrumental styles of teaching to respond to agency requirements for practitioners who know how to fill in forms
- lack of time to explore debates of principle, tease out policy links and explore some of the more challenging, exciting aspects of law
- concern that the assessment does not cover the breadth of law taught
- insufficient integration of law knowledge within practice learning
- the need to develop ways of using web-based resources and e-learning approaches generally, but associated with concern that less class-based time (or poorer attendance by students who can secure their resources elsewhere) may result in less well developed understanding of the complex relationships between law and practice.

A number of respondents referred to the constant evolution of teaching, learning and assessment, in part as a reflection of the rapid changes and development in the subject matter, but also as a result of recognition that there is probably no one best way of doing things.

## 3.3 Focus groups with students and practice teachers

### 3.3.1 Students' perspectives

Students were asked about their experiences of learning the law during the academic components of their programmes. In relation to expectations, students commonly described feeling daunted and apprehensive or even fearful of the subject, its perceived specialist nature and its technical jargon.

"I was really nervous."

Some had experience of friends failing law exams. Very few students had prior experience of the subject, and even if they did there was anxiety about transferring knowledge learned in a different context. Several described surprise at the level of structured learning they were expected to engage in and had not realised that taking on board new concepts would entail such a lot of work on their part.

"It's how much you've got to remember – do you need to know all of it?"

A minority of students felt more open minded about the subject, stimulated by the opportunity to engage with something new. There was some appreciation of what was perceived as its more structured and practical nature, in comparison to other curriculum areas, with the possibility of engaging in research that would bring practical results in terms of problem solving.

In relation to the experience of learning, many students felt rather overwhelmed by the volume of material to be squeezed into a short space of time.

"There wasn't enough time definitely. I wouldn't say now I know anything of the law."

Views on teaching and learning methods varied. There was appreciation of the case study approach in teaching, and the way in which this makes the law feel more 'real' and also enables students to draw on and share their own practice experience. Some felt, however, that more structured lecturer input was necessary in order to maximise the benefit of case studies – perhaps something akin to model answers after they had themselves done the work.

"Everyone tends to tell us 'these are the problems', but don't give us any solutions."

It was felt that lecturers should be prepared to repeat and revise information for students on request, and that the teaching schedule should be flexible enough to achieve this without students having to feel uncomfortable about asking what might appear naïve questions.

> "You need to feel its ok to ask a question, even if you know what you're saying is wrong."

Guided independent study drew positive comment, with appreciation of individual or group tasks that required students to research questions and report back.

> "This approach could not have been better – if [the lecturer] just stood there and told you the answers, you wouldn't really learn anything. Actually having to go and do it yourself I thought was good – even though we got muddled up in one bit, she directed you where you might have gone astray."

Conversely, other students found case studies and small group work a distraction, and felt there was a place for more 'talk and chalk'.

Students in the early stages of learning appeared to benefit from searching for tangible information that could then be used in a structured way to answer specific questions in a case study. If then, as they pieced it all together, they felt occasionally frustrated by the twists and turns of interpretation, they nonetheless developed a growing confidence in being able to locating their mandate for the exercise of power.

The downside of this approach was the difficulty for some students of doing the research. While some were confident they had fathomed the law library and electronic database systems, others were less sure, and tended to rely on textbooks. They were surprised at the range of sources of law, and felt that the task of accessing some of these was difficult, particularly in relation to case law and government circulars.

> "I think I tried to avoid the case law, because I just couldn't find how to access it sometimes."

Deciphering legal references was experienced as an alienating process, and students confessed to not knowing at times what they were searching for, or how to search by key terms of case references. They would have liked more time to review their research skills with a tutor.

Group-process problems might also intervene in small group independent learning. Groups were sometimes experienced as too large to facilitate participation and interaction. The discussion time was seen as vulnerable to a rather unfocused approach that strayed from the task in hand.

"Not everyone wants to get engaged in a discussion about other people's experiences."

Students were clear that if group work was the intention, it should be mandatory, and scheduled into the timetable at a specific place and time, rather than self-organised, to prevent some individuals becoming isolated and left out. The same applied to visits of observation, for example to court sessions.

Year 1 students generally were concerned at the prospect of no further discrete module of teaching in Year 2, but did feel they perhaps were getting the idea of applying their law learning in other modules. For this the discrete module was appreciated, albeit not long enough.

"This means you gain knowledge of structure, how it works, the jargon, and so you can transfer it."

There was a general view that law should be more integrated within other modules of learning, in addition to being covered in any discrete law module. It was commonly felt that more time for law was needed, students' current experience being that they could learn sufficient to get through the assignment but not to feel confident in practice. Curriculum time devoted to law was compared unfavourably with the time allocations for other aspects of the curriculum.

In relation to assessment, students were uncertain as to the best time for them to demonstrate competence in law. If the assessment is late in the programme some felt this encourages them not to take law learning as seriously earlier on, and possibly fail to engage with law learning opportunities. Others just felt it builds anxiety throughout the programme. Against this, sitting a law examination made more sense to some students during or after the placement, when they had had a chance to achieve more rounded learning about applying the law. There was also a view that more evidence of understanding the law in practice could be given if an assessment was embedded within one of the later placements.

Students whose assignment was based on a long case study felt they would have preferred to tackle several shorter pieces, finding the task of combining law knowledge in an essay-type assignment to be quite challenging. They wanted more guidance and perhaps examples of how to do this. They were also unclear about integrating anti-discriminatory perspectives within their law assignment and felt they need more guidance on this too.

A major concern for the future was how they would keep up to date in the context of workload pressures, and felt they would be very dependent on possibly unreliable team or organisational learning cultures to maintain the currency of knowledge they had acquired during training.

> "It depends on the caseload you're going to have as a social worker, if you're going to have time to go and read up on every case that comes out, because you're not really going to want to go home and spend your own time."

> "It depends what everyone else does in your workplace too ... if everybody's a little bit slack, I know myself I'd probably slip into that."

Students were also asked about their experiences of law learning during periods of practice learning. For many this had been a mixed experience. Those confident that they were encountering the law on placement included students placed in childcare, mental health and older people's teams in statutory agencies. Where law was being overly used in the teams, students felt they gained from this.

> "You can learn some of it in classes, but it's not till you're actually doing it, and you're in the situation, that you can understand it. Seeing it in practice makes it real."

> "I don't think we know how much we know until we apply it to practice. I think we know an awful lot more than we think."

Even so, their experiences were mixed, and in some cases had undermined their confidence. A student placed in a mental health team felt she was expected to know more than she did, and this had undermined her confidence. Another felt the law was used as a tool with which to blame practitioners.

> "If something goes wrong, you will be told 'you haven't done this under The Children Act', or whatever."

Conversely, a student in a childcare team had found herself able to quote relevant legislation to a qualified team member who was uncertain about it, and a student in an adult care management team found herself more law-conscious than long-qualified workers.

> "No one actually mentions law. It's more of an assumption that it's there. No one actually talks about it."

While they understood that their law learning continued on placement, and appreciated the practitioner perspective this exposed them to, this was accompanied by concern that their agency's interpretation and procedures tended to take centre stage rather than the legal framework itself. They were at times quite shocked by what they found.

> "I had a social worker ask me what section 47 was."

Some students were not impressed by the law learning opportunities on placement, finding out-of-date policies and procedures being used and key information not available without further enquiries at agency head office level. Getting accurate information through having access to statute or guidance was difficult, as these resources were commonly not available in agencies. Some students continued to use their academic tutors as sources of legal information while on placement and sometimes found themselves more aware than practitioners.

> "We have a real emphasis on law in this course – we know how much the law means. When you actually go on placement, people who completed courses before don't really see the relevance of knowing where policy guidance comes from."

"What alarms me is the lack of knowledge in practice – practitioners not knowing, as if it is not important."

"I felt they were wondering,'Why is she asking this about the law?'."

Other shortfalls related to the inter-linking of various aspects of legislation – knowledge in the agency appeared restricted to that relevant to a specific team focus (for example, section 17 of the Children Act 1989 provision for disabled children, or Approved Social Worker roles in relation to mental health admissions).

In some cases, students concluded that law was not a priority on placement because it did not figure large in the practice requirements.

Students did feel it was important to have a balance of academic and placement learning. They saw the taught input as a means of engaging with positive aspects of legislation – almost a benchmark or standard-setting exercise about how things should or could be. This was the subject of some ambivalence, for while it meant that the real world of practice might come as a shock, it did at least provide them with knowledge resources with which to hold their ground if necessary in practice. This was experienced as quite a daunting prospect.

"If that's the environment we're going to be moving into ... that's a big load to take on, to try and change that environment."

As a consequence, they would have liked more rehearsal of using the law to challenge the system.

One other gap identified by some students was their lack of learning about welfare benefits legislation. This related to the need to ensure that academic learning reflects the demands of the practice environment, in which students might often wish to ensure that service users are accessing the benefits to which they are entitled.

Finally, students were asked to reflect on the relationship between law and practice, and to identify any key message for teachers of law to social work students. The law as a mechanism of accountability was a key theme to emerge here.

"If you don't know the law then you come unstuck if something goes wrong."

A further theme was an appreciation of the complexity and grey areas or dilemmas in applying the law. These arose as a result of several factors: the wide range of sources that needed to be combined to produce usable 'legal knowledge'; the importance of interpretation; professional values and codes of ethics that also influence practice; and resource constraints in agencies. This last was causing disillusion, and making academic work feel more like an 'ideal world' exercise for some students.

"It was good to write about the law in that way, but you knew in your head that it was completely unrealistic, that you could never probably use the law in that way."

Others were happier to live with the tensions.

"We should be taught about how it should be, not how it actually is. It gives you something to work on."

A key message identified for law teachers was the importance of taking student learning styles into account, making sure that students get law somewhere in the style they most readily respond to. There was a firm student vote for a combination of discrete and integrated teaching. A second was to stress the importance of law learning on practice placements, and the need to ensure some standard of coverage that practice teachers are expected to provide, included in the placement agreement. Third, practitioner and service user contributions to classroom teaching were seen as very important. For one student, the contribution of people with learning disabilities about their experience of community care provision was the highlight that was going to stick in her mind. A further message was the importance of critical analysis of the legal framework, putting the factual knowledge in its context and encouraging students to engage in debate and analysis in the same way as would be expected in any other module of learning for social work. Finally, students wished to emphasise the importance of research skills to instilling a feeling of confidence for the future.

"I may not know the law in its entirety and in depth, but I know where to look and I know when I need to look."

### 3.3.2 Practice teachers

Practice teachers were asked first how they as practitioners use the law in their daily practice. Many practice teachers readily acknowledged that their practice as social workers is totally based in law, whatever their employing agency.

"What I say to students is 'we can't just go around doing as we like, we must act in accordance with the legal framework'."

Knowledge of the legal framework was seen as vital, although some practice teachers qualified this with the concept of 'working knowledge'.

"There's just the bits of it you use that would be relevant for your work. I have a broad underlying theory of it, and I know the reasons it was introduced, but there'd be great chunks of it I would never put into practice."

Others took a broader view, rejecting a narrow focus on disconnected aspects of legislation and emphasising the importance of crosscutting issues such as anti-discrimination legislation, human rights and disability. Several made the point that the impact of eligibility criteria in agencies was such that only people with complex needs were receiving services, and meeting their needs necessitated drawing on a wide range of legal knowledge.

"For me, that is part of the skill of a practitioner – to know sufficiently about what people are entitled to under the Act."

Some practice teachers in statutory agencies expressed the view that in terms of their organisational context law has much less of a profile than Performance Assessment Framework indicators*. The pursuit of star ratings, and the practices that had been introduced to support performance, were seen to have outweighed the fear of legal challenges from service users.

For many practice teachers, law elicited the same apprehension as for students, and they identified the same issue of accountability.

"I'd be very careful if I knew I was going to end up in court."

Some expressed the view that they could be caught out by law if they did not know how it required them to act in relation to some of the grey areas of practice, such as the disclosure of information.

They had a range of unmet needs in relation to developing and updating their legal knowledge, many feeling that it was left to individual, personal responsibility and that not everyone fulfils this. Some in adult services blamed the lack of explicit legal focus in their work for the absence of easily available knowledge updates. Those working in sectors where recent legislation had been introduced (adoption and leaving care services, for example) felt in a favoured position because recent training had been provided. Similarly, those in specialist legal roles, such as approved social workers, had good refresher mechanisms. Approved social worker training was held to be a model for post-qualification learning about the law, in contrast to the Post-Qualifying Child Care Award, where it was not experienced as having the same high profile.

E-mail alerts were sent out in one agency, and in other cases legal services could be approached for information, but

"You don't always get the answer you need, and it costs money."

"There is a charge every time you pick up the phone."

* Local authority performance against a range of indicators is judged as part of a system of Comprehensive Performance Assessment conducted by the Audit Commission, and results in the award of an annual star rating for the authority.

The constantly changing nature of law was experienced as a problem, along with the challenge posed by the complexity of legal information.

> "It's sometimes very difficult to find a particular section that you're actually looking for ... we do need something, a sort of Bible that has guidance, that you can just pick up easily and find what you're looking for."

This meant that legal information was often mediated through departmental interpretation.

> "[You have to be] guided by the policies and procedural guidelines that we are given, as opposed to having a handbook or a formal way of accessing the most up-to-date law on what we do."

There was awareness too that knowledge alone would not be enough; there was also the challenge of interpretation.

> "If you do go off doing your own research, knowing where to go is one thing, but your interpretation may be another thing – it's about understanding how it all works. It's not just law, it's statutory guidance on how that framework all hangs together."

Some practice teachers requested the opportunity to attend taught classes alongside students, as refresher training for themselves, or at least having access to the same handout material.

In terms of their role with students, practice teachers were generally confident that placements across all sectors do provide law-learning opportunities, from simple observation exercises to more complex tasks. Confidence varied, however, in the extent to which practice teachers could help students capitalise on their experience. They felt confident about the law in their own discrete area of practice, but did not feel sufficiently confident in other areas to give students a comprehensive learning experience. They felt too that their organisations were not set up to facilitate learning that crosses the boundaries of specialist adults and children's teams.

They were aware of students' anxieties about law, and were concerned to address these.

For students, knowledge of and skill in applying the law is a frightening experience because they think they must get it right, and they will be castigated if they do not. It ought to be a learning process.

They commented that anxiety makes it difficult for students to remember what they have learned. As practice teachers they have to tease out of students what their learning has been, and give structured ways of enabling them to apply this, reconnecting them to their academic learning, turning surface into deep learning. Practice teachers described two broad approaches to this. One would be to start with a piece of legislation that needed to be learned about and then find opportunities for students to apply it, or observe it being used (compulsory admission to psychiatric hospital under the Mental Health Act 1983 was an example here). An alternative approach would be starting with a practice situation and then ensuring that students reach back into the legal mandates to identify why they are taking a particular approach or making certain decisions.

Practice teachers felt they engaged in a lot of direct teaching, regardless of the approach they took, and that this could be quite challenging. They needed not only to identify the complexity of the integrated package that is their own practice, but also explain it to students and help them build it into their own understanding. Part of the role was making sure students can use resources available to them in practice, not just seeing books as something that belong in college.

"I remember having a debate with a student about 'What shall we do in this situation'. I said 'Where do you think we'd find the answer?' and she said 'In the Children Act'. We looked at the Act on the shelf for about 10 minutes, and I said 'Unless one of us lifts it off the shelf and gets it down, we'll never get anywhere!'. She got it down and went through it and in fact found the answer there, and then she said 'I can do this'."

They felt one of the distinctive law learning opportunities on placement was to help students develop judgement in interpreting the legal mandate in the context of real lives, which were inevitably more complex, finely tuned and dynamic than case studies could ever do justice to.

The vivid and immediate nature of practice learning was identified.

> "I don't think students realise how much power we have. You try and
> tell them, 'we have the power to take this person's liberty away from
> them' – they go 'oh, yeah'. Then you actually go out and you get the
> police and you get the ambulance and you take [the person] kicking
> and screaming somewhere they don't want to go. And that's reality.
> That makes a big impact."

Practice teachers identified some of the same tensions as students had
between 'ideal' and 'feasible' practice. Some felt their role was to encourage students to be realistic about what is achievable.

> "I've often said to social work students, when you're qualified you
> really can't go out there and change the world, you can only work
> within the requirements and statutes that your local authority allows
> you to."

Others felt that the role was to connect students to the potential both
for using the law to challenge poor decision making within agencies and
to argue against particularly restrictive interpretations of law.

> "The law is a dynamic thing, and social workers have helped change
> it. It's important students know the shortcomings of the law and also
> engage with the politics of social care."

Practice teachers named a number of mechanisms that supported their
efforts to enhance students' law learning, emphasising that different students need different approaches, depending on learning style. Practices
include:

- running group supervision sessions, bringing several students and
  practice teachers together to pool knowledge
- dedicating specific supervision sessions to teaching rather than to case
  management
- overtly reflecting on their own use of legal mandates in the broadest
  and not just the obvious sense

- using longer placements to phase students' learning
- requesting learning logs with specific sections on law; and ensuring agency policies are traced to their legal source.

Asked to identify key messages for teachers of law to social work students, they were clear that they wanted stronger connections with the university or college-based elements of programmes, to know where law appears in the curriculum and how it is taught. Some expressed a sense of insufficient connection and dialogue with academic tutors, which led to a lack of clarity about expectations related to law learning on placement.

A second message was if not to simplify the law (seen as 'mission impossible') at least to try and humanise, bring in the practitioners and service users who experience it in practice, so that students can hear first hand how it impacts on people's lives.

A third was to ensure that the spirit as well as the letter of the law is covered.

> "This [the spirit of the law] is the glue that holds it all together. This is where it starts from and if you find that the use of the Act doesn't benefit [people] then there's something very wrong with the way it is being used."

Where this meant preparing students to resist the impact of organisational culture that does not observe the spirit of the law, programmes should be doing this. Such an approach locates the law as one of the platforms, alongside other knowledge and resources, from which practitioners pursue goals that are consistent with their professional values and purpose. This was not a rosy view divorced from the realities of the practice environment. Practice teachers were well aware of the pressures, constraints and serious under-funding that affect implementation, yet retained commitment to educating students to be proactive in promoting service users' rights.

## 3.4 External assessors' views

External assessors, appointed by the Care Council for the country in question, make annual reports on Diploma in Social Work programmes. They are asked to comment to the Councils on how the programme has promoted effective learning and assessment arrangements for students to demonstrate "understanding and application of the law in social work with relevance to the country of training and practice".

As a contribution to this practice survey, inspectors from the Care Council for Wales, the Scottish Social Services Council, the Northern Ireland Social Care Council and the General Social Care Council provided summaries that drew on all external assessors' reports for the year 2002-2003. The reports do not represent a systematic analysis of the issues, but some common impressionistic themes can be identified.

The external assessors' comments show that most aspects of law teaching, learning and assessment drew positive comment across the four countries, with good outcomes achieved by students. In England, for example, standards were described as being either 'high' or 'a strength' in 38 cases (49% of all programmes), as 'good' in 26 cases (33%) and 'satisfactory' or 'reasonable' in 11 (14%). In the case of three programmes, standards were more problematic, but all had been remedied in consultation with the external assessor.

The following positive aspects of law teaching, learning and assessment were noted, combining data from all four countries.

### 3.4.1 Standards of learning and teaching arrangements

External assessors found law teaching to be relevant and up to date, allowing changes in law to be incorporated.

The location of law teaching prior to the first practice placement was felt to be appropriate, but it was also thought important that the early stages of study provided the foundation for an incremental approach, with law located throughout the Diploma programme.

Teaching was thought successfully to incorporate both the national and the UK-wide legislative framework, and the comprehensive nature of the curriculum drew positive comment. This related to:

- the range of service-user groups addressed
- the inclusion of human rights and equalities legislation
- attention to case law
- coverage of policies and procedures related to the legal framework.

In all countries, there was seen to be an appropriate focus on application to practice in both learning and assessment. This interlinking of knowledge, understanding and application in practice was one of the strongest themes to emerge from assessors' reports. It was believed to be facilitated in a number of ways:

- The use of interesting and challenging case studies was thought to encourage students to apply knowledge to a range of contemporary situations and circumstances
- The combination of good grounding in a specific law module, followed by a focus on understanding and application in a range of other assignments and modules, was found to produce positive results
- Carrying through the learning opportunities into placement was also seen as an important contribution
- Problem-based learning was seen as having something to offer students in relation to how they engage with the law/practice integration requirement, provided it is deeply enough embedded in the curriculum and is supported by sufficient taught content.

### 3.4.2 Standards of assessment

The appropriate challenge and rigour of assessments generally drew positive comment from external assessors. Many programmes were commended for their robust, systematic and consistent assessment of the subject.

A wide range of assessment methods is used. In England, law is the subject most frequently assessed by examination, a method used by 31 programmes, and indeed in most such programmes law is the only subject to be assessed in this way. Approaches include:

- seen and unseen examinations (where students do or do not receive the questions in advance)
- open or closed book approaches (where students are or are not allowed to take text books into the examination)
- multiple-choice test (where students choose from a range of pre-selected answers)
- examination questions based on case scenarios
- a mixture of these formats.

No particular method of assessment was seen by external assessors as more relevant or appropriate than others. However, one programme that had analysed the impact of introducing a law examination was commended by the external assessor for the students' learning outcomes, which were demonstrated across a broad range of service groups. Equally, however, the use of case studies/scenarios was positively commented upon in 24 programmes, and the evidence derived from practice portfolios and reports in 24 cases also.

The requirement for students to integrate legal knowledge and practice also drew positive comment from external assessors, with three particular aspects noted:

- the permeation of law assessment throughout the curriculum, encouraging law/practice integration within a range of assignments, in addition to the specific law module
- an incremental approach to assessment, requiring students to apply law to practice and integrate it with other knowledge in an increasingly sophisticated way as they progress through their programme
- the expectation that practice teachers routinely comment on students' understanding of law as demonstrated on placement, and in the context of agency procedures.

Problem areas relating to law teaching, learning and assessment, or areas for improvement, were identified as follows. It was noted that law is an area of difficulty for some students, who struggle to analyse, critically debate and apply the legislation. This was not unique to law, however, and external assessors commented equally on problems in the application of theory, anti-discriminatory practice, and critical analysis and reflection generally. In relation to law, the difficulty was seen to relate to:

- the challenge for students of moving on from merely listing legal 'facts' to meaningful application to practice situations
- the complexities of the law, which give rise to more learning support needs.

It was thought that the learning support needed by students, and the incremental nature of law learning, may also need to influence the timing of the assessment tasks.

Where external assessors raised concerns about specific programmes in England, this related to:

- the quality of teaching
- inconsistent standards in assessment, although even in these cases there was no doubt that students had met baseline requirements in law.

A number of external assessors in England commented on higher failure rates or lower marks profiles for law than for other modules. It was unclear whether this was due to the nature of the subject or the assessment method, which was often a seen or unseen examination. One suggestion from an assessor was to dispense with an unseen examination, another was to prepare students through learning about examination skills. Review of the assessment task was suggested in five cases, but for different reasons – to remedy poor success rates, to achieve more transparency in requirements or to ensure more comprehensive coverage of law. While greater transparency or consistency of marking was requested, this was not unique to law.

Specific suggestions for improvement included:

- Developing students' thinking on law, ethics and values, in particular:
    - > the ethical implications of using the law in practice
    - > the need for more attention to integrating anti-discriminatory practice issues within the law teaching (this was the most frequent improvement sought by external assessors in England)
    - > more focus on human rights and equality legislation
    - > analysis of the tensions between law and anti-discriminatory practice
    - > in the Wales context there was comment that further emphasis could be given to the Welsh Language Act.

- Ensuring more focus on specific areas of the law curriculum, for example:
    - > child care law and its application to child protection and work with children in need
    - > creating a balance between child care and community law.

- Giving more focus to governmental policy issues
- Achieving more integration between knowledge and practice
- Ensuring students have refresher sessions to maintain the currency of their knowledge
- Emphasising law in practice placements through:
  > preparation of practice teachers
  > specific report guidelines
- discussion of law learning during tutors' placement visits.

The extent to which external assessors' views mirror or differ from the perspectives of other stakeholders in law teaching, learning and assessment will be explored in the conclusion, which integrates and reviews the findings from the different sources used during this survey.

## 3.5 Consultation events

This section reports on the views and perspectives expressed at the two consultation events held during the course of the research, and incorporates a range of perspectives from people with experience of using services. The organisation of the data reflects the common questions and themes emerging from the literature (reported in the research review) and from the focus groups, questionnaire responses and external examiners' views (reported in this practice survey).

### 3.5.1 What is the purpose of law teaching for social workers?

**Are we aiming for students to become critical thinkers or people who can fix things, because they have hands-on skills?**

The consultation groups here concluded that we are training people to be fixers who think critically about what they are doing, termed as "plumbers plus"*. Fixers can be useful, but we also need people who will

---

*  The use of the term 'plumber' refers to the article by Twining[48] which posed the question of whether the purpose of law learning is to produce enlightened critical thinkers (like Pericles) or skilled technicians (like plumbers). The terminology was adopted by the consultation group during their discussion of the purpose of law teaching.

question the system, and service users need to be involved in deciding what needs fixing, as well as in how it is fixed.

**What should the core content of law teaching be?**

It followed then that the core content should include both knowledge and skills. The knowledge base was seen to include:

- the legal framework drawn from a wide range of sources, including case law, and the different status they have
- powers and duties – legislation relating to specific user groups but also about the connections between these in people's lives
- the historical development of legal frameworks – why and how they got there
- the relationship between law, policy and procedures, including consideration of local interpretation that may diverge from lawful practice
- the legal context for the work agencies do, including voluntary agencies
- court processes and procedures
- roles and accountability when providing social work services
- human rights and citizenship.

Participants were particularly concerned that students should not just think about the law in separate boxes relating to children or adults.

"Families don't fall into boxes."

There are areas of overlap, for example between child care and community care law in relation to disabled children, and there are also gaps in how social workers respond, for example in failing to consider community care law in working with disabled parents. This is made worse by the divisions within organisations into 'Adults' Services' and 'Children's Services'. Social workers must put all their fragmented knowledge together and see the whole picture.

It was thought important for the knowledge content to be reasonably comprehensive, at least as a map to guide students to what kind of information they do not necessarily cover in detail. They need to know what they do not know, to assist them in recognising and taking appropriate action on legal issues that arise in their work.

It was suggested that strong emphasis should be placed on enabling legislation such as the Race Relations (Amendment) Act 2000, the Disability Discrimination Act 1995 and the Special Educational Needs and Disability Act 2001.

Skills for students to learn in applying the law included:

- informing service users of their rights and advocating for these
- accessing information about the legal framework and learning the legal language
- using their own discretion in decision making
- challenging employers and other agencies
- record keeping
- oral and written communication with an emphasis on listening to service users
- 'disciplined thinking' – being able to analyse a situation and apply knowledge that is relevant and useful. Part of the skill is also being able to use knowledge to argue for best practice.

It was emphasised that knowledge gets out of date very quickly, and it is important that students learn skills in updating themselves. It may be more important that they learn what law is for and how to find information about it, rather than having to remember everything. This also has implications for how their understanding of law is assessed.

Regardless of knowledge and skills, it was emphasised that values and ethics should have a high profile. Students are being trained to take responsibility for their actions, and to exercise judgement to the best of their knowledge and ability in any given circumstances. In the US, law and ethics are more commonly linked together in teaching. This may reflect the greater emphasis there on law as a regulator of social work practice. It was anticipated this may develop in the UK too, as a result of changes in registration requirements for social work professionals.

### 3.5.2 How should law be taught?

**Should law be taught separately (discrete modules), or should it be taught alongside other subjects (integrated/infusion methods)?**

In reviewing the findings from the questionnaire survey of programmes, participants in the consultation events were surprised at the low number of hours spent teaching such an important topic, feeling it should be higher. They were additionally concerned that where law teaching is integrated with other subjects the dedicated time may be even less.

It was acknowledged there is a tension between breadth and depth of learning. If programmes allow students to choose their areas of in-depth study at some point later in their programme, then essential areas of law have to be taught earlier, to everyone. And if law is located in optional classes, which are perhaps related to specific areas of work such as child care, or adult services, how do students then learn about areas of law that cross these false boundaries? (Examples given included legal systems and complaints procedures.)

Surprise and concern were expressed about the number of programmes that appear not to teach in any detail about housing and homelessness legislation. It was pointed out that families lose children because of inadequate housing, and housing is central to community care provision, and to young people's aftercare.

Participants felt that a thematic approach to teaching may help students to 'join up' their knowledge so they can respond holistically in practice. Just learning and being tested on separate pieces of law such as the Children Act 1989 or the Mental Health Act 1983 may mean that their knowledge stays fragmented.

It was felt strongly that law learning should take place throughout the programme, not just in one year, and that phased learning is important. There was agreement that students needed to grasp the framework of legal rules, to know how law works, before moving on to specific duties and powers.

Equally, there were strong arguments for ensuring that law is integrated with other subjects in the curriculum. It could not be taught in isolation from working with people, for example, where trust and partnership skills were essential. It had to be linked into practice placements also.

There was discussion of the potential benefits of teaching law to students of social work and other professions together – for example, issues of capacity and consent, or law and ethics, are relevant to a range of professions.

## Who should do the teaching?

Service user involvement was thought to be essential. Case studies can ensure that service users' lives are placed centre-stage, and service users have an important role to play in developing appropriate case study material and in helping students to work on it. If service users are there when students are discussing what should be done in a case study, this can help students see it from their perspective. Service user perspectives on how the law affects them would broaden students' understanding. Service users may have different perspectives on what aspects of law are important, for example the value of social workers understanding complaints procedures and the use of law to challenge decision making. The recognition that service users and social workers are both frightened of the law might create a useful bridge for the development of partnership working under the legal framework.

An example was given of a system in which students present their findings on a case study to a 'panel' of service users, also adopting an advocacy role for service users' perspectives on the situation during the exercise. Service users could also be involved as co-learners – learning about the law alongside social work students, and in the process exchanging views and perspectives on law.

It was thought that both lawyers and social work academics and practitioners have important things to contribute to teaching, and also shortcomings in their approach. Information about legislation is empowering for social workers and service users alike, but lawyers need to understand how social work uses law in preparation for teaching it to social work students. Lawyers who teach on social work training may themselves be relatively new to some of the areas they are covering, because these areas are not central to mainstream legal training. It was thought there might be a new mix of skills required – a kind of 'new professional' – people who understand that middle ground, where law meets social work, and can bring together the principles and values they have in common.

Whoever teachers, it is also important that they stay up to date. Examples were given of service users, and sometimes social work students, being more up to date than practising social workers and their managers.

**What teaching and learning methods should be used?**

Any social work programme will have students with a mix of learning styles and needs. If problem-based learning is used, it is important that service users are involved in commenting on the definition of the problem that is being worked on, as well as on the possible solutions.

It was thought that students should be able to use a wide range of resources to help them in their learning. These would include:

- books, journals and agency literature
- websites
- video and audio tapes
- observation of court hearings
- shadowing practitioners undertaking legally mandated roles
- role play and simulations (mock courts)
- inter-professional learning (learning alongside law students, police officers)
- presentations from service users on their experiences of social workers and the law; from judges and legal practitioners on effective social work; from social workers on how they manage the dilemmas they encounter.

**How should students' learning in law be assessed?**

It was considered there could be value in adopting oral assessment, where students are questioned individually by assessors on their understanding of law, with service users involved as members of a panel.

### 3.5.3 How can we best connect law and social work to reflect the relationship between them?

There was a view that social workers can see law as something to be beaten over the head with. This can result in defensive practice, where social workers take action to avoid being criticised for not taking action. Teaching can help students see a more positive side of the law – as a tool to promote rights and empowerment.

It was felt to be very important that social workers see law as a positive part of their practice, rather than being defensive about it, or seeing it as something to be afraid of. Law should be seen, like values, as another 'lens' through which to examine practice – not just "Is what we are doing ethical and moral?" but also "Is it legal?".

A key question for practice is "can social workers and lawyers talk to each other?" and education practice needs to address this.

### 3.5.4 How can we combine theory and practice, academic learning and placement learning?

There was general recognition of the potential gap between 'law' and 'law-in-practice', with agreement that practice placements can help students to piece their knowledge together and apply it in a real situation. There is a real need for students to engage with 'real world' problems of the kind they are going to meet once qualified. Practice teachers have an important contribution in helping students do this.

Practice learning was seen as very important in enabling students to experience the tension between organisational rules and social work knowledge/values, and offering them opportunities to learn how to challenge this where necessary.

It was thought that the Department of Health requirement for students to undertake a placement involving statutory work should be interpreted widely, rather than as meaning 'in a statutory agency'. A student could get just as much, or more, experience of law in practice in a voluntary agency that is fulfilling statutory duties.

It was thought important for students to be able to learn about law both before and after their placements, as the ability to integrate learning from the two sources may well develop as this cycle of experience progresses.

There was agreement that students need practice in court work while on placement. Court was an arena in which the robustness of social workers' practice could make a key difference to service users' experiences. Examples were given of courts being very impersonal in how they represent people, with little recognition of the human side of people's lives. The 'person in the story' in court proceedings often appears to be lost. Law joins the lawyers together, whether they are appearing for the local authority or the service user, in a way that excludes non-lawyers, professionals and service users alike, and allows them to take over. There is a question about whether social workers have to join this system, or can change it. Through knowing the 'rules of the game' and standing up to what were termed 'legal tricks' they have the potential to make a difference to how service users experience the process.

There are also problems, however, with the consistency of quality in learning opportunities for students on practice placement. Examples were shared of agency procedures that were unlawful, or of lawyers not giving correct advice. Managers are important figures here, but sometimes they too are not up-to-date, and can seem obsessed by procedures. It was thought possible that law knowledge is hidden, ignored or forgotten in practice, with qualified social workers not realising that things they do everyday are unlawful.

It seems that not all practice teachers have knowledge and skills in law, and indeed the function of practice teaching was seen as under threat in the new degree, in which more emphasis is placed on practice assessment.

It was pointed out that with 'protected title' for the profession, meaning that social workers have to be registered with the Care Council in order to practise, they will be accountable as individuals. This may make it less likely that social workers will accept the compromise of knowing what's right but finding it easier to do what their agency tells them.

It was emphasised that at the end of the day, the university or college has to make sure that law is given enough importance in the placements that are used, and that this is consistent for all students. It cannot be left to chance and the knowledge of individual practice teachers.

Accurate guidance on the law in practice is essential; because the law does not provide crystal-clear rules, it has to be interpreted. The law gives people rights, and it gives social workers discretion, and students need to learn to be accountable for how they use this. Sound use of law can be another step on the way to getting things right for people.

## 3.6 Conclusions

In conclusion, we consider what the practice survey contributes to the task of identifying how teaching, learning and assessment of law in social work education might best be approached.

While the importance of law teaching is clearly recognised within programmes, the range of approaches to teaching, learning and assessment is very broad. This can be seen both as a strength and a challenge. It arises perhaps in part from the complex set of aims and learning outcomes commonly to be found in module outlines. We clearly ask a lot of students in their learning about the law. Not only do they need to become familiar with a large volume of legal knowledge; we expect them also to maintain a questioning and critical perspective on that knowledge, be technically proficient in its application to a range of situations encountered in practice, and to use it in a way consistent with professional ethics and values. Added to this, law appears to be one of the aspects of the curriculum about which students are most apprehensive.

It could be argued that law thus lends itself to a multi-faceted approach to teaching, learning and assessment, even beyond the flexibility required by good education practice with adult learners. We see this in the findings from the questionnaire survey, in which diversity of practice is perhaps the most striking theme.

Yet the diversity is neither random nor accidental. Responses show that educators have a clear and strong rationale for approaching teaching, learning and assessment in the ways that they do. By and large these are not based in research evidence on the effectiveness of different approaches in relation to law itself, but are drawn perhaps from a combination of custom and practice, experience of working with adult learners and shared ethos within programmes, alongside pragmatic considerations such as time and class size. There appears to be a process of sincere engagement with the task of making law interesting and manageable for students, while testing their learning rigorously, and a search for continuous improvement and development in the approaches taken. The lack of rigorous outcome evaluation is non untypical of social work education generally, or indeed of professional education more widely.[180]

The predominance of discrete teaching probably reflects the influence of a range of factors. There appears to be a view that law is a subject that must be 'taught' as opposed to merely 'learned'. This may reflect its position as a discipline distinct from other less easily identifiable sources of knowledge for practice. It is seen as having an identify of its own that is 'not social work', and is perhaps viewed as having a degree of clarity that other areas of the curriculum do not. In this way it lends itself to the assumption that the knowledge can be delivered and that students can 'get it right'.

The predominance of practice-led approaches such as case studies within the discrete teaching, and within assessment, may reflect the recognition that practitioners must ultimately use the law inductively – that is, they must be able to recognise legal issues that are embedded within the complex lives of people with whom they work. This will involve them in reaching back into their knowledge of legal mandates, powers and duties, to make decisions that are lawful and legally informed. It also requires them to integrate a range of knowledge from different legal sources if they are to meet the twin imperatives of ensuring safety and respecting autonomy, securing responsibility and promoting rights.

In terms of content, there appears to be a common core to the curriculum, but it is relatively small, and beyond it there is wide variation in terms of topics included and excluded by programmes. While programmes commonly identified some learning as 'core' and some as 'specialist', there were concerns expressed during the consultation about students being able to opt out of some specialist knowledge (through choice of modules). The difference between core and specialist knowledge was thought very difficult to determine and there was a danger that such decisions could change the balance of practice through giving a more widespread profile to certain aspects of the law (for example, those that mandate coercive action rather than promote entitlements).

One key development in the curriculum is the inclusion of human rights legislation. This is construed in two ways – as a core component of the legal framework within which decision making takes place (and therefore as a tool of accountability), but also as a means of strengthening anti-discriminatory and anti-oppressive approaches to practice (and therefore as a tool of empowerment). In this sense its inclusion is consistent with the interests and perspectives of service users in the consultation, although their perspectives were not confined to the human rights agenda and they were not alone in articulating the importance of this aspect of students' learning. However, it is true to say that programmes varied greatly in the amount of curriculum time dedicated to study on human rights as part of students' law learning.

Another key theme is the importance of presenting law as a positive tool for change in people's lives. Occasionally, law is presented in a negative light in programme documentation, and it is not uncommon for law and social work values to be placed at opposite ends of a spectrum, as if mutually exclusive. Students were certainly more aware of the potential for legal intervention to be experienced as oppressive than as empowering. Service users in contrast were concerned to encourage a more positive view among social workers, commenting that this might mean shifting the focus of what is defined as core legal knowledge to include empowering provision. They were concerned at poor relationships between lawyers and social workers, relating as adversaries rather than as allies, and courts being seen as an arena for castigating practitioners, rather than as an arena for joining in a process of challenging unfairness or upholding rights.

A key issue in education practice is that of alignment between aims, learning outcomes, teaching and learning methods and assessment methodologies. By and large, it appears that in the academic part of the curriculum these relationships are well conceived and strong. The variety in teaching and learning methods used addresses the diversity in the aims and learning outcomes. Law demands a lot of students, but educators make coherent attempts to facilitate the learning. Assessment methods too test the full range of learning outcomes, again due to the diverse range and combined methodologies that are commonly used. Base-line standards are thus seen to be being met, although it is more questionable whether the learning transfers to the challenges of practice environments and organisational contexts.

The task for law teachers arguably focuses on the need to motivate students to engage sufficiently with the topic early in the programme, with the benefits that then follow, in terms of confidence and integration of the subject within students' developing professional identity.

The significant demands of professional practice, however, make it imperative that the disjunction between academic and practice learning in relation to law receives attention. The neglect of law as a component of practice is another key theme to emerge from the practice survey.

There cannot be full alignment between aims, methods, assessment and outcomes until the neglect of law in practice learning is addressed.

The reasons for this neglect are no doubt complex, and reside probably as much in debates about the organisational base of the profession itself as in any distinctive features of the legal framework. Under the DipSW requirements,[12] law was clearly identified as a subsidiary requirement within one of the six practice requirements, yet this appears not to have been effective in consistently raising its profile. It remains to be seen how requirements for the new degrees will take this forward. In England, there is a view that law is conspicuous by its absence from the National Occupational Standards Key Roles. While it may be found in the lists of underpinning knowledge, the focus of students' placement learning may be more upon the behaviours as articulated in the Roles than upon the knowledge that underpins them. The existence of separate sets of requirements for the new degree in England (the QAA benchmark statement, the National Occupational Standards and Department of Health Requirements) perpetuates the potentially dangerous split between knowledge ('learned at college') and skills ('learned in the workplace'). In Scotland, Wales and Northern Ireland, where integrative frameworks have been developed, the potential to integrate law more fully in both academic and practice learning contexts is promising, and programmes in England will need to address this agenda independently in the absence of a national integrative framework.

Some programmes acknowledge that they must face the task of raising the profile of law learning with agencies offering practice learning opportunities and addressing the variable experience of students on placement in relation to this aspect of their experience. Programmes more broadly may need to address this through a combination of approaches, among which the overt inclusion of law in the practice curriculum, and proactive engagement with practice teachers and assessors could be two key developments. Practice teachers and practice assessors have a key role to play in raising the profile of law-related activity and learning by students on placement.

A tension in this respect is the relationship between law, policy and agency procedures. While students and practice teachers in this study were both, in different ways, dissatisfied with the profile of law in agencies, seeing agency procedures and targets as more influential in practice than the letter or the spirit of the law, employers have equally been critical of the legal and procedural knowledge base that students acquire during their training. A survey of employers,[181] conducted as part of a report on the enhancement of qualifying training for child and family social work in Wales, draws attention to the perceived superficial level of knowledge of the law achieved by students. While some employers felt that the level was sufficient, given that students did receive a basic framework within which to place the roles and responsibilities of social workers, others were more critical of students' technical and procedural knowledge. Employers' requirements of newly qualified social workers include a high degree of familiarity with national and agency policies, and the procedures devised to ensure their delivery. This tension is a practical example of the debate about the purpose of teaching law, and whether the aim is to produce critical thinkers or skilled technicians who can apply a set of rules. Yet agency policy and law are not one and the same, a point made by participants in the consultation when considering the role of complaints procedures and other procedures in law for challenging agency practice and decision making.

These tensions make it important to consider the timing of law teaching, and the importance of it appearing at all stages in the programme of learning, as part of the iterative processes of professional development.

It is clear that law teaching, learning and assessment, while established as a core area of learning for social work students, must undergo further development in order to achieve maturity as a component of professional education. The development agenda is likely to include, first, the need to review the range and depth of curriculum content, to ensure a rounded perspective on law and its relationship with professional practice. Second, there is a need for development of the practice curriculum in relation to law, and a focus on how students transfer the outcomes of academic learning into practice. Third, giving priority to the involvement of service users and carers will bring a contribution of perspectives currently largely absent from this area of the curriculum. Fourth, it is clear that in the absence of robust research evidence to underpin the choice of teaching, learning and assessment methods, systematic evaluation of the relationship between different approaches and the outcomes of student learning is an urgent priority.

# Integrative analysis

Suzy Braye and Michael Preston-Shoot

## 4.1 Introduction

This concluding chapter presents an integrative analysis of the findings from the research review, the practice survey and the consultation, which together constitute the knowledge review of learning, teaching and assessment of law in social work education. A number of key themes emerge.

## 4.2 The purposes of law teaching

There have been debates in parallel within legal and social work education about the purpose of teaching and learning. The debate concerns the balance to be struck between education and training, between the development of a critical breadth of perspective and the acquisition of technical skills and specialist knowledge. The literature from the US and the UK contains common responses to why social workers must know about, and be competent in, applying legal rules. Besides being a requirement of professional bodies in the UK, practice is legally regulated and social work intervention is often shaped or influenced by legal rules in statute and guidance. Cautionary notes are sounded, however, about the dangers of mechanistic jurisprudence and of teaching that divorces law from its social context.

Applied to teaching law to social workers, the professional requirement that practitioners can operate within statutory frameworks must be considered alongside the development of critical competence. By this is meant the ability to question agency procedures, professional roles and the interface between legal rules and social issues.

This duality is reflected in the learning outcomes sought for students, that they should not only become familiar with a large volume of legal knowledge, but will also maintain a questioning and critical perspective on it, be technically proficient in its application and use it in a way consistent with professional ethics and values. The purposes of law teaching have to date not significantly reflected the critical perspectives of services users and carers who experience the impact of legally mandated professional interventions. Those perspectives might broaden the definitions of what those interventions should be, as well as how they should be accomplished.

## 4.3   Core content of teaching

This balanced focus for teaching law to social workers leads to an emphasis on knowledge for practice and knowledge in practice. The former includes the functions of law in society and how legal rules are used in response to social issues. The latter focuses on substantive law about particular client groups and practice issues.

Here there is a tension between breadth and depth, particularly in the context of a crowded timetable. Beyond the common core of legal frameworks for community care, mental health and children's services, there is a wide range of included and excluded content. Focusing on a narrow range of legislation facilitates in-depth understanding, while mapping a broader territory gives students more comprehensive awareness as an aid to recognition of legal issues. A key challenge is to avoid fragmentation of knowledge, to ensure that students can respond holistically to service users' needs and rights by drawing on a range of appropriate legal provision. A further task is to ensure that the range of law includes those aspects deemed important by service users and carers, based on their experiences of service provision and legal contexts.

The balanced focus also requires an emphasis on skills for practice and skills in practice. The former embraces policy analysis and advocacy, and researching legal issues to inform decision making, vital to ensure that knowledge is kept up to date. The latter covers core social work skills, such as problem solving, decision making, advocacy, court work, recording and report writing. The notion of 'disciplined thinking' is important – being able to analyse a situation and use a range of relevant and useful knowledge, including law, in order to understand and to act appropriately.

Integration of knowledge and skills requires that teaching and learning should focus not just on substantive law but also on the contexts where decision making will be required. Students must develop an appreciation of how legal rules can impact on, but also empower their decision making.

## 4.4  Law, rights and ethics

The literature on teaching law both to law students and to social workers connects law and ethics, and law and human rights. These connections recognise the increasing centrality of ethical issues in the regulation of practice, and the increasing impact of the European Convention on Human Rights and Fundamental Freedoms on decision making by social work agencies.

Irrespective of the setting in which they practise, social workers require familiarity with statute and guidance in order to advise and advocate effectively for clients, and to communicate appropriately with other professionals and agencies. The literature also reminds social workers of their social change responsibilities and of the role of legal knowledge and skills in promoting social justice.

These concerns are reflected in education practice in a number of ways. There is a concern to use the law in a way that recognises its potential to oppress, and to minimise the negative constraints it might place upon people through coercion or restriction of autonomy. The concept of proportionality is important here. Beyond this, there is a concern to use the law proactively to promote rights and social justice, through tapping its potential to challenge oppression, or to secure access to beneficial resources. In this regard, educators share the concerns and priorities of service users, in inviting students to develop a perspective on the law that is not confined to coercive intervention. These agendas have implications for taught content around human rights and anti-discrimination legislation.

## 4.5  Curriculum organisation

One key debate in the literature is whether the academic curriculum for teaching and learning law in social work education should be organised around discrete modules and/or integrated alongside learning other knowledge and skills. Some research findings cast doubt on integrated models of curriculum design, suggesting that this results in lack of depth. However, by contrast, discrete modules must avoid divorcing knowledge of the legal rules from the social work context in which they might be applied.

A common pattern in education practice is an early discrete module, which provides foundational knowledge, followed by specialisation around client groups both through dedicated courses and through integration across the curriculum. The wide prevalence of some form of discrete teaching may reflect the perception of law as a distinct discipline that students must become familiar with before they are able to understand and integrate it within their own professional resources. It is viewed as having a degree of clarity lacking in other areas of the curriculum and discrete teaching is seen as allowing a degree of control over teaching inputs.

There is a small literature on the timing of inputs. This suggests that some knowledge of the legal system should precede the first practice learning opportunity and that some exposure to substantive law should be offered before students undertake direct work with clients. This is balanced by the experience of teachers that they can help students make more sense of the law after they have had some substantial practice experience. There is divergence in the literature relating to the degree to which some, more specialist client-group law should be covered in qualifying education. This covers mental health and adoption in particular.

Whatever model is adopted, to ensure that students develop knowledge and skills in applying the law, close coordination within the programme team is required to ensure integration of teaching and learning.

## 4.6 Methods of teaching and learning in the academic curriculum

A range of methods will help students to learn the content of the legal rules and to connect this knowledge with skills to apply it to decision making. The literature describes, but less often evaluates, the outcomes of a range of methods, including use of case law, case studies and critical incidents, analysis of source materials, and research and library tasks. Observation of legal procedures, project work and student presentations are described, alongside use of role-play, computer-assisted and web-based learning, self-audits and service user accounts.

A key concern of law teachers is to allay students' anxieties about the law, to make it more manageable and to ensure that it has a strong practice focus. Consequently extensive use is made of case study approaches, reflecting perhaps the recognition that practitioners must use the law inductively, identifying and responding to legal issues embedded in situations they encounter in practice.

The literature reports positive student evaluations for methods that encourage active involvement and deeper learning. Problem-based learning approaches are increasing in popularity with both students and educators. However, detail of data collection is often patchy and more rigorous, outcome-focused research designs are rare. More common are descriptive and theory-building conceptual accounts of the use of case studies, problem-based learning, and ecological or decision-making approaches to law learning.

## 4.7  Who teaches?

The literature contains variable approaches to this question. It ranges from unequivocal recommendations that lawyers must be involved, through examples of joint teaching by legal and social work academics, to the paramount need of ensuring that whoever facilitates learning and teaching has knowledge and empathic understanding of both law and social work. A careful use of guest speakers is encouraged but there is limited outcome-focused research on what combination best facilitates social work law learning.

Where teams of teachers are involved, the literature recommends preparation. This includes consideration of teaching styles appropriate to the student group and a review of the contribution, strengths and gaps that each participant brings.

Service user and carer involvement in law teaching is relatively uncommon, but there is ample scope for fruitful partnerships here to ensure that the teaching is based on a broader range of perspectives and incorporates the view of those who experience the impact of legal interventions by professionals. Service users have important perspectives also on the development of programme material, such as case studies and handouts, and the construction of the case-based 'problems' on which enquiry-based and problem-based learning rests

## 4.8 Assessment of law learning in the academic curriculum

One key theme to emerge from the literature is that of alignment between the methods of assessment and the practice context, the types of activities and judgements required of social workers in practice.

Case studies, extended scenarios, oral assessment and project work are all described in the context of this alignment. So too is student involvement in self and peer assessment, both of knowledge and of contributions to group discussion. Other assessment methods include observation reports, completion of workbooks, and computer-assisted fixed format and multiple-choice questions.

In education practice law learning is more commonly assessed through some form of coursework, using one or more of the above formats. Examinations are also widely used, often in combination with coursework. Assessments of all kinds commonly target legal knowledge and the ability to apply it to practice scenarios. Less consistently, critical analysis and social work values appear in the assessment criteria.

The literature contains student evaluations of assessment methods that they have experienced and, less frequently, detailed evaluations of the effectiveness of different methods in assessing knowledge. Research to investigate the most effective means of enabling students to retain knowledge learned is missing.

There is a small literature on the timing of assessment, more conceptual than empirical, which indicates that assessment should ideally occur when students have undertaken some practice learning and benefited from both specialist client group law teaching and integration of law in the wider curriculum.

## 4.9 Connecting law and social work

Both US and UK commentators agree that relationships between social workers and lawyers can be strained, and that students frequently are apprehensive about law learning and interaction with legal systems and processes. Law can be seen as something with which to castigate the social work profession, resulting in defensive practice.

Commentators also agree that the basic objective of law teaching and learning is not to create legal experts but to enable students to operate effectively in their context – social work – using a thorough knowledge of legal concepts and rules. A key task is to locate law as a positive element of social work practice, and for it to be seen, like values, both as a core mandate and a lens though which practice is evaluated.

The US literature in particular contains reports of successful joint working between legal and social work practitioners. This experience leads some US and UK writers to identify a practice or role continuum, at different points along which law or social work will be more influential in contributing to decision making.

A logical development of connecting law and social work is the development of law and social work students learning together. Here, published accounts are few, despite the increasing policy emphasis on inter-agency and inter-professional collaboration, with papers offering descriptive and conceptual accounts rather than evaluated outcomes.

Another natural development is an analysis of similarities and differences between the skills used by legal and social work practitioners. The literature does recognise that issues of status and power have to be overcome to facilitate joint working. However, from a conceptual analysis of roles and tasks, it also emphasises common approaches to effectiveness, problem solving, communication and evidence, with parallel skills in, for example, advocacy, engagement, solution-focused interventions and system change. Within this territory, where law meets social work, there may be a new mix of skills that brings together the principles and values of both professions and applies them to the task of developing lawful, ethical social work practice. Service users are keen to witness such a development, and for social workers and lawyers to see themselves as allies in the task of promoting rights and justice.

## 4.10 Practice curriculum

The literature on teaching, learning and assessment in the practice curriculum is less extensive. Research evidence suggests, moreover, that practice teachers are apprehensive about their competence to facilitate student learning of law and concerned about their own knowledge of the legal rules. Research also suggests that practice teachers vary quite widely in their recognition of legal issues in their work and that the agency context is crucial in supporting this aspect of practice learning.

The literature provides illustrations of what a practice curriculum might contain. Some examples explicitly link core social work skills and competences with different elements of legal knowledge and skills. Some distinguish between interim and final competence, and offer ideas about what students should be able to do at different assessment points in their practice learning. Some offer teaching and assessment methods, such as case studies, workbooks, and agency-based exercises.

It is, however, relatively uncommon for students to be addressing specific, law-related learning outcomes on placement. While it is expected that practice teachers will help students be aware of the legal context for their casework, and written assignments commonly contain some legal content, there is inconsistency and variation in the extent and depth of learning. Students are not satisfied with this aspect of their law learning, and practice teachers observe their difficulties in connecting academic learning with the placement experience.

There is thus emerging concern about the degree to which placement learning preserves the alignment between aims, methods and outcomes of students' law learning. The neglect of law as a component of practice is a key theme from this review.

## 4.11 Continuing professional development

The literature contains several examples of exhortations on the importance of social workers remaining up-to-date in terms of legal knowledge but fewer examples of how universities and agencies might facilitate on-going law learning. The findings in the practice survey on the ways in which law learning can be eroded for students on placement in agency contexts where legal frameworks do not have a high profile, or where policy and procedural concerns have taken precedence, have a direct relevance to the needs of qualified workers who experience those agency contexts as the daily locus of practice.

## 4.12 Conclusion

This research into teaching, learning and assessment of law in social work education began with four objectives. The first was to offer an overview of approaches to teaching, learning and assessment, and this integrative summary reports some of the headlines from the literature, the practice survey and the consultations.

The second was to examine the effectiveness of different approaches to teaching, learning and assessment. Here, empirical evidence has been found to be limited, with the majority of literature offering descriptive and conceptual accounts, practice wisdom rather than research-based evidence of inputs and outcomes. Equally in education practice there has been no systematic evaluation of the effectiveness of the different approaches that are used, although there is clear feedback from students about what they find helpful.

The third was to explore the extent to which current education practice reflects evidence on effectiveness. This integrative summary demonstrates that education practice in relation to law in social work education generally reflects the themes and debates that can be found in the literature. Law teaching, learning and assessment is carefully conceived, with a clear rationale advanced for the approaches that are taken. There is sincere engagement with the task of making law learning manageable and accessible for students, while maintaining high expectations of their performance in assessment. Approaches are not based on systematically researched evidence of effectiveness, however, and it is difficult for educators to exercise informed judgement about the value of certain approaches over others.

The fourth objective was to identify future directions for research-informed organisation of teaching, learning and assessment of law in social work education. Theory building in respect of social work law now needs to move beyond delineating the field of study to research systematically what enables students to acquire and to retain knowledge of the legal rules and skills in practising social work law. There remain questions about the range and depth of core curriculum content needed to prepare students to be confident that they can use the law effectively in addressing the complexities of professional practice. The place of law in practice learning, alongside the academic curriculum, must be a core focus of development. The participation of service users and carers as key contributors to the process, and primary stakeholders in the outcomes, of students' learning must be more fully reflected in education practice, and the impacts of such participation included in the future research agenda.

# References

1   SCIE (Social Care Institute for Excellence) (2003) *Interim guidelines for SCIE systematic knowledge reviews*, London: SCIE.

2   Beckford Report (1985) *A child in trust*, London: London Borough of Brent.

3   Stevenson, O. (1988) 'Law and social work education: a commentary on "The Law Report"', *Issues in Social Work Education*, vol 8, pp 37-45.

4   Braye, S. and Preston-Shoot, M. (1990) 'On teaching and applying the law in social work: it is not that simple', *British Journal of Social Work*, vol 20, no 4, pp 333-53.

5   Marsh, P. and Triseliotis, J. (1996) *Ready to practise? Social workers and probation officers: Their training and first year in work*, Aldershot: Avebury.

6   Barnes, J. (2002) *Focus on the future: Key messages from focus groups about the future of social work training*, London: DH.

7   Roche, J. (2001) 'Social work values and the law', in L.-A. Cull and J. Roche (eds) *The law and social work*, Basingstoke: Palgrave.

8   Phillips, A. (1979) 'Social work and the delivery of legal services', *Modern Law Review*, no 42, pp 29-41.

9   Preston-Shoot, M. (2000) 'Making connections in the curriculum: law and professional practice', in R. Pierce and J. Weinstein (eds) *Innovative education and training for care professionals: A providers' guide*, London: Jessica Kingsley Publishers.

10  Clarke, A. (1999) *Community nurses and the law*, London: Community Practitioners and Health Visitors Association.

11  Ridley, A. (1994) 'Legal skills for non-law students: added value or irrelevant diversion?', *The Law Teacher*, vol 28, pp 281-91.

12  CCETSW (Central Council for Education and Training in Social Work) (1995) *Assuring quality in the Diploma in Social Work – 1. Rules and requirements for the DipSW*, London: CCETSW.

13  Care Council for Wales (2004) *Approval and visiting of degree courses in social work (Wales) Rules 2004*, Cardiff: Care Council for Wales (www.ccwales.org.uk).

14. DH (Department of Health) *Requirements for social work training*, London: DH.

15. Northern Ireland Social Care Council (2003) *Framework specification for the Degree in Social Work*, Belfast: Department of Health, Social Services and Public Safety.

16. Scottish Executive (2003) *Standards in social work education: Framework for social work education in Scotland*, Edinburgh: Scottish Executive.

17. QAA (Quality Assurance Agency) (2000) *Subject benchmark statements: Social policy and administration and social work*, Gloucester: QAA for Higher Education.

18. DHSSPS (Department of Health, Social Services and Public Safety) (2003) *Framework specification for the Degree in Social Work*, Belfast: DHSSPS.

19. TOPSS (Training Organisation for the Personal Social Services) (2002) *The National Occupational Standards for Social Work*, Leeds: TOPSS.

20. Preston-Shoot, M. (2000) 'What if? Using the law to uphold practice values and standards', *Practice*, vol 12, no 4, pp 49-63.

21. Preston-Shoot, M. (2001) 'Regulating the road of good intentions: observations on the relationship between policy, regulations and practice in social work', *Practice*, vol 13, no 4, pp 5-20.

22. Ball, C., Harris, R., Roberts, G. and Vernon, S. (1988) *The law report: Teaching and assessment of law in social work education*, London: CCETSW.

23. Grace, C. and Wilkinson, P. (1978) *Negotiating the law: Social work and legal services*, London: RKP.

24. Ball, C., Preston-Shoot, M., Roberts, G. and Vernon, S. (1995) *Law for social workers in England and Wales*, London: CCETSW.

25. Wallis-Jones, M. and Lyons, K. (2003) *2001 Employment Survey: Newly qualified social workers*, Research Report for Department of Health, Dagenham: University of East London.

26. Preston-Shoot, M., Roberts, G. and Vernon, S. (1997) '"We work in isolation often and in ignorance occasionally": on the experiences of practice teachers teaching and assessing social work law', *Social Work Education*, vol 16, no 4, pp 4-34.

27  Jankovic, J. and Green, R. (1981) 'Teaching legal principles to social workers', *Journal of Education for Social Work*, vol 17, no 13, pp 28-35.

28  Lemmon, J. (1983) 'Legal content in the social work curriculum', *Journal of Education for Social Work*, vol 19, no 2, pp 71-6.

29  Lynch, R. and Brawley, E. (1994) 'Social workers and the judicial system: looking for a better fit', *Journal of Teaching in Social Work*, vol 10, no 1/2, pp 65-82.

30  Kopels, S. and Gustavsson, N. (1996) 'Infusing legal issues into the social work curriculum', *Journal of Social Work Education*, vol 32, no 1, pp 115-25.

31  Madden, R. (2000) 'Legal content in social work education: preparing students for interprofessional practice', *Journal of Teaching in Social Work*, vol 20, no 1/2, pp 3-17.

32  Swain, P. (1999) 'Reflections on teaching law in social work – if only it were that simple', in J. Fook, F. Lindsay and M. Ryan (eds) *Advances in Social Work and Welfare Education*, vol 2, no 2, pp 124-38, Victoria: Australian Association of Social Workers.

33  Carlile Report (1987) *A child in mind*, London: London Borough of Greenwich.

34  Reith, M. (1998) *Community care tragedies: A practice guide to mental health inquiries*, Birmingham: Venture Press.

35  Stanley, N. and Manthorpe, J. (2001) 'Reading mental health inquiries: messages for social work', *Journal of Social Work*, vol 1, no 1, pp 77-99.

36  Reder, P., Duncan, S. and Gray, M. (1993) *Beyond blame: Child abuse tragedies revisited*, London: Routledge.

37  Preston-Shoot, M., Roberts, G. and Vernon, S. (1998) 'Social work law: from interaction to integration', *Journal of Social Welfare and Family Law*, vol 20, no 1, pp 65-80.

38  Lavery, R., McAuley, C., McGolgan, M., McKeown, A. and Higgins, P. (1997) *Law for social workers in Northern Ireland*, Loondon: CCETSW.

39  Brammer, A. (2003) *Social work law*, Harlow: Longman.

40  Brayne, H. and Broadbent, G. (2002) *Legal materials for social workers*, Oxford: Oxford University Press.

41  Brayne, H. and Carr, H. (2003) *Law for social workers* (8th edn), Oxford: Oxford University Press.

[42] Johns, R. (2003) *Using the law in social work*, Exeter: Learning Matters.

[43] *Social Work Education* (2003) vol 22, no 5, October.

[44] Cull, L.-A. and Roche, J. (2001) *The law and social work*, Basingstoke: Palgrave.

[45] Baillie, D., Cameron, K., Cull, L.-A., Roche, J. and West, J. (2003) *Social work and the law in Scotland*, Basingstoke: Palgrave.

[46] Braye, S. and Preston-Shoot, M. (1999) 'Accountability, administrative law and social work practice: redressing or reinforcing the power imbalance?', *Journal of Social Welfare and Family Law*, vol 21, no 3, pp 235-56.

[47] Preston-Shoot, M., Roberts, G. and Vernon, S. (2001) 'Values in social work law: strained relations or sustaining relationships?', *Journal of Social Welfare and Family Law*, vol 23, no 1, pp 1-22.

[48] Twining, W. (1967) 'Pericles and the plumber', *Law Quarterly Review*, vol 83, pp 396-426.

[49] Campbell, R., Pound, P., Pope, C., Britten, N., Pill, R., Morgan, M. and Donovan, J. (2003) 'Evaluating meta-ethnography: a synthesis of qualitative research on lay experiences of diabetes and diabetes care', *Social Science & Medicine*, no 56, pp 671-84.

[50] NHSCRD (NHS Centre for Reviews and Dissemination) (2001) *Understanding systematic reviews of research on effectiveness: CRD's guidance for those carrying out or commissioning reviews*, Report 4, York: NHSCRD (www.york.ac.uk/inst.crd/report4.htm).

[51] Secker, J. and Clark, C. (1990) *A bibliography of relevant research in social work education and training*, Edinburgh: University of Edinburgh.

[52] Boaz, A., Ashby, D. and Young, K. (2002) *Systematic reviews: What have they got to offer evidence based policy and practice?*, Working Paper 11, London: ESRC UK Centre for Evidence-based Policy and Practice.

[53] Pawson, R., Boaz, A., Grayson, L., Long, A. and Barnes, C. (2003) *Types and quality of knowledge in social care*, London: Social Care Institute for Excellence.

[54] Boaz, A. and Ashby, D. (2003) *Fit for purpose? Assessing research quality for evidence based policy and practice*, London: ESRC UK Centre for Evidence-based Policy and Practice.

55   Bradney, A. (1992) 'Ivory towers and satanic mills: choices for university law schools', *Studies in Higher Education*, vol 17, no 1, pp 5-21.

56   Boon, A. (1998) 'History is past politics: a critique of the legal skills movement in England and Wales', *Journal of Law and Society*, vol 25, no 1, pp 151-69.

57   Bergman, P. (2003) 'Reflections on US clinical education', *International Journal of the Legal Profession*, vol 10, no 1, pp 109-21.

58   Diesfeld, K. (1994) 'Mental health law: innovations in education and representation', *Disability and Society*, vol 9, no 3, pp 375-82.

59   Jones, P. (1995) 'Developing alternative models of professional education', *International Journal of the Legal Profession*, vol 2, no 2/3, pp 281-5.

60   Jones, P. (2000) 'Theory and practice in professional legal education', *International Journal of the Legal Profession*, vol 7, no 3, pp 239-59.

61   Hinett, K. (2002) *Developing reflective practice in legal education*, Coventry: UK Centre for Legal Education.

62   Byles, L. and Soetendorp, R. (2002) 'Law teaching for other programmes', in R. Burridge, K. Hinett, A. Paliwala and T. Varnava (eds) *Effective learning and teaching in law*, London: Kogan Page.

63   Howe, D. (1986) 'Welfare law and the welfare principle in social work practice', *Journal of Social Welfare Law*, pp 130-43, May.

64   Madden, R. and Wayne, R. (2003) 'Social work and the law: a therapeutic jurisprudence perspective', *Social Work*, vol 48, no 3, pp 338-47.

65   King, M. and Trowell, J. (1992) *Children's welfare and the law: The limits of legal intervention*, London: Sage Publications.

66   Cameron, K. (2003) 'Social work practice and accountability', in D. Baillie, K. Cameron, L.-A. Cull, J. Roche and J. West (eds) *Social work and the law in Scotland*, Basingstoke: Palgrave.

67   Dutt, R. (2001) 'Racism and social work practice', in L.-A. Cull and J. Roche (eds) *The law and social work*, Basingstoke: Palgrave.

68   Dewees, M. and Roche, S. (2001) 'Teaching about human rights in social work', *Journal of Teaching in Social Work*, vol 21 nos 1/2, pp 137-55.

69   Foster, H. (1964) 'Social work, the law, and social action', *Social Casework*, vol 45, no 7, pp 383-92.

70   Gangoli, G. and Solanki, G. (1998) 'Reining women's sexuality through law: implications for social work education', *Indian Journal of Social Work*, vol 59, no 4, pp 1011-18.

71   Toddington, S. (1995) *The emperor's new skills: The academy, the profession and the idea of legal education*, Hull: University of Hull.

72   Sherr, A. and Sugarman, D. (2000) 'Theory in legal education', *International Journal of the Legal Profession*, vol 7, no 3, pp 165-77.

73   Cull, L.-A. and Roche, J. (2002) 'Developing a responsive curriculum for health and social welfare professionals', Paper presented at the European Distance Education Network, second research workshop, Hildesheim, March.

74   ButleRitchie, D. (2003) 'Situating "thinking like a lawyer" within legal pedagogy', *Cleveland State Law Review*, vol 50, no 1, pp 29-56.

75   Hess, G. (2002-03) 'Learning to think like a lawyer: reflective journals for legal educators', *Gonzaga Law Review*, vol 38, pp 129-53.

76   Ogloff, J., Lyon, D., Douglas, K. and Rose, G. (2000) 'More than "learning to think like a lawyer": the empirical research on legal education', *34 Creighton Law Review 73*.

77   Braye, S. and Preston-Shoot, M. (1997) *Practising social work law* (2nd edn), London: Macmillan.

78   Schottland, C. (1968) 'Social work and the law: some curriculum approaches', *Buffalo Law Review*, vol 17, pp 719-31.

79   Miller, J. (1980) 'Teaching law and legal skills to social workers', *Journal of Education for Social Work*, vol 16, no 3, pp 87-95.

80   Alcock, P. (1977) 'Law in society: problems of course construction for social work students', *The Law Teacher*, vol 11, no 1, pp 11-17.

81   Blyth, E., Dunkley, A., Hodgson, A., Milner, J., Platt, C. and Wilson, J. (1995) *Education, social work and the law: Preparing for professional practice*, London: CCETSW.

82   Bogolub, E. (1998) 'Infusing content about discharging legal responsibilities into social work practice classes: the example of mandated maltreatment reporting', *Journal of Teaching in Social Work*, vol 17, nos 1/2 , pp 185-99.

[83] Howling, P. and Wodarski, J. (1992) 'Legal requisites for social workers in child abuse and neglect situations', *Social Work*, vol 37, no 4, pp 330-6.

[84] Henderson, J., Lloyd, P. and Scott, H. (2002) '"In the real world we're all put on the spot at some time or other, so you need to be prepared for it": an exploratory study of an oral method of assessing knowledge of mental health law', *Social Work Education*, vol 21, no 1, pp 91-103.

[85] Woodcock, A. (1988) 'Methods of law teaching on BTEC courses', *The Law Teacher*, vol 22, no 1, pp 14-27.

[86] Vernon, S. (1998) *Social work and the law* (3rd edn), London: Butterworths.

[87] Dickson, D. (1997) 'Law, ethics and social work with the elderly: self-determination', *Journal of Law and Social Work*, vol 7, no 2, pp 105-25.

[88] Roche, J. (1997) 'Law, ethics and social work practice: a critical curriculum', *Liverpool Law Review*, vol 19, no 2, pp 121-42.

[89] Watkinson, A. (2001) 'Human rights laws: advocacy tools for a global civil society', *Canadian Social Work Review*, vol 18, no 2, pp 267-86.

[90] Rhode, D. (1992) 'Ethics by the pervasive method', *Journal of Legal Education*, no 42, pp 31-56.

[91] Webb, J. (1998) 'Ethics for lawyers or ethics for citizens? New directions for legal education', *Journal of Law and Society*, vol 25, no 1, p 134.

[92] Webb, J. (2000) 'Developing ethical lawyers: can legal education enhance access to justice?', *The Law Teacher*, vol 34, pp 284-97.

[93] Blechner, B., Hager, C. and Williams, N. (1994) 'The Jay Haley technique: teaching law and ethics to medical and dental students', *American Journal of Law and Medicine*, vol 20, no 4, pp 163-83.

[94] Cooper, A. (1992) 'Anxiety and child protection work in two national systems', *Journal of Social Work Practice*, vol 6, no 2, pp 117-28.

[95] Laming, H. (2003) *Inquiry into the death of Victoria Climbié*, London: The Stationery Office.

[96] Parkinson, C. and Thompson, P. (1998) 'Uncertainties, mysteries, doubts and Approved Social Worker training', *Journal of Social Work Practice*, vol 12, no 1, pp 57-64.

[97] Preston-Shoot, M., Roberts, G. and Vernon, S. (1998d) 'Developing a conceptual framework for teaching and assessing law within training for professional practice: lessons from social work', *Journal of Practice Teaching*, vol 1, no 1, pp 41-51.

[98] Nash, P. (1984) 'Mental health legislation in psychiatric nurse training: survey of nurse tutors', *Nurse Education Today*, vol 4, no 3, pp 69-72.

[99] Cox, C. (2001) 'The legal challenges facing nursing', *Journal of Orthopaedic Nursing*, vol 5, no 2, pp 65-72.

[100] Barker, R. (1989) 'Independent social workers and legal training', *Journal of Independent Social Work*, vol 3, no 3, pp 1-5.

[101] Harvey, A. (1974) 'Legal studies for social workers?', *New Law Journal*, no 124, p 869.

[102] Terry, J. (1977) 'Problems of teaching professional law to social workers', *The Law Teacher*, vol 11, no 1, pp 1-10.

[103] Tingle, J. (2001) 'Patient power and litigiousness', *Practice Nursing*, vol 12, no 12, pp 487-8.

[104] Cowley, S. and Andrews, A. (2001) 'A scenario-based analysis of health visiting dilemmas', *Community Practitioner*, vol 74, no 4, pp 139-42.

[105] Broadbent, G. and White, R. (2003) 'Identifying underlying principles in social work law: a teaching and learning approach to the legal framework of decision making', *Social Work Education*, vol 22, no 5, pp 445-59.

[106] Carter, G. (1989) 'Inclusion of law in the social work curriculum', *Journal of Law and Social Work*, vol 1, no 2, pp 44-47.

[107] Forgey, M. and Colarossi, L. (2003) 'Interdisciplinary social work and law: a model domestic violence curriculum', *Journal of Social Work Education*, vol 39, no 3, pp 459-77.

[108] Gustavsson, N. and Kopels, S. (1996) 'Law and social work: an infusion model', *Journal of Law and Social Work*, vol 6, no 1, pp 3-14.

[109] Preston-Shoot, M., Roberts, G. and Vernon, S. (1998b) 'Working together in social work law', *Journal of Social Welfare and Family Law*, vol 20, no 2, pp 137-50.

[110] IASSW (International Association of Schools of Social Work) (2001) *International definition of social work*, Copenhagen: IASSW and the International Federation of Social Workers.

[111] Sparer, E. (1968) 'The place of law in social work education: a commentary on Dean Schottland's article', *Buffalo Law Review*, vol 17, pp 733-40.

[112] Ward, D. and Hogg, B. (1993) 'An integrated approach to the teaching of social work law', in M. Preston-Shoot (ed) *Assessment of competence in social work law*, London: Whiting and Birch/Social Work Education.

[113] Katz, J. (1988) 'Reflections on teaching law and medicine', *Houston Law Review*, vol 25, no 3, pp 475-92.

[114] Finley, C. and Goldstein, M. (1991) 'Curriculum survey: ethical and legal instruction – a report from the APTA Department of Education and the APTA Judicial Committee', *Journal of Physical Therapy Education*, vol 5, no 2, pp 60-4.

[115] Endeshaw, A. (2002) 'Teaching law to business students: an inquiry into curriculum methodology', *The Law Teacher*, vol 36, no 1, pp 24-43.

[116] Skwarok, L. (1995) 'Business law for non-lawyers: setting the stage for teaching, learning and assessment at Hong Kong Polytechnic University', *The Law Teacher*, vol 29, no 2, pp 189-212.

[117] Wong, Y. (2003) 'Harnessing the potential of problem-based learning in legal education', *The Law Teacher*, vol 37, no 2, pp 157-73.

[118] Bailey, S. (2004) *Using problem-based learning to teach company law*, Coventry: United Kingdom Centre for Legal Education.

[119] Eadie, T. and Ward, D. (1995) 'Putting a scenario approach to teaching social work law into practice: one year's experience on a Probation APP', *Social Work Education*, vol 14, no 2, pp 64-84.

[120] Smith, C. (1997) 'Mutual respect or mutual distrust: social workers and the courts in child care decisions', *Liverpool Law Review*, vol xix, no 2, pp 159-79.

[121] Ward, J. and Salter, M. (1990) 'Law for professional accounting education', *The Law Teacher*, vol 24, no 3, pp 208-28.

[122] Ehrlich, I. and Ehrlich, P. (1979) 'Social work and legal education: can they unite to serve the elderly?', *Journal of Education for Social Work*, vol 15, no 2, pp 87-93.

[123] Moskowitz, M. (1992) 'Beyond the case method: it's time to teach with problems', *Journal of Legal Education*, vol 42, pp 241-70.

[124] Davies, G., Marshall, E. and Robertson, N. (1998) *Child abuse: Training investigating officers*, Police Research Series Paper 94, London: Home Office.

[125] Dickens, J. (2004) 'Teaching childcare law: key principles, new priorities' *Social Work Education*, vol 23, no 2, pp 217-30.

[126] Roberts, G. (1974) 'Teaching law to social workers', *Social Work Today*, vol 5, no 12, p 353.

[127] Johns, R. (2003) 'Application of web-based learning in teaching social work law', *Social Work Education*, vol 22, no 5, pp 429-43.

[128] Oliver, J. and Huxley, P. (1985) 'The development of computer assisted learning for the teaching of mental health legislation', *Social Work Education*, vol 4, no 2, pp 20-1.

[129] Sarnoff, S. (2003) 'Considerations of web teaching in social work: one instructor's experience', *Journal of Teaching in Social Work*, vol 23, nos 1/2, pp 21-33.

[130] Adams, R. (1993) 'Using the law in social work: a flexible learning initiative', in M. Preston-Shoot (ed) *Assessment of competence in social work law*, London: Whiting and Birch/Social Work Education.

[131] Debreceniova, J. and Kolikova, M. (2003) 'Schola Ludus: new ways of teaching law in Slovakia', *The Law Teacher*, vol 37, no 3, pp 260-72.

[132] Greenbaum, E. (2003) 'Problem solving in legal education', *International Journal of the Legal Profession*, vol 10, no 1, pp 69-91.

[133] Braye, S., Lebacq, M., Mann, F. and Midwinter, E. (2003) 'Learning social work law: an enquiry based approach to developing knowledge and skills', *Social Work Education*, vol 22, no 5, pp 479-92.

[134] Munby, T. (1997) 'Immigration, nationality and asylum law for social workers: why and how it should be taught', *Liverpool Law Review*, vol XIX, no 2, pp 193-202.

[135] Braye, S. and Preston-Shoot, M. (1991) 'On acquiring law competence for social work: teaching, practice and assessment', *Social Work Education*, vol 10, no 1, pp 12-29.

[136] Oliver, J. and Huxley, P. (1986) 'The effectiveness of teaching mental health legislation to social workers seeking approval under the 1983 Mental Health Act', *Issues in Social Work Education*, pp 101-17.

[137] Oliver, J. and Huxley, P. (1988) 'Fixed response assessment (MCQ and TFQ): some research findings relevant to planning for approved social worker training and assessment', in P. Wedge (ed) *Social work: Research into practice*, Birmingham: BASW.

[138] Oliver, J. and Huxley, P. (1988) 'The development of computer assisted learning (CAL) materials for teaching and testing mental health social work in Great Britain: a review of four years progress', *Journal of Teaching in Social Work*, vol 2, no 2, pp 21-34.

[139] Swain, P. and Evans, S. (1999) 'Law and social work practice multimedia project', *New Technology in the Human Services*, vol 12, nos 3/4, pp 47-54.

[140] Maharg, P. and Muntjewerff, A. (2003) 'Through a screen darkly: electronic legal education in Europe', *The Law Teacher*, vol 36, no 3, pp 307-32.

[141] Alldridge, P. and Mumford, A. (1998) 'Gazing into the future through a VDU: communications, information technology and law teaching', *Journal of Law and Society*, vol 25, no 1, pp 116-33.

[142] Moodie, P. (1997) 'Law courseware and IOLIS: assessing the present and constructing the future', *The Journal of Information, Law and Technology*, vol 1 (http://elj.warwick.ac.uk/jilt/cal/971mood/).

[143] Homer, M. (1992) 'Child protection agencies: multidisciplinary, post-qualification legal training', *The Law Teacher*, pp 36-42.

[144] Preston-Shoot, M., Roberts, G. and Vernon, S. (1998c) '"I am concerned at the possible level of legal input expected from practice teachers": developing expertise in teaching and assessing social work law', *Social Work Education*, vol 17, no 2, pp 219-31.

[145] Campbell, J., Britton, F., Hamilton, B., Hughes, P., Manktelow, R. and Wilson, G. (2001) 'The management and supervision of approved social workers: aspects of law, policy and practice', *Journal of Social Welfare and Family Law*, vol 23, no 2, pp 155-72.

[146] Ball, C., Roberts, G., Trench, S. and Vernon, S. (1991) *Teaching, learning and assessing social work law: Report of the Law Improvements Project group*, London: CCETSW.

[147] Lancashire Polytechnic (1991) *Work-based learning in legal studies*, Preston: Faculty of Health, Department of Social Work and Community Studies.

148 Braye, S. (1993) 'Building competence in social work law for the Diploma in Social Work', in M. Preston-Shoot (ed) *Assessment of competence in social work law*, London: Whiting and Birch/Social Work Education.

149 Blumenfield, S., Simon, E.P. and Bennett, C. (1991) 'The legal clinic: helping social workers master the legal environment in health care', *Social Work in Health Care*, vol 16, no 2, pp 5-17.

150 Hogg, B., Kent, P. and Ward, D. (1992) *The teaching of law in practice placements*, Nottingham: School of Social Studies, University of Nottingham.

151 Preston-Shoot, M. (1993) 'Whither social work law? Future questions on the teaching and assessment of law to social workers', in M. Preston-Shoot (ed) *Assessment of competence in social work law*, London: Whiting and Birch/Social Work Education.

152 Bone, A. and Hinett, K. (2002) *Assessment for learning: A guide for law teachers*, Coventry: United Kingdom Centre for Legal Education.

153 Ball, C. (1989) 'From classroom to casework', *Community Care*, 26 January, Supplement, i-ii.

154 Wilson, K. and James, A. (1989) 'Looking into the law report: a two-dimensional affair', *Social Work Today*, 16 March, pp 12-13.

155 Katkin, D. (1974) 'Law and social work: a proposal for interdisciplinary education', *Journal of Legal Education*, vol 26, pp 294-317.

156 Oneglia, S. and Orlin, M. (1978) 'A model for combined private practice: attorneys and social workers in domestic relations', *Journal of Applied Social Science*, pp 37-46.

157 Slaght, E. (2002) 'Revisiting the relationship between social work and law enforcement', *Social Work*, pp 86-93.

158 Wilson, J., Setterlund, D. and Tilse, C. (2003) '"I know I signed something": older people, families and social workers' understanding of the legal aspects of entry to residential care', *Australian Social Work*, vol 56, no 2, pp 155-65.

159 Vernon, S., Harris, R. and Ball, C. (1990) *Towards social work law: Legally competent professional practice*, London: CCETSW.

[160] Braye, S. and Preston-Shoot, M. (1994) 'Partners in community care? Rethinking the relationship between the law and social work practice', *Journal of Social Welfare and Family Law*, vol 2, pp 163-83.

[161] Weil, M. (1982) 'Research on issues in collaboration between social workers and lawyers', *Social Service Review*, pp 393-405.

[162] Sklar, R. and Torczyner, J. (1991) 'Lawyers and social workers: a new joint law MSW degree programme at McGill University', *Canadian Social Work Review*, pp 97-105.

[163] White, C. (2002) 'Reassessing the social worker's role as an appropriate adult', *Journal of Social Welfare and Family Law*, vol 24, no 1, pp 55-65.

[164] Brayne, H. (1998) 'Counselling skills for the lawyer: can lawyers learn anything from counsellors?', *The Law Teacher*, vol 32, no 2, pp 137-56.

[165] Galowitz, P. (1999) 'Collaboration between lawyers and social workers: re-examining the nature and potential of the relationship', *Fordham Law Review*, no 67, pp 2123-54.

[166] Family and Child Care Law Training Group (1989) *Children Act 1989: Training together. A training and curriculum model for the Children Act 1989,* London: Family and Child Care Law Training Group.

[167] Preston-Shoot, M. (2003) 'Teaching and assessing social work law: reflections from a post-qualifying programme', *Social Work Education*, vol 22, no 5, pp 461-78.

[168] Craige, H., Saur, W. and Arcuri, J. (1982) 'The practice of social work in legal services programs', *Journal of Sociology and Social Welfare*, vol 9, no 2, pp 307-17.

[169] Secker, J. and Hill, K. (2002) 'Mental health training and development needs of community agency staff', *Health and Social Care in the Community*, vol 10, no 5, pp 323-30.

[170] GSCC (General Social Care Council) (2002) *Codes of practice for social care workers and employers*, London: GSCC.

[171] Fakhoury, W. and Wright, D. (2004) 'A national survey of approved social workers in the UK: information, communication and training needs', *British Journal of Social Work*, vol 34, no 5, pp 663-75.

[172] Randall, J. (2002) 'The practice-research relationship: a case of ambivalent attachment?', *Journal of Social Work*, vol 2, no 1, pp 105-22.

[173] Read, J. and Clements, L. (1999) 'Research, the law and good practice in relation to disabled children: an approach to staff development in a local authority', *Local Governance*, vol 25, no 2, pp 87-95.

[174] Fisher, M. (2001) 'Educational input to improve documentation skills', *Nursing Times*, vol 97, no 8, pp 35-6.

[175] Duncan, T., Piper, C. and Warren-Adamson, C. (2003) 'Running rings round law? An ecological approach to teaching law for child-centred practice', *Social Work Education*, vol 22, no 5, pp 493-503.

[176] Crisp, B., Anderson, M., Orme, J. and Green Lister, P. (2003) *Learning and teaching in social work education: Assessment*, London: Social Care Institute for Excellence.

[177] Pithouse, A. and Scourfield, J. (2002) 'Ready for practice? The DipSW in Wales: views from the workplace on social work training', *Journal of Social Work*, vol 2, no 1, pp 7-27.

[178] QAA (Quality Asssurance Agency) (2001) *The framework for higher education qualifications in England, Wales and Northern Ireland*, London: QAA for Higher Education.

[179] QAA (Quality Asssurance Agency) (2001) *The framework for higher education qualifications in Scotland*, London: QAA for Higher Education.

[180] Carpenter, J. (2005) *Evaluating outcomes in social work education*, London/Dundee: Social Care Institute for Excellence/Scottish Institute for Excellence in Social Work Education.

[181] SIS (Social Information Systems) Ltd (2001) *Report to develop guidance to establish a common knowledge base and outcomes for social work training with children and families*, Knutsford: SSI Ltd.

[182] Ball, C. (1988) 'Conspicuous by its absence', *Community Care*, 7 April, pp 17-18.

[183] Banks, S. (1999) 'Pedagogy and ideology: teaching law as if it matters', *Legal Studies*, vol 19, no 4, pp 445-67.

[184] Bates, StJ. and Bates, M. (1975) 'The legal education of social workers', *Social Work Today*, vol 5, no 23, pp 710-12.

[185] Gwenlan, C. (1993) Law teaching learning outside the college and assessment, in M. Preston-Shoot (ed) *Assessment of competence in social work law*, London: Whiting and Birch/Social Work Education.

[186] Hill, M., Lockyer, A., Morton, P., Batchelor, S. and Scott, J. (2003) 'Safeguarding children's interests in welfare proceedings: the Scottish experience', *Journal of Social Welfare and Family Law*, vol 25, no 1, pp 1-21.

[187] Matthew, V. (1993) 'College based assessment of competency in social work law', in M. Preston-Shoot (ed) *Assessment of competence in social work law*, London: Whiting and Birch/Social Work Education.

[188] Schwartz, M. (2001) 'Teaching law by design: how learning theory and instructional design can inform and reform law teaching', *San Diego Law Review*, vol 38, no 2, pp 347-63.

[189] Scott, A. (2004) *Using problem-based learning to teach constitutional and administrative law*, Coventry: United Kingdom Centre for Legal Education.

# Appendix 1: Search strategies

All databases were searched from 1967-2004, unless otherwise stated.

**Index to Theses**
**08/01/04**
#1 legal education
#2 law teaching
#3 law skills
#4 education and law
#5 education and social work

**Legal Journals Index**
**10/01/04**
#1 legal education
#2 vocational training
#3 practitioner
#4 vocational qualifications
#5 teaching legal skills
#6 academic skills
#7 study skills
#8 legal study skills
#9 legal profession
#10 legal skills
#11 legal theory
#12 undergraduate legal education
#13 university legal education
#14 vocational education
#15 law education
#16 legal skills training

**Westlaw**
**08/01/04**
#1 social work
#2 social work and education

#3 social work and training

#4 social work and practice

#5 social work and child abuse

#6 care proceedings

#7 social work and care proceedings

#8 social services

#9 social services and theory

#10 social welfare

#11 social work practice

#12 social work law

#13 social work values

#14 law and social work practice

#15 Children Act and education

#16 Children Act and training

#17 social work and children

#18 social work and child care or childcare

#19 community care and law

## Ebscohost Research Databases – Academic Search Elite 08/01/04

#1 social work

#2 law

#3 social work and law

#4 social work practice

#5 communication

#6 communication and social work

#7 telecommunication and social work

#8 education

#9 education and social work

#10 social work education

#11 legal education

## SIGLE 1980-2003 (Index to Grey Literature) 26/02/04

#1 social work education

#2 legal education

#3 law education and theory

#4 law and social work education

#5 child protection and law and educat*
#6 family and law and educat*
#7 family and law and train*
#8 adoption and law and train*
#9 adoption and law and educat*
#10 adoption and law
#11 disab* and law and educat*
#12 disab* and law and train*
#13 mental health and law and train*
#14 law and mental health and educat*
#15 nurs* and legal and educat*
#16 health service* and law and train*
#17 health service* and law and educat*
#18 communit* and law and educat*
#19 educat* and law and nurs*
#20 educat* and law
#21 law and nurs*

## ASSIA (Applied Social Sciences Index and Abstracts) 16/02/04

#1 social work/de and law/de
#2 social work/de
#3 social work/de and computer assisted instruction/de
#4 social work/de and education/de

## Cambridge Scientific Abstracts
## Social Services Abstracts
## 13/02/04

#1 law/de and social work/de
#2 law and clinical social work
#3 law and international social work
#4 law and occupational social work
#5 social work research
#6 social work theory

## Ovid Social Work Abstracts
## 29/02/04

#1 disab* and law and educat*

#2 educational programs/de
#3 institutional ethnography/de
#4 disabilities/de
#5 colleges/de
#6 legislation/de
#7children/de
#8 civil rights/de
#9 special education/de
#10 education supervision and training/de
#11 social work education/de
#12 undergraduate education/de
#13 social work practice/de and education
#14 law and education and training/de
#15 social work and educat* and law
#16 law/de and social work/de
#17 interdisciplinary education/de
#18 interdisciplinary education/de and law
#19 ethical and legal issues/de
#20 social work students/de
#21 educational preparedness/de
#22 legal issues/de and social work education/de
#23 law and teaching
#24 undergraduate education/de and social work education
#25 social work students/de
#25 legal system and social work
#26 social workers/de and lawyers/de
#27 school social workers/de and law

## British Nursing Index
## 19/02/04
#1 nursing education/de
#2 law and nursing education/de
#3 ethics and law
#4 midwifery and education and law
#5 education, nursing [Legislation and Jurisprudence]
#6 training support financial [Legislation and Jurisprudence]
#7 legislation
#8 legislation and health policy

**JSTOR**
**10/2/04**

\# 1 legal education
\# 2 legal and education
\# 3 teaching law
\# 4 health and teaching law

**INGENTA**
**05/4/04**

\# 1 health and teaching law
\# 2 health professional*
\# 3 educ*

# Appendix 2:
## Annotated bibliography of key references for *Teaching, learning and assessment of law in social work education*

### Reference
Adams, R. (1993) 'Using the law in social work: a flexible learning initiative', in M. Preston-Shoot (ed) *Assessment of competence in social work law*, London: Whiting and Birch/Social Work Education.[130]

### Country
UK

### Learning and teaching and social work law
Reports on a distance and open learning approach to law learning.

### Evaluation
Descriptive account of six unit module and work books. No evaluation.

### Reference
Alldridge, P. and Mumford, A. (1998) 'Gazing into the future through a VDU: communications, information technology and law teaching', *Journal of Law and Society*, vol 25, no 1, pp 116-33.[141]

### Country
UK

### Learning and teaching and social work law
Considers the technical achievements of communications and information technology (CIT) in the practice and teaching of law, and challenges assumptions about the theory, practice and teaching of law.

The contribution of CIT to the teaching of law is considered and the authors suggest that it has redefined teaching and learning interaction.

## Evaluation

Considers different methods in terms of how they can be used for imaginative ways of teaching but the authors recognise that research is required on the relative effects on students of use of communications and information technology as compared with face-to-face teaching.

## Reference

Bailey, S. (2004) *Using problem-based learning to teach company law*, Coventry: United Kingdom Centre for Legal Education.[118]

## Country

UK

## Learning and teaching and social work law

Very clear and practical exposition of methods of facilitating and assessing problem-based learning.

## Evaluation

Descriptive and conceptual, building on theory from teaching experience. Records positive student feedback but does not provide details.

## Reference

Ball, C. (1988) 'Conspicuous by its absence', *Community Care*, 7 April, pp 17-18 April.[182]

## Country

UK

## Learning and teaching and social work law

Reports research findings from the Law Report (Ball et al, 1988).[22]

## Evaluation

Essentially a summary of key research findings that set the framework for subsequent debates and theory building.

**Reference**

Ball, C. (1989) 'From classroom to casework', *Community Care*, 26 January, Supplement, i-ii.[153]

**Country**

UK

**Learning and teaching and social work law**

Summary of the Law Report findings and some proposals.

**Evaluation**

Essentially a summary of key research findings that set the framework for subsequent debates and theory building.

**Reference**

Ball, C., Harris, R., Roberts, G. and Vernon, S. (1988) *The Law Report: Teaching and assessment of law in social work education*, London: CCETSW.[22]

**Country**

UK

**Learning and teaching and social work law**

Research findings on teaching and assessment of law in social work programmes in the UK. Sharply critical of educational practices and of the level of legal knowledge and skills demonstrated by social work students at the point of qualification. Makes recommendations for improving law teaching on social work programmes.

**Evaluation**

An empirical study that set the framework for subsequent debates in the UK.

**Reference**

Ball, C., Preston-Shoot, M., Roberts, G. and Vernon, S. (1995) *Law for social workers in England and Wales*, London: CCETSW.[24]

**Country**
UK

**Learning and teaching and social work law**
Offers an academic and practice curriculum.

**Evaluation**
Limited discussion of research findings indicating an improvement in outcomes of law teaching. Useful ideas relating to teaching and assessment methods.

**Reference**
Ball, C., Roberts, G., Trench, S. and Vernon, S. (1991) *Teaching, learning and assessing social work law*, Report of the Law Improvements Project Group. London: CCETSW.[146]

**Country**
UK

**Learning and teaching and social work law**
Offers a curriculum and discusses aims of law teaching.

**Evaluation**
Only limited discussion of the practice curriculum. Essentially a contribution to theory building surrounding teaching, learning and assessment of law in social work education.

**Reference**
Banks, S. (1999) 'Pedagogy and ideology: teaching law as if it matters', *Legal Studies*, vol 19, no 4, pp 445-67.[183]

**Country**
UK

**Learning and teaching and social work law**
Law must be taught within the context of the society in which it operates. Learning the law is not just about learning legal rules and procedures but is about learning and understanding law's internal point of view

and subjecting that viewpoint to critical analysis. Context may also be understood to be that which is framed by professional standards and requirements. A broader exposure to differing perspectives and contexts will assist critique as well. Explores how to make legal education more meaningful, with obvious parallels with social work education. Argues for the integration of differing legal and cultural perspectives in rhe curriculum. Provides a strong argument for cross-cultural and cross-experiential curricula.

## Evaluation

The article sets out a framework for teachers to use in creating a cross-cultural and experiential law curriculum. Teaching the law is a social process and is neither objective nor content neutral. Teachers and students are both influenced by ideological and pedagogical assumptions. Being aware of this enables a more critical examination and engagement with people and information. Law needs to be taught in a cross-cultural and cross-experiential fashion to make it matter to all students.

## Reference

Barker, R. (1989) 'Independent social workers and legal training', *Journal of Independent Social Work*, vol 3, no 3, pp 1-5.[100]

## Country

USA

## Learning and teaching and social work law

An editorial and exhortation that bemoans the absence of material in journals on this topic.

## Evaluation

Useful for parallels between the UK and US and draws on informal research to support the argument. Covers some of what social workers need to know, why they need to know it, and refers to the importance of continuing professional development.

## Reference

Bates, StJ. and Bates, M. (1975) 'The legal education of social workers', *Social Work Today*, vol 5, no 23, pp 710-12.[184]

## Country

UK

## Learning and teaching and social work law

A review of what areas of law to teach so that social workers recognise legal problems and assess the strengths and needs of clients.

## Evaluation

Descriptive and conceptual. No formal evaluation of what is proposed, although this draws on earlier research.

## Reference

Blechner, B., Hager, C. and Williams, N. (1994) 'The Jay Haley technique: teaching law and ethics to medical and dental students', *American Journal of Law and Medicine*, vol 20, no 4, pp 163-83.[93]

## Country

USA

## Learning and teaching and social work law

The article describes a curriculum that combines law and ethics. It consists of 56 actual and hypothetical cases from which legal and ethical issues are extracted. The aim is to provide students with an understanding of the legal and ethical underpinnings of the decisions they make. The authors set out reasons why it is important to study legal and ethical aspects of practice and to undertake such study as early as possible in the professionalisation process. The article gives a broad outline of course content, the teaching strategies employed, and the assessment strategies used.

## Evaluation

Feedback from students suggests that they have learned to weigh and balance legal and ethical issues. No evaluation has been undertaken to measure the impact of the course on practice.

## Reference

Blumenfield, S., Simon, E.P. and Bennett, C. (1991) 'The legal clinic: helping social workers master the legal environment in health care', *Social Work in Health Care*, vol 16, no 2, pp 5-17.[149]

## Country

USA

## Learning and teaching and social work law

Focuses as much on continuing professional development as on qualifying training. Sees a legal clinic as a practice curriculum intervention – legal consultation on cases and issues.

## Evaluation

Evaluated by staff but no data given.

## Reference

Blyth, E., Dunkley, A., Hodgson, A., Milner, J., Platt, C. and Wilson, J. (1995) *Education, social work and the law: Preparing for professional practice*, London: CCETSW.[81]

## Country

UK

## Learning and teaching and social work law

Outlines a minimum level of legal competence for education social work. Covers knowledge, skills, assessment, and methods of teaching and learning.

## Evaluation

A contribution to theory building. Curriculum guidance.

**Reference**

Bogolub, E. (1998) 'Infusing content about discharging legal responsibilities into social work practice classes: the example of mandated maltreatment reporting', *Journal of Teaching in Social Work*, vol 17, nos 1/2, pp 185-99.[82]

**Country**

USA

**Learning and teaching and social work law**

An infusion model with a particular focus on how – cases, role-play. Reference to practice teacher support, and to integrating legal knowledge with skills.

**Evaluation**

No empirical element. A conceptual contribution to developing methods of teaching and learning law in social work education.

---

**Reference**

Bone, A. and Hinett, K. (2002) *Assessment for learning: A guide for law teachers*, Coventry: United Kingdom Centre for Legal Education.[152]

**Country**

UK

**Learning and teaching and social work law**

Very clear and practical exposition of assessment.

**Evaluation**

Descriptive and conceptual, building on the theory and practice of assessment. No formal evaluation.

---

**Reference**

Boon, A. (1998) 'History is past politics: a critique of the legal skills movement in England and Wales', *Journal of Law and Society*, vol 25, no 1, pp 151-69.[56]

## Country
UK

## Learning and teaching and social work law
Historical overview that includes analysis of trends in legal education, synopsis of pedagogical debates regarding skills teaching and course content, and extent of professional bodies' control over this. Critique of Law Society model of vocational training, 'failure' of skills movement.

## Evaluation
Useful summary of debate about responsibility for skills teaching and implications of professional dominance of the skills curriculum, but no direct reference to social work although obvious parallels.

## Reference
Bradney, A. (1992) 'Ivory towers and satanic mills: choices for university law schools', *Studies in Higher Education*, vol 17, no 1, pp 5-21.[39]

## Country
UK

## Learning and teaching and social work law
Theoretical discussion of issues emerging from history of law teaching in UK. Summary of history of law teaching with special reference to the relationship between universities and 'industry', that is, the legal profession. Broad historical approach.

## Evaluation
Concise summary of the debates which has parallels with social work although these are not indicated in the article.

## Reference
Braye, S. (1993) 'Building competence in social work law for the Diploma in Social Work', in M. Preston-Shoot (ed) *Assessment of competence in social work law*, London: Whiting and Birch/Social Work Education.[148]

## Country
UK

### Learning and teaching and social work law

Outlines contribution practice placements can make to developing student competence. Focus on learning processes in placement. Gives indicators for emerging competence in law, integrated with processes of social work.

### Evaluation

Descriptive and conceptual. Offers useful guidance for assessing the development of students' competence as they progress through a practice curriculum.

### Reference

Braye, S. and Preston-Shoot, M. (1990) 'On teaching and applying the law in social work: it is not that simple', *British Journal of Social Work*, vol 20, no 4, pp 333-53.[4]

### Country

UK

### Learning and teaching and social work law

Presents case for teaching social work law, conceptual framework and teaching examples. Explores framework of tensions between various factors.

### Evaluation

Argues powerfully for the teaching of social work law in principle and offers example of how law might be taught using case study approach.

### Reference

Braye, S. and Preston-Shoot, M. (1991) 'On acquiring law competence for social work: teaching, practice and assessment', *Social Work Education*, vol 10, no 1, pp 12-29.[135]

### Country

UK

## Learning and teaching and social work law

Justifies law teaching in social work, providing teaching examples. Concerned with assimilation of law into practice.

## Evaluation

Argues for integration and partnership in teaching social work law. Contains examples of social work law teaching.

## Reference

Braye, S. and Preston-Shoot, M. (1994) 'Partners in community care? Rethinking the relationship between the law and social work practice', *Journal of Social Welfare and Family Law*, vol 2, pp 163-83.[160]

## Country

UK

## Learning and teaching and social work law

The focus of the article is that there must be greater clarity about how the law contributes to and concerns itself with the major contemporary themes of professional practice. It provides a framework for clarifying the relationship between law and social work, and for translating this into practice at levels of policy formation and contact with service users.

## Evaluation

Argues for partnership between law and social work in relation to community care service provision. Very relevant to exposition of role of law and social work.

## Reference

Braye, S. and Preston-Shoot, M. (1999) 'Accountability, administrative law and social work practice: redressing or reinforcing the power imbalance?', *Journal of Social Welfare and Family Law*, vol 21, no 3, pp 235-56.[46]

## Country

UK

### Learning and teaching and social work law
Application of law to social work practice. Explores issues of accountability. Exploration of service user rights, rights-based approach.

### Evaluation
Summary of areas in which accountability principles apply to social work.

### Reference
Braye, S., Lebacq, M., Mann, F. and Midwinter, E. (2003) 'Learning social work law: an enquiry based approach to developing knowledge and skills', *Social Work Education*, vol 22, no 5, pp 479-92.[133]

### Country
UK

### Learning and teaching and social work law
Pedagogical example. Argues for enquiry-based approach. Problem-based learning compared to enquiry based and action learning.

### Evaluation
Presents teaching examples and explains how they are used, relating these to theory. Directly relevant to the teaching of social work law.

### Reference
Broadbent, G. and White, R. (2003) 'Identifying underlying principles in social work law: a teaching and learning approach to the legal framework of decision making', *Social Work Education*, vol 22, no 5, pp 445-59.[105]

### Country
UK

### Learning and teaching and social work law
Outlines use of the legal framework of decision making to facilitate student social work law learning. Offers a teaching and learning strategy.

## Evaluation

A descriptive and conceptual paper that clearly lays out the framework of an approach to law teaching to social work students.

## Reference

Byles, L. and Soetendorp, R. (2002) 'Law teaching for other programmes', in R. Burridge, K. Hinett, A. Paliwala and T. Varnava (eds) *Effective learning and teaching in law*, London: Kogan Page.[62]

## Country

UK

## Learning and teaching and social work law

Descriptive account of what works on the basis of experience. Focus on approaches to teaching, learning outcomes, assessment strategies and tasks, content and skills.

## Evaluation

Does not include social work but does include nursing. A descriptive and conceptual account that can easily be applied to social work law teaching, learning and assessment.

## Reference

Campbell, J., Britton, F., Hamilton, B., Hughes, P., Manktelow, R. and Wilson, G. (2001) 'The management and supervision of Approved Social Workers: aspects of law, policy and practice', *Journal of Social Welfare and Family Law*, vol 23, no 2, pp 155-72.[145]

## Country

UK

## Learning and teaching and social work law

Argues strongly for the need for a more consistent approach to training and reapproval of Approved Social Workers.

## Evaluation

An empirical study, finding high levals of satisfaction with training in order to prepare Approved Social Workers for statutory duties.

### Reference

Carter, G. (1989) 'Inclusion of law in the social work curriculum', *Journal of Law and Social Work*, vol 1, no 2, pp 44-7.[106]

### Country

USA

### Learning and teaching and social work law

Descriptive think piece that contains statements on why, how, skills and assessment.

### Evaluation

Contains a very basic reporting of student evaluation but gives no details of data collection.

### Reference

Cowley, S. and Andrews, A. (2001) 'A scenario-based analysis of health visiting dilemmas', *Community Practitioner*, vol 74, no 4, pp 139-42.[104]

### Country

UK

### Learning and teaching and social work law

A useful approach clearly described of how to enable students to explore acccountability and practice dilemmas. Teaching scenarios given.

### Evaluation

Descriptive and conceptual. No formal evaluation but an example of a similar teaching approach from another discipline.

### Reference

Cox, C. (2001) 'The legal challenges facing nursing', *Journal of Orthopaedic Nursing*, vol 5, no 2, pp 65-72.[99]

### Country

UK

## Learning and teaching and social work law

A theoretical overview of law relevant to medical care. It covers the legal principles within capacity and consent to treatment, acccountability and record keeping. There are clear parallels to social work but these are not made explicit in the paper.

## Evaluation

Descriptive and conceptual. No formal evaluation.

## Reference

Cull, L.-A. and Roche, J. (2002) 'Developing a responsive curriculum for health and social welfare professionals', Paper presented at the European Distance Education Network Second Research Workshop, Hildesheim, 21-23 March.[73]

## Country

UK

## Learning and teaching and social work law

The article outlines the issues involved in developing a curriculum in law for social work students in two jurisdictions (England and Wales, and Scotland) and considers the challenges in delivering supported open learning materials for social work students as well as students from other professions, service users and the 'general interest' market. The article also considers the issues in relation to online delivery of courses, for the students, the tutors and for the authors of such materials. It concludes with a consideration of the issues that apply to teaching law to non-lawyers.

## Evaluation

Useful overview of some of the issues raised by supported open learning and online learning.

## Reference

Davies, G., Marshall, E. and Robertson, N. (1998) *Child abuse: Training investigating officers*, Police Research Series Paper 94, London: Home Office.[124]

**Country**
UK

**Learning and teaching and social work law**
Empirical study based on focus group interviews. Looks at curriculum, joint training, trainers.

**Evaluation**
Evidence-based monograph, the messages from which can be applied to qualifying and post-qualifying education.

**Reference**
Dewees, M. and Roche, S. (2001) 'Teaching about human rights in social work', *Journal of Teaching in Social Work*, vol 21, nos 1/2, pp 137-55. [68]

**Country**
USA

**Learning and teaching and social work law**
An account of teaching human rights. Answers the question how to provide teaching and facilitate learning in particular, using readings, case examples, videos and social action projects.

**Evaluation**
No evaluation offered. A descriptive and conceptual paper.

**Reference**
Dickens, J. (2004) 'Teaching childcare law: key principles, new priorities', *Social Work Education*, vol 23, no 2, pp 217-30. [125]

**Country**
UK

**Learning and teaching and social work law**
Presents findings from research on the role of lawyers and social workers, research based on 54 interviews split between social services and legal staff in local authorities. Itemises four principles of teaching law in social work.

### Evaluation

Presents clear and persuasive arguments relevant to social work law teaching childcare, evidence based. Offers four principles on which social work law teaching should be based.

### Reference

Diesfeld, K. (1994) 'Mental health law: innovations in education and representation', *Disability and Society*, vol 9, no 3, pp 375-82.[58]

### Country

UK

### Learning and teaching and social work law

Chronicles the development of a mental health law clinic established to enable law students to apply theory to practice and engage with real problems in the mental health field. Advantages include learning skills through hands-on representation, which enables students to form a bridge between legal theory and practice. This clinical approach to legal education empowers students as they participate in evolving curriculum based on cases, relevant research, issue spotting, case management and development of relationships with clients.

### Evaluation

Provision of legal services through a client-directed law clinic provides fertile ground for students and their clients to develop a meaningful professional partnership. Students learn skills in collaboration.

### Reference

Duncan, T., Piper, C. and Warren-Adamson, C. (2003) 'Running rings round law? An ecological approach to teaching law for child-centred practice', *Social Work Education*, vol 22, no 5, pp 493-503.[175]

### Country

UK

### Learning and teaching and social work law

Pedagogical example. Presents practice example of teaching in social work law based on ecological theory.

### Evaluation

Presents examples of material used and demonstrates its application to teaching practice. Excellent linkage of theory to practice.

### Reference

Eadie, T. and Ward, D. (1995) 'Putting a scenario approach to teaching social work law into practice: one year's experience on a Probation APP', *Social Work Education*, vol 14, no 2, pp 64-84.[119]

### Country

UK

### Learning and teaching and social work law

A scenario approach to teaching and assessment, located in research on both outcomes for student learning of academic and practice curricula. Provides examples of the approach in the academic curriculum, with suggestions of how learning may be consolidated in practice.

### Evaluation

Provides student comments as evaluation but no detail of numbers or how data collected.

### Reference

Ehrlich, I. and Ehrlich, P. (1979) 'Social work and legal education: can they unite to serve the elderly?', *Journal of Education for Social Work*, vol 15, no 2, pp 87-93.[122]

### Country

USA

### Learning and teaching and social work law

Briefly reports the literature on outcomes of joint programmes. Focuses on the how of interdisciplinary law and social work education. Emphasises importance of preparation of law and social work staff first to shift attitudes and develop joint work with students.

## Evaluation

A descriptive and conceptual paper. The recommended approach is not evaluated.

## Reference

Endeshaw, A. (2002) 'Teaching law to business students: an inquiry into curriculum methodology', *The Law Teacher*, vol 36, no 1, pp 24-43.[115]

## Country

Singapore

## Learning and teaching and social work law

Outlines content, teaching methods and assessment. While the focus is on teaching law to business students, clear parallels may be drawn with social work.

## Evaluation

Empirical paper with student views reported.

## Reference

Fakhoury, W. and Wright, D. (2004) 'A national survey of Approved Social Workers in the UK: information, communication and training needs', *British Journal of Social Work*, vol 34, no 5, pp 663-75.[171]

## Country

UK

## Learning and teaching and social work law

A study assessing the training needs of Approved Social Workers and making recommendations for training and for continuing professional development.

## Evaluation

An empirical study using postal questionnaires. The article derives themes from what respondents report but it does not fully interrogate the data. It is possible that the expression of need for more knowledge is actually an expression of anxiety about never having sufficient legal knowledge.

### Reference

Family and Child Care Law Training Group (1989) *Children Act 1989: Training together. A training and curriculum model for the 1989 Children Act.* [166]

### Country

UK

### Learning and teaching and social work law

Identifies knowledge requirements, skills needs and target groups.

### Evaluation

A conceptual monograph with recommendations for the curriculum.

### Reference

Finley, C. and Goldstein, M. (1991) 'Curriculum survey: ethical and legal instruction – a report from the APTA Department of Education and the APTA Judicial Committee', *Journal of Physical Therapy Education*, vol 5, no 2, pp 60-4. [114]

### Country

USA

### Learning and teaching and social work law

Focuses on what a survey of courses found relating to teaching ethics and legal issues. Describes in outline the content of courses, the hours devoted to them, and the profile of teachers.

### Evaluation

Does not evaluate infusion versus a modular approach. Does not focus on outcomes.

### Reference

Fisher, M. (2001) 'Educational input to improve documentation skills', *Nursing Times*, vol 97, no 8, pp 35-6. [174]

### Country

UK

### Learning and teaching and social work law

Brief description of a post-qualifying course for nurses on record keeping, including its legal significance. Whether knowledge has been applied is tested by requiring participants to audit their practice and to report back on their findings.

### Evaluation

Descriptive and conceptual. No formal evaluation although the article states that written evaluations were collected from participants.

### Reference

Forgey, M. and Colarossi, L. (2003) 'Interdisciplinary social work and law: a model domestic violence curriculum', *Journal of Social Work Education*, vol 39, no 3, pp 459-77.[107]

### Country

USA

### Learning and teaching and social work law

Presentation of model curriculum for teaching about domestic violence in USA. Interdisciplinary approach with an exploration of outcomes.

### Evaluation

Example of joint teaching of legal and social work students.

### Reference

Galowitz, P. (1999) 'Collaboration between lawyers and social workers: re-examining the nature and potential of the relationship', *Fordham Law Review*, vol 67, pp 2123-54.[165]

### Country

USA

### Learning and teaching and social work law

A paper that focuses on issues of collaboration between two professions and unusually devotes much attention to what social work practitioners can offer lawyers to assist them in their practice. Briefly covers questions of inter-professional education.

## Evaluation

Descriptive and conceptual. No formal evaluation.

## Reference

Gangoli, G. and Solanki, G. (1998) 'Reining women's sexuality through law: implications for social work education', *Indian Journal of Social Work*, vol 59, no 4, pp 1011-18.[70]

## Country

India

## Learning and teaching and social work law

Feminist critique of law in India related to sexuality and sexual offences, with an exploration of implications for social work and social education.

## Evaluation

A short and very general article, adopting a feminist approach.

## Reference

Gustavsson, N. and Kopels, S. (1996) 'Law and social work: an infusion model', *Journal of Law and Social Work*, vol 6, no 1, pp 3-14.[108]

## Country

USA

## Learning and teaching and social work law

Covers what should be taught, why and how. Provides an infusion model with examples of different issues or client groups. No discussion of assessment.

## Evaluation

Description without empirical evidence.

## Reference

Gwenlan, C. (1993) 'Law teaching learning outside the college and assessment', in M. Preston-Shoot (ed) *Assessment of competence in social work law*, London: Whiting and Birch/Social Work Education.[185]

## Country

UK

## Learning and teaching and social work law

Discusses problems and concerns for practice teachers. Argues that practice teaching structure in agencies may need to develop. Considers what this may mean for assessment – some focus on what, why and when of learning and assessment.

## Evaluation

A conceptual paper that offers a contribution to theory building surrounding the practice curriculum for social work law.

## Reference

Henderson, J., Lloyd, P. and Scott, H. (2002) '"In the real world we're all put on the spot at some time or other, so you need to be prepared for it": an exploratory study of an oral method of assessing knowledge of mental health law', *Social Work Education*, vol 21, no 1, pp 91-103.[84]

## Country

UK

## Learning and teaching and social work law

Evaluation of pedagogical method: results of using oral examinations in testing knowledge of student Approved Social Workers. Draws on student evaluations and quotes their comments. Oral examinations are challenging but reflective of practice situations, "supportive and fair" yet "terrifying and inquisitorial".

## Evaluation

Includes evaluation of pedagogical methods and promotes the case for using oral examinations.

### Reference

Hill, M., Lockyer, A., Morton, P., Batchelor, S. and Scott, J. (2003) 'Safeguarding children's interests in welfare proceedings: the Scottish experience', *Journal of Social Welfare and Family Law*, vol 25, no 1, pp 1-21.[186]

### Country

UK

### Learning and teaching and social work law

A paper that researches what training is provided to safeguarders which, while tangential to teaching law in social work education, raises issues concerned with continuing professional development and with how much law non-lawyers should know in order to perform their roles.

### Evaluation

An empirical study in which questionnaires, interviews and analysis of case records are used to clearly identify current practice. Recommendations are drawn directly from the data that is presented.

### Reference

Hogg, B., Kent, P. and Ward, D. (1992) *The teaching of law in practice placements*, University of Nottingham, School of Social Studies.[150]

### Country

UK

### Learning and teaching and social work law

Focuses on research encounters between practice teachers and students. Lack of knowledge of legislation, confusion about the nature of law, and inconsistent approaches to teaching in college and on placement amongst the findings. Practice teachers have widely differing attitudes to what are legal issues in social work.

### Evaluation

A valuable empirical study focusing on the somewhat neglected area of the social work law practice curriculum.

## Reference
Homer, M. (1992) 'Child protection agencies: multidisciplinary post-qualification legal training', *The Law Teacher*, pp 36-42.[143]

## Country
UK

## Learning and teaching and social work law
A short paper focusing on continuing professional development. It identifies the challenges involved in inter-agency training but also the benefits to be gained. It is critical of the short course format for in-service training.

## Evaluation
Descriptive and conceptual. No formal evaluation but includes a very brief discussion of the difficulties of evaluating such training.

## Reference
Howe, D. (1986) 'Welfare law and the welfare principle in social work practice', *Journal of Social Welfare Law*, pp 130-43, May.[63]

## Country
UK

## Learning and teaching and social work law
Theoretical analysis of relationship between welfare law and social work. Suggests that social work practice remains essentially tied and specific to the client group, reflecting the perceptual outlook that the law imposes on each client group.

## Evaluation
Not specifically about learning and teaching but underlines the importance of law in social work. Macro-level analysis.

## Reference
Howling, P. and Wodarski, J. (1992) 'Legal requisites for social workers in child abuse and neglect situations', *Social Work*, vol 37, no 4, pp 330-6.[83]

## Country
USA

## Learning and teaching and social work law
Summary of what US social workers need to know about child abuse law.

## Evaluation
Relates to US practice. General summary of law.

## Reference
Jankovic, J. and Green, R. (1981) 'Teaching legal principles to social workers', *Journal of Education for Social Work*, vol 17, no 13, pp 28-35. [27]

## Country
USA

## Learning and teaching and social work law
Theoretical overview, mainly historical. Presents case for greater attention to legal concepts in social work education. A model is presented for integrating legal concepts.

## Evaluation
Very general and quite weak in coverage of the debates, almost superficial.

## Reference
Johns, R. (2003) 'Application of web-based learning in teaching social work law', *Social Work Education*, vol 22, no 5, pp 429-43. [127]

## Country
UK

## Learning and teaching and social work law
Focuses on how – a method of teaching and learning.

### Evaluation

A partly descriptive and conceptual, and partly empirical paper. It draws on student evaluations but without detail of how many were involved in the data collection.

### Reference

Jones, P. (1995) 'Developing alternative models of professional education', *International Journal of the Legal Profession*, vol 2, nos 2/3, pp 281-5.[59]

### Country

UK

### Learning and teaching and social work law

Distinguishes between learning to work and learning about work. Reviews developments in legal education and is sharply critical of a technocratic approach to training.

### Evaluation

Conceptual paper that offers useful ideas about the purpose of vocational education.

### Reference

Jones, P. (2000) 'Theory and practice in professional legal education', *International Journal of the Legal Profession*, vol 7, no 3, pp 239-59.[60]

### Country

UK

### Learning and teaching and social work law

Overview of theoretical approaches to competence-based education and training. Presents a critique of Schön's work and points to limitations of competence-based approaches.

### Evaluation

Useful critique, applied only to law teaching.

### Reference

Katkin, D. (1974) 'Law and social work: a proposal for interdisciplinary education', *Journal of Legal Education*, vol 26, pp 294-317.[155]

### Country

USA

### Learning and teaching and social work law

Curriculum critique and proposal for bringing social work and law education together. Overview of roles of lawyers and social workers with particular reference to youth justice in the US.

### Evaluation

Presents curriculum proposal but no bibliography included and now somewhat dated.

---

### Reference

Kopels, S. and Gustavsson, N. (1996) 'Infusing legal issues into the social work curriculum', *Journal of Social Work Education*, vol 32, no 1, pp 115-25.[30]

### Country

USA

### Learning and teaching and social work law

Survey of law teaching in US social work courses. Questionnaire of all courses teaching social workers. Quantitative: 52% response rate. Sample frame: all 112 MSW courses accredited by the Council on Social Work Education.

### Evaluation

Valuable quantitative research demonstrating lack of interest in law and that it is not accorded great importance in the US social work curriculum.

---

## Reference

Lancashire Polytechnic (1991) *Work-based learning in legal studies*, Preston: Faculty of Health, Department of Social Work and Community Studies.[147]

## Country

UK

## Learning and teaching and social work law

Survey and course development research for learning law in practice. Focus on practice curriculum but also on academic curriculum, teaching and assessment methods.

## Evaluation

An important contribution to theory building in respect of teaching, learning and assessment of law in social work education in the academic and practice curricula. Offers useful ideas for teaching and assessment.

## Reference

Lemmon, J. (1983) 'Legal content in the social work curriculum', *Journal of Education for Social Work*, vol 19, no 2, pp 71-6.[28]

## Country

USA

## Learning and teaching and social work law

National survey of law courses in social work programmes. Some reference to continuing professional development and to methods of teaching, fieldwork placements, and law as social change.

## Evaluation

Empirical research, applying findings on current education practice to a previously devised conceptual model.

### Reference
Lynch, R. and Brawley, E. (1994) 'Social workers and the judicial system: looking for a better fit', *Journal of Teaching in Social Work*, vol 10, nos 1/2, pp 65-82.[29]

### Country
USA

### Learning and teaching and social work law
Clearly demonstrates that the challenge of facilitating students' social work law learning is not just a UK problem. Argues that social workers need better preparation. Offers core curriculum content, additionally specialised in criminal justice. Focuses on why teaching and assessing student competence in law is important.

### Evaluation
Conceptual paper, relying on assertion and argumentation.

### Reference
Madden, R. (2000) 'Legal content in social work education: preparing students for interprofessional practice', *Journal of Teaching in Social Work*, vol 20, nos 1/2, pp 3-17.[31]

### Country
USA

### Learning and teaching and social work law
Describes a dedicated course combined with an infusion approach. Focus is also on continuing professional development. Some consideration of how and why to teach social work and the law, also some focus on what to include, particularly skills for practice.

### Evaluation
Conceptual rather than empirical.

### Reference
Madden, R. and Wayne, R. (2003) 'Social work and the law: a therapeutic jurisprudence perspective', *Social Work*, vol 48, no 3, pp 338-47.[64]

## Country

USA

## Learning and teaching and social work law

Focuses on an approach to law in practice but with relevance to what is taught, especially roles for social workers in and around legal systems and why such teaching is essential.

## Evaluation

Conceptual rather than empirical.

## Reference

Maharg, P. and Muntjwereff, A. (2003) 'Through a screen darkly: electronic legal education in Europe', *The Law Teacher*, vol 36, no 3, pp 307-32.[140]

## Country

UK/Netherlands

## Learning and teaching and social work law

An exploration of the use of ICT in legal education via a description of several initiatives. The article describes a range and variety of e-teaching models with the different kinds of electronic materials employed classified as either 'communication', 'information' or 'instructional' tools. More detailed description of two initiatives is provided: the coaching system used by the University of Amsterdam and the transactional learning approach used by the Faculty of Law at the University of Strathclyde. Raises a number of issues in relation to electronic learning including that managed learning environment (MLE) technology can enable teachers to avoid difficult questions about how they organise their teaching and can be used to support shallow learning. Benefits are, however, that the web environment enables a more integrated approach of using technologies in legal education. It can open up new ways of teaching and learning the law, by providing students with an environment in which they can manage legal information and legal knowledge for their personal professional use.

**Evaluation**

Electronic learning has the capacity to extend and develop educational ideas. MLEs do not support any single approach, however, and it is important for development of software and staff development to take place concurrently, and for both to be informed by research findings.

**Reference**

Marsh, P. and Triseliotis, J. (1996) *Ready to practise? Social workers and probation officers: Their training and first year in work*, Aldershot: Avebury.[5]

**Country**

UK

**Learning and teaching and social work law**

Research with newly qualified practitioners, and with supervisors, on the effectiveness of training and perceived readiness to practise. Contains analysis of results on law teaching in programmes.

**Evaluation**

An empirical study that covers much more than just the outcomes of social work law teaching, learning and assessment.

**Reference**

Matthew, V. (1993) 'College based assessment of competency in social work law', in M. Preston-Shoot (ed) *Assessment of competence in social work law*, London: Whiting and Birch/Social Work Education.[187]

**Country**

UK

**Learning and teaching and social work law.**

Considers what is competence, what law to teach and different types of assessment.

**Evaluation**

A descriptive contribution to theory building surrounding the curriculum for social work law.

## Reference
Miller, J. (1980) 'Teaching law and legal skills to social workers', *Journal of Education for Social Work*, vol 16, no 3, pp 87-95.[79]

## Country
USA

## Learning and teaching and social work law
Presents ideas about the content of teaching and learning law relating to social work. Focuses too on how to deliver this content, proposing a foundation/basic course followed by expansion. Passing reference to assessment.

## Evaluation
Conceptual with no empirical data.

## Reference
Moodie, P. (1997) 'Law courseware and IOLIS: assessing the present and constructing the future', *The Journal of Information, Law and Technology*, vol 1 (http://eli.warwick.ac.uk/jilt/cal/97_mood/).[142]

## Country
UK

## Learning and teaching and social work law
The paper explores the impact of IOLIS on the teaching of law in the UK. This product delivers a law curriculum online. It is the experience of lecturers using IOLIS that informs this article, although the author also offers a number of observations on the limitations of the courseware and the potential for its future development. Moodie describes the different teaching and assessment strategies that the courseware supports, arguing that it allows students their first experience with 'real' legal material.

## Evaluation
HEFCE evaluation indicated that usage of teaching and learning technology programme materials is sparse and this also seemed to be true of IOLIS.

## Reference

Moskovitz, M. (1992) 'Beyond the case method: it's time to teach with problems', *Journal of Legal Education*, vol 42, pp 241-70.[123]

## Country

USA

## Learning and teaching and social work law

The article focuses on the case law method of teaching law and contends that since the main purpose of legal education today is to train lawyers, rather than to examine the 'science of law', that teachers should instead adopt the problem method to train professionals. Other professional schools in business and medicine use it so lawyers should too. He argues that problem solving is the single intellectual skill on which all law practice is based. While the case method shows the students how others solve problems, the problem method lets students learn to solve problems by finding, framing and analysing issues themselves.

## Evaluation

Moskovitz argues that knowledge used is better remembered and that the problem method motivates students to work harder, for it challenges them with the very situations they will face in their elected professional field. He suggests the method has further advantages, including broadening the range of matters open to the student's consideration, increasing effectiveness of instruction where case law is inadequate and providing stimulus to student interest.

## Reference

Munby, T. (1997) 'Immigration, nationality and asylum law for social workers: why and how it should be taught', *Liverpool Law Review*, vol XIX, no 2, pp 193-202.[134]

## Country

UK

## Learning and teaching and social work law
Focuses on teaching a specialist area and covers content and method of teaching.

## Evaluation
No evaluation. A descriptive and conceptual paper.

## Reference
Nash, P. (1984) 'Mental health legislation in psychiatric nurse training: a survey of nurse tutors', *Nurse Education Today*, pp 69-72.[98]

## Country
UK

## Learning and teaching and social work law
An article which identifies the varying amounts of time allocated to mental health law teaching, the differing teaching methods used, and the limited knowledge held by some tutors. Some parallels may be drawn with social work but these are not made explicit in the paper

## Evaluation
A small-scale empirical survey. The findings are clearly presented but the implications of the findings could have been developed.

## Reference
Oliver, J. and Huxley, P. (1985) 'The development of computer assisted learning for the teaching of mental health legislation', *Social Work Education*, vol 4, no 2, pp 20-1.[128]

## Country
UK

## Learning and teaching and social work law
Initial report of a research study of assessment methods evaluated by ASW candidates (65). Evaluates a means of assessment – multiple choice questions. Evaluates a means of teaching.

### Evaluation

An empirical paper, the findings in which are further developed in subsequent publications by the authors.

### Reference

Oliver, J. and Huxley, P. (1988) 'Fixed response assessment (MCQ and TFQ): some research findings relevant to planning for approved social worker training and assessment', in P. Wedge (ed) *Social work: Research into practice*, Birmingham: BASW.[137]

### Country

UK

### Learning and teaching and social work law

Empirical study of assessment methods evaluated by ASW candidates (65). Evaluates different methods of assessment – multiple choice questions, true/false questions. Evaluates a means of teaching.

### Evaluation

A detailed description of the research undertaken into assessment methods. A detailed analysis of the findings.

### Reference

Oliver, J. and Huxley, P. (1988) 'The development of computer assisted learning (CAL) materials for teaching and testing mental health social work in Great Britain: a review of four years progress', *Journal of Teaching in Social Work*, vol 2, no 2, pp 21-34.[138]

### Country

UK

### Learning and teaching and social work law

Empirical study of teaching and assessment methods evaluated by ASW candidates (65). Evaluates a means of assessment – multiple choice questions – and the use of computer programmes to facilitate learning and to test knowledge acquired by students.

## Evaluation

A useful empirical paper that offers an evidence base for approaches to assessment of social work law learning, knowledge and skills.

## Reference

Oliver, J. and Huxley, P. (1986) 'The effectiveness of teaching mental health legislation to social workers seeking approval under the 1983 Mental Health Act', *Issues in Social Work Education*, pp 101-17.[136]

## Country

UK

## Learning and teaching and social work law

Controlled experiment with 83 social workers. Claims to show that students benefited from training using quantitative data; showed positive response to computer-assisted learning.

## Evaluation

One of the few empirical studies of actual teaching methods in social work law. Evidence-based.

## Reference

Oneglia, S. and Orlin, M. (1978) 'A model for combined private practice: attorneys and social workers in domestic relations', *Journal of Applied Social Science*, pp 37-46.[156]

## Country

USA

## Learning and teaching and social work law

Theoretical discussion of relationship between law and social work in the US. Argues that lawyers should take on board counselling skills and social workers should enhance their role in court. Uses case examples.

## Evaluation

Limited applicability to UK context but one of a few examples in US of joining law and social work together in practice.

### Reference

Parkinson, C. and Thompson, P. (1998) 'Uncertainties, mysteries, doubts and Approved Social Worker training', *Journal of Social Work Practice*, vol 12, no 1, pp 57-64.[96]

### Country

UK

### Learning and teaching and social work law

Strongly asserts that knowledge alone is insufficient for the approved social worker role. The paper presents ideas about how to develop reflection for practice, and about formative and summative assessment in training. Issues of continuing professional development are prominent.

### Evaluation

Descriptive and conceptual. The paper reports on feedback from course participants and tutors but without directly presenting what they expressed.

### Reference

Phillips, A. (1979) 'Social work and the delivery of legal services', *Modern Law Review*, vol 42, 29-41.[8]

### Country

UK

### Learning and teaching and social work law

A paper that is sharply critical of social workers' attitudes towards law and legal practitioners. It explores possible reasons for this state of affairs. The paper does not discuss directly teaching, learning and assessment of law in social work education but does refer to contemporary debates about what social workers should know in order to practise effectively.

### Evaluation

A paper based on the author's observations of social workers in teams. However, no account of the observational method is given.

## Reference

Preston-Shoot, M. (1993) 'Whither social work law? Future questions on the teaching and assessment of law to social workers', in M. Preston-Shoot (ed) *Assessment of competence in social work law*, London: Whiting and Birch/Social Work Education.[151]

## Country

UK

## Learning and teaching and social work law

Addresses seven themes arising from a conference, on what should be taught and assessed, and how.

## Evaluation

Essentially an account of where development of the discipline of teaching, learning and assessment of law in social work education had reached.

## Reference

Preston-Shoot, M. (2000) 'Making connections in the curriculum: law and professional practice', in R. Pierce and J. Weinstein (eds) *Innovative education and training for care professionals: A providers' guide*, London: Jessica Kingsley Publishers.[9]

## Country

UK

## Learning and teaching and social work law

Offers suggestions for academic and practice curricula. Details some research evidence on how social workers experience the law in practice and how practice teachers approach teaching and assessing students' knowledge of, and skills in using the law.

## Evaluation

A descriptive and conceptual paper, which provides detail of exercises for use in academic and practice curricula to facilitate students' law learning. Detail is also provided of what might be included in the practice curriculum and how the challenge of learning and assessment might be approached.

### Reference

Preston-Shoot, M. (2003) 'Teaching and assessing social work law: reflections from a post-qualifying programme', *Social Work Education*, vol 22, no 5, pp 461-78.[167]

### Country

UK

### Learning and teaching and social work law

Teaching example. Report on social work law teaching for practice teachers. Sets out teaching programme with qualitative evaluation of attitudes of participants. Primarily about practice teachers' attitudes and the agency context for achieving social work law learning in practice placements.

### Evaluation

Directly about social law teaching in the UK: focuses on practice teachers and what can be achieved through practice learning. One of the few studies of law component of practice learning.

### Reference

Preston-Shoot, M., Roberts, G. and Vernon, S. (1997) '"We work in isolation often and in ignorance occasionally": on the experiences of practice teachers teaching and assessing social work law', *Social Work Education*, vol 16, no 4, pp 4-34.[26]

### Country

UK

### Learning and teaching and social work law

Presents the findings of a survey of practice teachers in terms of their felt readiness to engage with students in teaching and assessing knowledge of, and skills in implementing legal rules.

### Evaluation

An empirical study of practice teacher views of teaching and assessment of law in the practice curriculum.

## Reference

Preston-Shoot, M., Roberts, G. and Vernon, S. (1998) '"I am concerned at the possible level of legal input expected from practice teachers": developing expertise in teaching and assessing social work law', *Social Work Education*, vol 17, no 2, pp 219-31.[144]

## Country

UK

## Learning and teaching and social work law

Research-based examination of teaching of social work law in practice placements. Reports on research into practice teachers' views of law content.

## Evaluation

Offers evidence of issues encountered by practice teachers in teaching law in social work practice placements. One of the few studies of law component of practice learning.

## Reference

Preston-Shoot, M., Roberts, G. and Vernon, S. (1998) 'Developing a conceptual framework for teaching and assessing law within training for professional practice: lessons from social work', *Journal of Practice Teaching*, vol 1, no 1, pp 41-51.[97]

## Country

UK

## Learning and teaching and social work law

Uses a case study to review the development of teaching and assessment of social work law. It reviews the evidence on the interactions between the law and practice, and for the skills necessary for competence. Proposals are made for assisting practice teachers to facilitate and assess a student's law learning while on placement. The paper concludes with how the theory surrounding teaching, learning and assessment of law in social work education might be taken up by health and welfare professions.

### Evaluation

A summary of progress in respect of identifying the discipline of social work law and of building an academic and practice curriculum to meet the demands of practice.

### Reference

Preston-Shoot, M., Roberts, G. and Vernon, S. (1998) 'Social work law: from interaction to integration', *Journal of Social Welfare and Family Law*, vol 20, no 1, pp 65-80.[37]

### Country

UK

### Learning and teaching and social work law

Theoretical discussion and acknowledgement of emergence of new academic discipline of social work law. Explores the nature and structure of social work law and how the social work curriculum needs to prepare students for the content of practice – law, and social work knowledge, values and skills; and for the context of practice – managing the organisational location.

### Evaluation

Sets out the conceptual framework for integrating social work law teaching. The theoretical base provides a framework that may be applied to individual cases and is capable of coping with complex situations and dilemmas.

### Reference

Preston-Shoot, M., Roberts, G. and Vernon, S. (1998) 'Working together in social work law', *Journal of Social Welfare and Family Law*, vol 20, no 2, pp 137-50.[109]

### Country

UK

## Learning and teaching and social work law

Theoretical exploration of commonalities between law and social work; maps out social work law terrain. Analyses causes of misunderstandings: related to loyalties, legalism, concepts and mutual expectations. It argues that a mutually recognised and comprehensible set of meanings will result in more effective services but that this requires a reflective, critical and analytical examination and definition of core principles and characteristics.

## Evaluation

A conceptual paper with practice examples that directly addresses the law/social work relationship, presenting a convincing explanation of mutual misunderstanding.

## Reference

Preston-Shoot, M., Roberts, G. and Vernon, S. (2001) 'Values in social work law: strained relations or sustaining relationships?', *Journal of Social Welfare and Family Law*, vol 23, no 1, pp 1-22.[47]

## Country

UK

## Learning and teaching and social work law

Explores the nature and structure of social work law and considers the relationship between social work values and social work law. Tracing certain trends in social work law and human rights legislation, the article considers how rights can be grounded more clearly in values. The article focuses on the challenge of maintaining an ethically informed practice and a learning culture that enables the promotion of quality decisions and the confident and credible exercise of authority, autonomy and discretion.

## Evaluation

A theoretical contribution to the definition of the discipline of social work law. The potential connections between values, rights, legal provisions and practice dilemmas are explored in order to demonstrate that an articulation of a clear value base might draw support from, but also seek to critique and develop the legal mandate

## Reference
Read, J. and Clements, L. (1999) 'Research, the law and good practice in relation to disabled children: an approach to staff development in a local authority', *Local Governance*, vol 25, no 2, pp 87-95.[173]

## Country
UK

## Learning and teaching and social work law
A paper that describes an approach to continuing professional development and in-service training that seeks to connect teaching and learning with policy and practice development. The paper outlines a four-stage process, involving training, performance review conducted between individual participants and their managers, consultation for participants on specific issues or questions with the trainers, and follow-up. Law is seen as a tool to support social work decision making based on research and professional judgement. The involvement of managers in performance review and follow-up is seen as valuable in connecting training with policy and practice development.

## Evaluation
A descriptive paper of an approach to continuing professional development that summarises an evaluation by participants without giving details of how their views were sought and what they actually reported. Participants are reported to have valued this approach to learning.

## Reference
Ridley, A. (1994) 'Legal skills for non-law students: added value or irrelevant diversion?', *The Law Teacher*, vol 28, pp 281-91.[11]

## Country
UK

## Learning and teaching and social work law
Useful material on teaching law to non-lawyers. The paper includes material on skills, links to knowledge and co-teaching.

## Evaluation

Mainly descriptive and conceptual. Student involvement in evaluation is noted but not reported in depth.

## Reference

Roberts, G. (1974) 'Teaching law to social workers', *Social Work Today*, vol 5, no 12, p 353.[126]

## Country

UK

## Learning and teaching and social work law

A review of the relationship between law and social work. The paper briefly explores different teaching methods and areas of law that need to be covered in the curriculum

## Evaluation

Descriptive and conceptual. No formal evaluation but draws on published research for its analysis.

## Reference

Roche, J. (1997) 'Law, ethics and social work practice: a critical curriculum', *Liverpool Law Review*, vol 19, no 2, pp 121-42.[88]

## Country

UK

## Learning and teaching and social work law

Theoretical discussion of interconnection between ethics, law and social work to argue for greater attention to jurisprudence in social work law. Strong focus on ethics, empowerment and rights. Argues that more attention needs to be paid in social work law to broader discussions about the role of law.

## Evaluation

Strong theoretical and ethical argument. Directly addresses social work law teaching principles.

### Reference
Sarnoff, S. (2003) 'Considerations of web teaching in social work: one instructor's experience', *Journal of Teaching in Social Work*, vol 23, nos 1/2, pp 21-33.[129]

### Country
USA

### Learning and teaching and social work law
Uses a social welfare law course as an example for web use.

### Evaluation
This is a methods article at a very general level. Not much focus on the law itself and little empirical evaluation.

### Reference
Schottland, C. (1968) 'Social work and the law: some curriculum approaches', *Buffalo Law Review*, vol 17, pp 719-31.[78]

### Country
USA

### Learning and teaching and social work law
Theory-building paper that offers views on course content, how law may be taught to social workers, and attitudes towards law(yers). Itemises 13 knowledge areas and 6 skill areas for coverage.

### Evaluation
An early contribution to what law should be taught to social workers and for what purpose. Relies on opinion, providing no empirical evidence for the conclusions that are drawn.

### Reference
Schwartz, M. (2001) 'Teaching law by design: how learning theory and instructional design can inform and reform law teaching', *San Diego Law Review*, vol 38, no 2, pp 347-63.[188]

## Country
USA

## Learning and teaching and social work law
An overview of why law school teaching (in America) has stagnated and in particular in relation to the pressure to conform to the vicarious learning model (that is, one-on-one, teacher-on-student dialogues). Vicarious instruction assumes some sort of rebound learning effect; that somehow the teacher's comments, questions and corrections will not only help the selected student but will rub off on all the students in the class. The article offers a 'dramatically different approach' to law school instruction to produce effective, efficient and appealing law school instruction – a model of instructional design, described as a reflective, systematic and comprehensive approach to creating instruction and one which is 'learner centred, active and meaningful'. The author points out that numerous media comparison studies reveal that, while certain media are more effective than others in certain contexts, with certain learners and for certain tasks, no single medium – not computers, texts, or live teachers – has ever been shown to be superior overall.

## Evaluation
An example lesson plan is included in what is otherwise a conceptual paper.

## Reference
Scott, A. (2004) *Using problem-based learning to teach constitutional and administrative law*, Coventry: United Kingdom Centre for Legal Education.[189]

## Country
UK

## Learning and teaching and social work law
A clear description of problem-based learning, with an emphasis on skills for practice.

## Evaluation
Descriptive and conceptual. No formal evaluation.

## Reference
Sklar, R. and Torczyner, J. (1991) 'Lawyers and social workers: a new joint law MSW degree programme at McGill University', *Canadian Social Work Review*, pp 97-105.[162]

## Country
Canada

## Learning and teaching and social work law
Curriculum critique and proposal for bringing social work and law education together. Example of joint teaching of lawyers and social workers. Presents a rationale and curriculum in detail. The basis of information about how the joint course is taught.

## Evaluation
Interesting example with specific curriculum details in tabular format.

## Reference
Skwarok, L. (1995) 'Business law for non-lawyers: setting the stage for teaching, learning and assessment at Hong Kong Polytechnic University', *The Law Teacher*, vol 29, no 2, pp 189-212.[116]

## Country
China

## Learning and teaching and social work law
Outlines how the academic law for business students curriculum was modified and then delivered. Offers an account of curriculum building, with a focus on teaching methods, learning and assessment.

## Evaluation
Descriptive account with limited evaluation, that is, no details given of how data collected from students. Contains some messages that are pertinent for social work law teaching and assessment.

**Reference**
Slaght, E. (2002) 'Revisiting the relationship between social work and law enforcement', *Social Work*, pp 86-93.[157]

**Country**
USA

**Learning and teaching and social work law**
Curriculum critique and proposal for bringing social work and law enforcement agents together. Presents general argument that law enforcers need social work skills and that law enforcement context of much of social work needs to recognised. Includes some examples of places where law enforcement agents are taught alongside social workers.

**Evaluation**
Limited applicability to UK context but one possibly unique example of joining law enforcement agents and social workers together in US.

**Reference**
Smith, C. (1997) 'Mutual respect or mutual distrust: social workers and the courts in child care decisions', *Liverpool Law Review*, vol XIX, no 2, pp 159-79.[120]

**Country**
UK

**Learning and teaching and social work law**
Focus is not teaching, learning and assessment of law in social work education but does argue for the need for social workers to understand judicial perspectives and to be aware of when courts may intervene. Concludes with the use of case law to inform and educate social workers because case law offers a real situation, illustrates how courts may intervene in social work planning, and emphasises the importance of cooperation between local authorities and courts.

### Evaluation

A conceptual paper focusing mainly on the law in practice but with some relevance for teaching social work law.

### Reference

Sparer, E. (1968) 'The place of law in social work education: a commentary on Dean Schottland's article', *Buffalo Law Review*, vol 17, pp 733-40.[111]

### Country

USA

### Learning and teaching and social work law

Theoretical debate. Refutation of Schottland's arguments concerning the role of law in social work education. Asserts the importance of examining social welfare practices and using the law to challenge these.

### Evaluation

Not really relevant to the UK – practice examples relate to income support and policing of responsibility for maintenance payments.

### Reference

Stevenson, O. (1988) 'Law and social work education: a commentary on "The Law Report"', *Issues in Social Work Education*, vol 8, pp 37-45.[3]

### Country

UK

### Learning and teaching and social work law

Contribution to theoretical debate about teaching social work law and CCETSW guidelines. Challenges some of the Law Report (Ball et al, 1988).[22] Argues for an integrated approach to teaching social work law.

### Evaluation

Part of the debate about social work law teaching in UK, specifically in relation to the integration or discrete teaching issue.

## Reference
Swain, P. (1999) 'Reflections on teaching law in social work – if only it were that simple', in J. Fook, F. Lindsay and M. Ryan (eds) *Advances in Social Work and Welfare Education*, vol 2, no 2, pp 124-38, Victoria: Australian Association of Social Workers.[32]

## Country
Australia

## Learning and teaching and social work law
Reports on a curriculum review at two universities. The paper provides an overview of what is taught and how student learning is assessed. The paper questions problem-based learning and infusion models.

## Evaluation
Descriptive and conceptual but also presents the results of student evaluation of the delivery and assessment methods used.

## Reference
Swain, P. and Evans, S. (1999) 'Law and social work practice multimedia project', *New Technology in Human Services*, vol 12, nos 3/4, pp 47-54.[139]

## Country
Australia

## Learning and teaching and social work law
Offers examples of innovative teaching including in social work law. Describes use of multimedia and points to some of its limitations.

## Evaluation
Very limited discussion and disappointingly little information on what is taught.

## Reference
Twining, W. (1967) 'Pericles and the Plumber', *Law Quarterly Review*, vol 83, pp 396-426.[48]

## Country
UK

## Learning and teaching and social work law
This paper concentrates on the purposes of teaching law to law students. It debates the relationship between education and training, which has obvious parallels with similar discussions about the purpose of social work education. The focus is on the question 'for what purposes should what be taught to whom, by whom and how?'.

## Evaluation
A highly theoretical and conceptual paper from which messages for teaching, learning and assessment of law in social work education can be drawn.

## Reference
Vernon, S., Harris, R. and Ball, C. (1990) *Towards social work law: Legally competent professional practice*, London: CCETSW.[159]

## Country
UK

## Learning and teaching and social work law
This monograph continues to develop the themes initially presented in the Law Report (Ball et al, 1988[22]). It also introduces a new theme by reviewing possible parallels with, and lessons to be taken from legal education. It reviews progress in establishing a subject area – social work law.

## Evaluation
Further conceptual work on the relationship between social work(ers) and law(yers). Some further research findings on students' competence for practice are presented.

## Reference
Wallis-Jones, M. and Lyons, K. (2003) *2001 Employment Survey: Newly qualified social workers*, Research Report for Department of Health, Dagenham: University of East London.[25]

## Country
UK

## Learning and teaching and social work law
A survey of newly qualified social workers. The focus is on their experiences of social work education and their felt readiness to practise.

## Evaluation
Empirical findings from newly qualified students that includes feedback on law teaching.

## Reference
Ward, D. and Hogg, B. (1993) 'An integrated approach to the teaching of social work law', in M. Preston-Shoot (ed) *Assessment of competence in social work law*, London: Whiting and Birch/Social Work Education.[112]

## Country
UK

## Learning and teaching and social work law
Reviews the debate about law training for social workers and presents a model programme. This covers basic concepts, content areas and skills. Some consideration is given to assessment.

## Evaluation
The paper is descriptive. It draws on research findings for support for the ideas being developed but it does not contain an evaluation of any outcomes of the approach being taken.

## Reference
Ward, J. and Salter, M. (1990) 'Law for professional accounting education', *The Law Teacher*, vol 24, no 3, pp 208-28.[121]

## Country
UK

### Learning and teaching and social work law

A useful paper that offers observations on continuing professional development and on methods of teaching law to non-lawyers. It cautions about the dangers of a translation process when attempting to make law accessible to non-lawyers.

### Evaluation

Descriptive and conceptual, building theory on the basis of teaching experience and student feedback.

### Reference

Watkinson, A. (2001) 'Human rights laws: advocacy tools for a global civil society', *Canadian Social Work Review*, vol 18, no 2, pp 267-86.[89]

### Country

Canada

### Learning and teaching and social work law

Theoretical discussion about human rights and social work. Outlines some human rights cases considered to be relevant to social work and argues that human rights education should be central to social work education.

### Evaluation

Theoretical discussion using case law examples but demonstrates that human rights education is important in social work law education. Interesting theoretical discussion that mainly pertains to Canadian context.

### Reference

Weil, M. (1982) 'Research on issues in collaboration between social workers and lawyers', *Social Service Review*, pp 393-405.[161]

### Country

USA

## Learning and teaching and social work law

Research study of attitudes towards interprofessional collaboration between US social workers and lawyers after joint training in courtwork.

## Evaluation

Includes valuable literature review and evidence-based evaluation of training in specific practice area in US.

## Reference

White, C. (2002) 'Reassessing the social worker's role as an appropriate adult', *Journal of Social Welfare and Family Law*, vol 24, no 1, pp 55-65.[163]

## Country

UK

## Learning and teaching and social work law

Refers to the lack of training for this role and indicates what should be included. Draws on research into the role for the recommendations it offers.

## Evaluation

Descriptive and conceptual. No formal evaluation.

## Reference

Wilson, J. Setterlund, D. and Tilse, C. (2003) '"I know I signed something": older people, families and social workers' understanding of the legal aspects of entry to residential care', *Australian Social Work*, vol 56, no 2, pp 155-65.[158]

## Country

Australia

## Learning and teaching and social work law

Empirical research from Australia involving service users and social workers, concerning the vulnerability of older people and their entry to the care system. Postal survey of practitioners, focus group and individual interviews of service users; sample of 377 social workers. Concludes that social workers failed to acknowledge the importance of law in their everyday practice with older people.

## Evaluation
Practice focused in an Australian context, but useful example of research that demonstrates the importance of law in social work. Evidence based.

## Reference
Wilson, K. and James, A. (1989) 'Looking into the law report: a two-dimensional affair', *Social Work Today*, pp 12-13, 16 March.[154]

## Country
UK

## Learning and teaching and social work law
Theoretical discussion about social work law teaching. Critique of well-known Law Report (Ball et al, 1988)[22] arguing that it takes a 'two-dimensional' view and is wrong about the centrality of law in social work.

## Evaluation
Important contribution to the debate about the role of law in social work and consequences for social work law teaching.

## Reference
Wong, Y. (2003) 'Harnessing the potential of problem-based learning in legal education', *The Law Teacher*, vol 37, no 2, pp 157-73.[117]

## Country
Singapore

## Learning and teaching and social work law
Provides an overview of problem-based learning (PBL) and its application to legal education. Too often the law is taught as if all problems are to be solved with legal solutions. Traditional law teaching emphasises learning the law rather than learning how to learn the law. Areas of law arising

from a client's problems are often not readily apparent and may involve overlapping areas of law and even other disciplines. The real world and traditional legal education are at odds. PBL is one approach that can be adopted to bring the two closer together.

### Evaluation
The paper defines what is meant by PBL and describes the essential features of a PBL curriculum, including peer learning and feedback.

### Reference
Woodcock, A. (1988) 'Methods of law teaching on BTEC courses', *The Law Teacher*, vol 22, no 1, pp 14-27.[85]

### Country
UK

### Learning and teaching and social work law
A useful paper that clearly describes some innovative approaches to teaching and learning. Teaching and assessment methods are clearly described.

### Evaluation
Empirically based paper that draws on student and tutor evaluation of different teaching and assessment methods.

# Appendix 3:
## Practice survey questionnaire

Commissioned by the Social Care Institute for Excellence (SCIE)

**Why we need your help**

Law is an essential component of the social work curriculum. This questionnaire seeks information on how students learn about law on your social work qualifying programme(s). It is part of a review of good practice commissioned by SCIE. In addition, we are undertaking a review of the literature, and consulting with service users, carers and others who have an interest in social workers' understanding of law. SCIE will subsequently publish guidance and materials that will support programmes in law teaching, learning and assessment.

**What we would like you to do**

We recognise that the new degree will be at varying stages of development.

- If you have already started to deliver the new degree, we would like you to give us information about law within your new degree programme(s).
- If your plans for the new degree are not yet complete, please tell us about your DipSW programme(s).

We would be very grateful if you could complete all sections of the questionnaire – this will take about 30 minutes. If you would prefer to complete an electronic version, please request a proforma from ruth1@liv.ac.uk

We are interested also to look at module outlines, examples of syllabus content and assessments. Please attach any documentation that amplifies your responses. All information will be held in confidence.

**When you have completed the questionnaire**

Please return it, together with any supporting documentation, to: Ruth Melville, Department of Sociology, Social Policy and Social Work, Eleanor Rathbone Building, Bedford St South, Liverpool L69 7ZA.

**RESPONSE DEADLINE - 5th APRIL 2004**

Many thanks indeed for your help with this project. We are grateful for your time, and we will make sure that you receive information about the outcomes. If you would like any further detail or clarification, please do contact us.

**Suzy Braye, s.braye@liv.ac.uk,
Michael Preston-Shoot, michael.preston-shoot@luton.ac.uk**

## Section 1: Background Information

1.1    Name of institution

1.2    Contact details of person completing this form: ......................

Name ..............................................................................................

Phone .......................................... E-mail .....................................

Role..............................................................................................
(*eg law module leader, programme head, please specify*)

1.3  Are you responding to this questionnaire in relation to your

New degree programmes........ DipSW programmes ............

**If New degree, please continue with Q1.4.  If DipSW, please go to Q1.5.**

1.4 New degree programme(s) offered: (please enter all that apply)

| Level of award | Date of first intake | Full-time numbers (annual intake) | Part-time numbers (annual intake) |
|---|---|---|---|
| Undergraduate Degree | | | |
| Postgraduate Diploma | | | |
| Postgraduate Masters | | | |

**If you are responding about your new degree please now go to Section 2 and answer all subsequent questions with information from your new degree programme(s).**

1.5 Diploma in Social Work programmes offered: (*please enter all that apply*)

| Level of award | Date of final intake | Full-time numbers (Annual intake) | Part-time numbers (Annual intake) |
|---|---|---|---|
| Dip/HE | | | |
| Undergraduate Degree | | | |
| Postgraduate Diploma | | | |
| Postgraduate Masters | | | |

**If you are responding about your DipSW programme(s), please now continue with Section 2 and answer all subsequent questions with information from your DipSW programme(s)**

## Section 2: Content, structure and location of teaching and learning

*This section is about the academic taught element of the programme. We will ask about practice learning later.*

2.1 Do you have a discrete law module or modules in your programmes?

Yes ☐ No ☐

**If yes, please continue with Q2.2  If no, please go to Q2.7**

2.2 If Yes, where in your programmes do the discrete module(s) appear? (*Please enter all that apply – if you have more than one discrete module, use columns 2/3 to give us information about each one separately.*)

| Stage of learning | Discreet Law Module 1 | | Discreet Law Module 2 | | Discreet Law Module 3 | |
|---|---|---|---|---|---|---|
| | Contact hours | credit | Contact hours | credit | Contact hours | credit |
| Certificate level (1st level undergraduate) | | | | | | |
| Intermediate level (2nd level undergraduate) | | | | | | |
| Honours level (3rd level undergraduate) | | | | | | |
| Masters level Year 1 of study (4th level postgraduate) | | | | | | |
| Masters level Year 2 of study (4th level postgraduate) | | | | | | |

2.3   What are the aims of the discrete law module(s)?
*Please list aims separately for each module if you have identified more than one module in question 2.2 above. Please also attach module outlines if available.*

2.4   What are the learning outcomes?
*Please list aims separately for each module if you have identified more than one module in question 2.2 above. Please also attach module outlines if available.*

2.5   What is your rationale for locating some or all law teaching/ learning in a discrete module or modules?

2.6   Is legal content taught/learned on any module other than a law module?

Yes ☐        No ☐

If yes, please specify the modules and level

| Module | Level (eg, 1/2/3 undergraduate; 1/2 postgraduate) | Contract hours relating to law |
|--------|--------------------------------------------------|-------------------------------|
|        |                                                  |                               |
|        |                                                  |                               |
|        |                                                  |                               |
|        |                                                  |                               |
|        |                                                  |                               |
|        |                                                  |                               |

**Now please go to Q2.11**

**If there is no discrete law module on your programme:**

2.7    Where in your programmes does law teaching/learning appear?

| Module Please indicate subject area and module credit rating | Certif-icate (level 1 under-graduate) | Inter-mediate (level 2 under-graduate) | Honours (level 3 under-graduate) | Masters Year 1 (level 4 post-graduate) | Masters Year 2 (level 4 post-graduate) |
|---|---|---|---|---|---|
| | Contract hours relating to law | Contract hours relating to law | Contract hours relating to law | Contract hours relating to law | Contract hours relating to law |
| | | | | | |
| | | | | | |
| | | | | | |
| | | | | | |
| | | | | | |
| | | | | | |

2.8 What are the aims of the **law** teaching/learning in these modules?

*Please list aims separately for each module if you have identified more than one module in question 2.7 above. Please also attach module outlines if available.*

```
┌──────────────────────────────────────────────────────────┐
│                                                          │
│                                                          │
│                                                          │
│                                                          │
│                                                          │
│                                                          │
└──────────────────────────────────────────────────────────┘
```

2.9   What are the learning outcomes attached to students' learning of **law** in these modules? *Please list aims separately for each module if you have identified more than one module in question 2.7 above. Please also attach module outlines if available.*

```
┌──────────────────────────────────────────────────────────┐
│                                                          │
│                                                          │
│                                                          │
│                                                          │
│                                                          │
└──────────────────────────────────────────────────────────┘
```

2.10 Why do you believe it is important to teach law solely within other modules?

```
┌──────────────────────────────────────────────────────────┐
│                                                          │
│                                                          │
│                                                          │
│                                                          │
│                                                          │
└──────────────────────────────────────────────────────────┘
```

**Regardless of whether law teaching is in discrete or integrated modules...**

2.11  Please tick to indicate the core law curriculum content covered.

| Law content (NB This is not an 'ideal' list!) | Level | | | | |
|---|---|---|---|---|---|
| | Certif-icate (level 1 under-graduate | Inter-mediate (level 2 under-graduate | Honours (level 3 under-graduate | Masters Year 1 (level 4 post-graduate | Masters Year 2 (level 4 post-graduate |
| Legal system | | | | | |
| Court structures | | | | | |
| Human rights | | | | | |
| Anti-discrimination legislation | | | | | |
| Family support | | | | | |
| Child protection | | | | | |
| Adoption | | | | | |
| Community care/older people | | | | | |
| Community care/disability | | | | | |
| Adult protection | | | | | |
| Mental health | | | | | |
| Youth justice | | | | | |
| Adult criminal justice | | | | | |

| Law content (NB This is not an 'ideal' list!) | Level | | | | |
|---|---|---|---|---|---|
| | Certif-icate (level 1 under-graduate | Inter-mediate (level 2 under-graduate | Honours (level 3 under-graduate | Masters Year 1 (level 4 post-graduate | Masters Year 2 (level 4 post-graduate |
| Domestic abuse | | | | | |
| Education | | | | | |
| Healthcare | | | | | |
| Employment | | | | | |
| Housing | | | | | |
| Immigration and asylum | | | | | |
| Welfare benefits | | | | | |
| Data protection and records | | | | | |
| Complaints | | | | | |
| Quality and statndards | | | | | |
| Others (please add) | | | | | |
| | | | | | |
| | | | | | |
| | | | | | |
| | | | | | |

2.12 Are there any specific areas of relevant law that you have chosen to exclude?  If so, please tell us what they are, and why you have excluded them.

```



```

2.13 If you have ticked anti-discrimination legislation in the list above, please tell us what particular legislation is included.

```



```

2.14 Please add any comments you wish to make about the choice of content, structure and location of law teaching within your programme.

```



```

## Section 3 : Teaching and learning processes

*This section is about teaching and learning. We will come to assessment later.*

3.1   Is all the law on your programme taught by one person?

Yes ☐          No ☐

If no, how many people are involved? ........................

3.2   For each person who teaches law, please identify their location within or outside the teaching team, and use the codes below to indicate their professional background.

| | Member of core social work team | Member of different team in same institution | Lecturer from another institution | Someone else (please specify) |
|---|---|---|---|---|
| Person 1 | | | | |
| Person 2 | | | | |
| Person 3 | | | | |
| Person 4 | | | | |
| Person 5 | | | | |
| Person 6 | | | | |
| Person 7 | | | | |
| Person 8 | | | | |

Background: (if an individual falls into more than one category, please enter all that apply)

1 = academic lawyer  2 = practising lawyer  3  =  social  work academic      4 = social work practitioner   5 = service user
6 = carer       7 = other (please specify)

3.3  If service users and carers are involved in teaching law, please tell us more about what they contribute.

```
┌─────────────────────────────────────────────────────────┐
│                                                         │
│                                                         │
│                                                         │
│                                                         │
│                                                         │
│                                                         │
└─────────────────────────────────────────────────────────┘
```

3.4  If practitioners are involved in teaching law, please tell us more about what they contribute.

```
┌─────────────────────────────────────────────────────────┐
│                                                         │
│                                                         │
│                                                         │
│                                                         │
│                                                         │
│                                                         │
└─────────────────────────────────────────────────────────┘
```

3.5  What teaching and learning methods do you use? Please tick all that apply.

lectures ☐                              lecture with small group exercises ☐

seminars – tutor led ☐                  seminars – student led ☐

video material ☐                        simulation exercises ☐

independent individual study ☐          independent group study ☐

visits/observations ☐                   individual tutorials ☐

e-learning (campus-network) ☐           e-learning (web-based) ☐

distance learning ☐                     other (please specify).............................

3.6 What is the rationale behind your choice of teaching and learning methods for law? (*We are interested in any philosophy of teaching and learning/pedagogy that underpins your approach.*)

3.7 What materials do you expect students to use in learning about the law? (*please tick all that apply*)

| | | | |
|---|---|---|---|
| law textbooks written for social workers | ☐ | general law textbooks | ☐ |
| critical social work texts/journals | ☐ | critical legal texts/journals | ☐ |
| class handouts | ☐ | electronic databases | ☐ |
| online journals | ☐ | websites | ☐ |

other (specify) ................................................................................................

3.8 What sources of law do you expect students to become familiar with in their studies? (*please tick all that apply across the curriculum as a whole, recognising that the souces may vary depending on the area of law under consideration*)

| | | | |
|---|---|---|---|
| statutes | ☐ | regulations | ☐ |
| guidance | ☐ | case law | ☐ |
| codes of practice | ☐ | local authority circulars | ☐ |

other (specify) ................................................................................................

3.9 Please add any comments you wish to make about the process of teaching and learning of law within your programme.

<br><br><br><br><br>

## Section 4: Practice learning

4.1 Where are practice learning days located in your programme(s)? (*ie the programme(s) that are the subject of your answers in this questionnaire*)

|  | Number of days |  | Number of days |
|---|---|---|---|
| 1st level undergraduate |  | Year 1 study postgraduate |  |
| 2nd level undergraduate |  | Year 2 study postgraduate |  |
| 3rd level undergraduate |  |  |  |

4.2 Do you have specific learning objectives relating to law on practice placement?

Yes ☐        No ☐

If Yes, please tell us what they are

<br><br><br><br>

4.3 How is the teaching and learning of law incorporated into students' practice learning? (*please tick all that apply*)

overt inclusion in placement contracts/learning objectives ☐

legal components in casework to be undertaken ☐

specific tasks built into placement ☐

specified element of written work produced during placement ☐

other (*please specify*) .........................................................................

4.4 Do you undertake any specific activities or provide any guidance to practice teachers to support their role in students' learning of law?

    Yes ☐        No ☐

    If Yes, please tell us what you do

4.5 Only if you are responding in relation to the new degree, how do you interpret the requirement that students gain experience of statutory work?

4.6   Please add any comments you wish to make about law with the practice learning elements of your programme(s).

```



```

## Section 5: Assessment

5.1   How is students' law learning assessed? (*please tick all that apply*) *Please send us examples of assessments that you have undertaken.*

| Examination | Open book** | Closed book** |
|---|---|---|
| Law exam | | |
| Seen* | | |
| Unseen* | | |

| Other exam | Open book** | Closed book** |
|---|---|---|
| Seen* | | |
| Unseen* | | |

| Coursework | |
|---|---|
| Case study | |
| Essay | |
| Assesses seminar | |
| Assessed presentation | |
| Other law project | |
| Integrated in other assingnments | |
| Other (please specify) | |

*Seen/unseen relates to whether questions are given to students in advance.

** Open/closed book relates to whether students may use textbooks during the exam.

5.2  If you use examinations, do these contain: (*please tick all that apply*)

Multiple choice  ☐          Case studies  ☐          Essays  ☐

Other (Please specify) ................................................................................

5.3  What are you looking for in assessing student's learning? (*Please also append your assessment criteria if available.*)

Accurate knowledge of content of legal framework.............................

Use of varied sources of law (ie statute/case law, etc).........................

Knowledge of historical development of legal framework..................

Critical analysis of legal framework.........................................................

Application of law to social work practice...............................................

Professional ethics and values

Other criteria (please explain).................................................................

5.4   What is your rationale for assessing law in the way(s) you do.

```



```

5.5   Please add any comments you wish to make about the assessment of law within your programme(s).

```



```

## Section 6: Evaluation of teaching, learning and assessment of law

6.1   How do you evaluate the teaching, learning and assessment of law? (*please tick all that apply*)

feedback from:

| | | |
|---|---|---|
| students ☐ | teaching staff ☐ | service users/ ☐ carers |
| practice teachers ☐ | employers ☐ | external ☐ examiners |
| institutional quality ☐ monitoring | GSCC ☐ | |

other (*please specify*) ...............................................................................

6.2 Please summarise the key messages from any evaluation undertaken in relation to students' learning of law.

```
┌────────────────────────────────────────────────────────┐
│                                                        │
│                                                        │
│                                                        │
│                                                        │
│                                                        │
└────────────────────────────────────────────────────────┘
```

## 7 General Comments

7.1 Have there been any factors that have particularly influenced your approach to the teaching, learning and assessment of law?

external guidance (*if so which*)..................................................

research (*if so, which ?*)..................................................

literature (*If so , which ?*)..................................................

7.2 Have you undertaken in the past, or are you undertaking, any outcome study of students' law learning?

Yes ☐          No ☐

If Yes, please give us details

(*If a report or publication is available, please send us a copy or the reference.*)

```
┌────────────────────────────────────────────────────────┐
│                                                        │
│                                                        │
│                                                        │
│                                                        │
│                                                        │
└────────────────────────────────────────────────────────┘
```

7.3 Can you summarise any changes and developments in your approach in the last few years? *We are particularly interested to know of any changes you have made or anticipate making during the transition from DipSW to the new degree, and why.*

```



```

7.4 How satisfied are you with your current approach to the teaching, learning and assessment of law?

very satisfied ☐ reasonably satisfied ☐

a little dissatisfied ☐ very dissatisfied ☐

Please indicate in the box below any particular areas of satisfaction or dissatisfaction:

```



```

7.5 Would you be prepared to talk to us further about your responses to this questionnaire? *If yes, we may contact you by phone. If there is someone else we should speak to, please give their contact details.*

Yes ☐ No ☐

Thank you very much for your cooperation in completing this questionnaire. If our questions have omitted to ask about important aspects of law in social work education, please continue your comments below.

Please return the completed questionnaire, together with any supporting documentation, by 5th April 2004, to:

Ruth Melville, Department of Sociology, Social Policy and Social Work, Eleanor Rathbone Building, Bedford St South, Liverpool L69 7ZA.   ruth1@liv.ac.uk

# Appendix 4:
## Format for focus group discussion with students: *Teaching, learning and assessment of law in social work education*

**A. Law teaching during the academic component of the programme**

1. Think back to before you started your law teaching – what did you feel and what were you expecting?

    *prompts:*
    did you know anything about law?
    did you think it was an important part of social work?
    did you feel confident/eager/apprehensive/uncertain?

2. Thinking about the law teaching, what did you feel you had learnt by the time you had finished the module(s) and handed in your assignment(s)?

    *prompts:*
    do you feel it gave you an understanding of the legal system?
    did you learn about law in relation to key service user groups?
    did you get a sense of the relationship between law and social work practice?
    do you feel you know how to keep your knowledge up to date?

3. How did you learn what you learnt, and did you feel the teaching methods were appropriate?

    *prompts:*
    how helpful were the teaching/learning methods (lectures,

seminar tasks, case studies, assessed work, service user input)?

what helped the most?

was the curriculum content appropriate – anything you were surprised to find included or omitted?

## B. Practice placement

4. Have you been able to make use of your law learning now you are on placement?

> *prompt:* in what way?

5. Have you learnt anything more/different about law on your placement?

> *prompt:* what? how?

6. Does the law make more, or less, sense now you are on placement?

> *prompt:* in what way?

## C. Reflection

7. What would you now say is the relationship between law and social work practice?

> *prompts:* legal mandates; law and ethics; accountability

8. What has made the biggest contribution to your understanding of that relationship?

> *prompts:* different elements of taught course; practice experience

9. What would be your key message to law teachers?

> *prompts:*
> curriculum content/teaching and learning methods
> discrete or integrated teaching or both
> barriers to learning/what is a struggle/what helps

# Appendix 5:
# Format for focus group discussion with practice teachers

**A. Using the law in your own practice**

1. How do you as practitioners use the law in your daily practice?
   *prompts:*
   do you think it is an important part of social work?
   do you feel confident/apprehensive/uncertain?

2. How did you learn what you know about the law?
   *prompts:*
   social work qualification training/in-servicetraining/ shortcourses/PQ training/agency briefings/agency procedural guidance?
   do you feel you know how to keep your knowledge up to date?

3. What would you say is the relationship between law and social work practice?
   *prompts:*
   legal mandates; law and ethics; accountability

**B. Helping students learn about the law**

4. Is helping students to learn about the law one of your aims as a practice teacher?
   *prompts:*
   if Yes, why?
   if No, why?

5. How knowledgeable/skilled are students in this area of learning when they come out on placement?
*prompts:*
what are their knowledge/skills?
what gaps?

6. What opportunities do you think exist to learn about the law on placement?
*prompts:*
legal content in cases
agency policies/procedures
if no obvious opportunities, how can these be created?

7. How confident are you that you can help students in this area of learning?
*prompts:*
what helps/hinders

## C. Reflection

8. What makes the biggest contribution to students' understanding of the relationship between law and social work practice?
*prompts:* different elements of taught course; practice experience

9. What would be your key message to law teachers?
*prompts:*
curriculum content/teaching & learning methods
barriers to students' learning/what is a struggle/what helps

# Appendix 6:
# First briefing paper

## Preparation for the first consultation event on 29 March 2004

### What is this piece of work?

The Social Care Institute for Excellence (SCIE) has a programme of research underway to support the introduction of the new social work degree in the UK. SCIE have asked us to do a 'Knowledge Review' – this is a piece of research to find out what is known about effective ways for social work students to learn about the law. SCIE will be producing guidance for new degree programmes.

### Why is law important in social work?

Law affects social work practice in all sorts of ways. It provides the legal framework for many of the things that social workers do, particularly:

- promoting people's rights
- challenging oppression and discrimination
- assessing people's needs
- making sure that services are provided to meet needs
- protecting people from harm.

Law has been a required part of social work training for many years. It is one of the core requirements for the new social work degree.

## How much do social workers know?

As long ago as 1988, research identified that there were gaps and shortcomings in social workers' knowledge and understanding of the law. This led to:

- interest in how social work students learn about the law
- interest in how the law affects social work practice.

A number of books have been written specifically for social workers. Despite this we know relatively little about the most effective ways of helping students to learn, or to use law in practice. Worryingly, more recent research has reported:

- a continued lack of confidence in legal knowledge among qualifying social workers
- a loss of knowledge in the first year of practice, especially in areas that are not regularly used.

This piece of work for SCIE will try to fill some of the gaps in our knowledge about what works in teaching, learning and assessing law in social work education.

## How are we doing the knowledge review?

We are doing three things in our work for SCIE:

1. A review of published research: This involves searching libraries and databases for research into law teaching in social work education. We are also searching for research on teaching law to other professions, including student lawyers. Once we find publications, we will assess whether they provide good evidence of what approaches to teaching work best.
2. A survey of what is happening in practice on training programmes: This involves sending a questionnaire to all universities and colleges where social workers are trained, to ask questions about how they approach law teaching. This information will add to our knowledge of what works well, and may give us pointers to good practice.

3. Consultation with a wide range of people who have experience of and interest in social workers' understanding of the law: This is why we are holding the two consultation events.

**What will the first consultation event be about?**

At this first event, we would like to hear your experiences of social workers' understanding of the law, and the relationship between law and social work practice. We would like your ideas on:

- What should students learn about law and its importance for social work?
- What helps students learn about the law?
- How does law learning affect professional practice?

We would like to give you more details about our review of published research. We would like to ask for your ideas on:

- Are we searching for research on law teaching in the right ways?
- Where else we might look for published information on law teaching?
- How should we judge the quality of what we find?

We would like also to ask for your guidance on the survey of current teaching. Once we receive responses to the questionnaire we have sent to social work programmes, we will be doing some telephone interviews with teachers of law. We may also meet with students.

- What questions should we be asking teachers and students?

We are looking forward to seeing you in Luton on the 29th March.

# Appendix 7:
## Second briefing paper

### Preparation for the second consultation event
### on 21 May 2004

This piece of work for SCIE will try to fill some of the gaps in our knowledge about what works in teaching, learning and assessing law in social work education.

**What was the first consultation event about?**

At the first event on 29th March 2004, participants' shared experiences of social workers' knowledge and use of the law. We considered:

- what students should learn about law and its importance for social work
- what helps students learn about the law
- how law learning affects professional practice.

In relation to the research for SCIE, we discussed:

- where we might look for published information on law teaching
- how should we judge the quality of what we find
- what we should be asking law teachers, practitioners and students.

The notes of this first consultation are enclosed with this briefing pack.

**What will the second consultation event be about?**

At the second event on 21st May 2004, we hope to:

- confirm whether the notes from the first meeting are accurate
- present early findings from the review of published research and literature on the teaching and learning of law
- present early findings from the survey of current teaching and learning practice on social work education programmes
- work together to decide what are the themes emerging from these early findings
- decide together what further analysis would be useful.

We are looking forward to seeing you in Luton on the 21st May.

# Index

# Other knowledge reviews available from SCIE

**LEARNING AND TEACHING IN SOCIAL WORK EDUCATION: ASSESSMENT**
Beth R. Crisp, Mark R. Anderson, Joan Orme and Pam Green Lister
1 904812 00 7
November 2003

**THE ADOPTION OF LOOKED AFTER CHILDREN: A SCOPING REVIEW OF RESEARCH**
Alan Rushton
1 904812 01 5
November 2003

**TYPES AND QUALITY OF KNOWLEDGE IN SOCIAL CARE**
Ray Pawson, Annette Boaz, Lesley Grayson, Andrew Long and Colin Barnes
1 904812 02 3
November 2003

**INNOVATIVE, TRIED AND TESTED: A REVIEW OF GOOD PRACTICE IN FOSTERING**
Clive Sellick and Darren Howell
1 904812 03 1
November 2003

**FOSTERING SUCCESS: AN EXPLORATION OF THE RESEARCH LITERATURE IN FOSTER CARE**
Kate Wilson, Ian Sinclair, Claire Taylor, Andrew Pithouse and Clive Sellick
1 904812 04 X
January 2004

**TEACHING AND LEARNING COMMUNICATION SKILLS IN SOCIAL WORK EDUCATION**
Pamela Trevithick, Sally Richards, Gillian Ruch and Bernard Moss with Linda Lines and Oded Manor
1 904812 12 0
May 2004

**IMPROVING THE USE OF RESEARCH IN SOCIAL CARE PRACTICE**
Isabel Walter, Sandra Nutley, Janie Percy-Smith, Di McNeish and Sarah Frost
1 904812 13 9
June 2004

**LEARNING AND TEACHING IN SOCIAL WORK EDUCATION: TEXTBOOKS AND FRAMEWORKS ON ASSESSMENT**
Beth R. Crisp, Mark R. Anderson, Joan Orme and Pam Green Lister
1 904812 21 X
April 2005

# Join SCIE's update list

If you are interested in a particular element of SCIE's work, or perhaps all of it, you can register your interest with us by filling out this form and posting it or faxing it back to us.

When a new publication, new information, a new event or a new commission become available we will let you know either by email or by post.

Please enter your details here

Name _____

Job title _____

Organisation _____

Address _____

Telephone _____  Facsimile _____

Email _____

Please tick what areas of SCIE's work you are interested in:

☐ adult services
☐ children and families services
☐ e-learning
☐ electronic Library for Social Care
☐ human resource development
☐ knowledge in social care
☐ participation
☐ social work education

SCIE commissions out much of its work. If you are interested in applying for SCIE's commissions, please tick here ☐

**Data protection**
The information you provide on this booking form will be held on a database so that we can keep you up-to-date with relevant publications and other SCIE news. We will not pass your details on to any other company.

**Please fill out the form overleaf and return to SCIE at:**

Communications Team
Social Care Institute for Excellence
Goldings House
2 Hay's Lane
London SE1 2HB

or fax it to 020 7089 6841